A JOURNAL OF CONTEMPORARY WRITING

IRISH PAGES
DUILLÍ ÉIREANN

IRISH PAGES is a biannual journal (Spring-Summer, Autumn-Winter), edited in Belfast and publishing, in equal measure, writing from Ireland and overseas. It appears at the end of each six-month period.

Its policy is to publish poetry, short fiction, essays, creative non-fiction, memoir, essay reviews, nature-writing, translated work, literary journalism, and other autobiographical, historical, religious and scientific writing of literary distinction. There are no standard reviews or narrowly academic articles. Irish language and Ulster Scots writing are published in the original, with English translations or glosses. IRISH PAGES is a non-partisan, non-sectarian, culturally ecumenical, and wholly independent journal. It endorses no political outlook or cultural tradition, and has no editorial position on the constitutional question. Its title refers to the island of Ireland in a purely apolitical and geographic sense, in the same manner of The Church of Ireland or the Irish Sea.

The sole criteria for inclusion in the journal are the distinction of the writing and the integrity of the individual voice. Equal editorial attention will be given to established, emergent and new writers.

The views expressed in IRISH PAGES are not necessarily those of the Editors. The magazine has no editorial or financial connection to the Linen Hall Library or its Directors. It is published by Irish Pages Ltd, a non-profit organisation.

Submissions are welcome but must be accompanied by return postage or an international reply coupon. No self-addressed envelope is required. Reporting time is nine months. If work is accepted, a copy on disk may be requested.

Your subscription is essential to the independence and survival of the journal. Subscription rates are £16stg/€26/$45 for one year. Visit our website at www.irishpages.org for a subscription form or to order online. Credit cards are welcome.

IRISH PAGES
The Linen Hall Library
17 Donegall Square North
Belfast BT1 5GB

Legal Advice: Kathy Mathews, Johnsons Law, Belfast/Dublin/London

*IRISH PAGES is designed by Alicia McAuley Publishing Services and
set in 12/14.5 Monotype Perpetua. It is printed in Belfast by Nicholson & Bass.*

*This issue has been generously asssisted by Foras na Gaeilge
and the Arts Councils of Northern and Southern Ireland.*

ISBN 978-0-9561046-7-0

IRISH PAGES

CHRIS AGEE, *Editor*

CATHAL Ó SEARCAIGH, *Irish Language Editor*

SEÁN MAC AINDREASA, *Managing Editor*

LYNLEY EDMEADES, RÍONNAGH SHERIDAN, ELIZABETH SWITAJ
Editorial Assistants

EDITED IN BELFAST
VOLUME 6, NUMBER 1

IRISH PAGES
DUILLÍ ÉIREANN

VOLUME 6, NUMBER 1

CONTENTS

Ireland in Crisis

After a Poetry Reading, City Hall, Dublin
By Mark Granier

WHAT HAPPENED TO IRELAND?
(THE 2011 HUBERT BUTLER ANNUAL LECTURE)

Morgan Kelly

Insolvent majesty.

The meteoric trajectory of the Irish economy over the past 25 years from basket case to superstar and back to basket case raises a natural question: what happened to Ireland? In my talk this evening I want to discuss where the Irish economy came from, where we are now, and where we are likely heading.

For most of its history, the Irish state has been an economic failure. Ireland went from being one of the highest income countries in Western Europe at independence to an income of half the European average by the 1980s, and even this dismal performance was only achieved through mass emigration. Things suddenly changed in the 1990s, when Irish incomes rapidly rose to average European levels, and unemployment more or less disappeared. Like all overnight successes, Ireland's was decades in the making, going back at least to the introduction of free secondary education and the expansion of the university system in the 1970s, the growing realization in the 1980s that Ireland could only survive if costs were kept at a competitive level, and the currency devaluations of the early 1990s.

This rapid growth in incomes and employment had extraordinary benefits for Irish society. Most social problems disappear as people find work – being able to afford a car, to take your family on holiday, to buy toys for your kids at Christmas, transforms a person's self-respect – and rates of alcoholism, suicide, teenage pregnancy all fell while life expectancy rose from one of the lowest in Europe to one of the highest. The grinding poverty that had always been a feature of Irish life disappeared, and so, as the need to blame others for our failure as a society, did our resentment of Britain.

The one group in Irish society that failed to benefit from the real prosperity of the 1990s (apart from the Catholic Church, whose self-destruction stemmed from other causes) were politicians. Irish politics had always been based on clientelism, where the extensive electioneering of proportional representation campaigns was undertaken by volunteers in return for menial public service jobs or being moved to the top of local authority housing lists. Suddenly political patronage lost its value – who wanted a job in the post office when they could work for Dell instead? – and politicians were left looking for a new source of funding for elections.

Through the 1990s employment and competitiveness rose together. By 2000 Irish incomes had converged to average European levels, there was full employment, and competitiveness began to fall as wages were bid up faster than productivity rose. At this stage it might have been expected that Irish growth rates would fall back to ordinary European levels. Instead, growth continued at the rapid rates of the 1990s with one difference, that it was now driven by a credit-fuelled building boom rather than by competitiveness.

In the 1990s, Ireland got around five per cent of its national income from building – the usual level for an industrialized economy – but by 2006 this had reached 15 per cent. During 2006–2007, we built half as many houses as the UK, which is 15 times our size. In effect, after 2000, Ireland decided that competitiveness no longer mattered and that we could get rich by selling houses to each other. The immediate cause of the building boom was the rise in house prices, which made building very profitable: in the late 1990s, the average cost of a house, new or second-hand, in Dublin or elsewhere, was around four times the average industrial wage. By 2006, the average new house cost 10 years' wages, while Dublin second-hand houses cost 16 years' wages.

However, this rise in house prices was driven in turn by one thing: no, not rising incomes, or falling interest rates; but bigger mortgages. Between 1995 and 2006 the average mortgage for a first time buyer rose from three times the average industrial wage, to nine times average wages, and house prices moved in perfect synchrony. You can download a paper of mine from University College Dublin called "The Irish Credit Bubble" which shows exactly how house prices were driven by rising mortgages.

So, rising bank lending drove up house prices, which led to more house building, and this is what drove the Irish economy between 2000 and 2008. This lending bonanza represented a complete change for Irish banks. Right through the 1990s, their lending had been very conservative and tightly controlled by a Central Bank which needed to protect an independent currency. So tight was lending in fact, that house prices actually rose a lot more slowly during the early 1990s than people's incomes.

While most banks abroad lent about 80 per cent of national income, Irish banks in 2000 lent only 60 per cent. Between 2000 and 2008, during what economists used to call the "Great Moderation", banks found that they could borrow almost any amount on international markets without security at rates only slightly above central bank rates. This led to an international lending boom where bank lending in most European economies rose to around 100 per cent of national income. In Ireland lending rose from 60 to nearly 200 per cent, and most of this was funded by borrowing from overseas banks. Everything that happened in Ireland between 2000 and 2008 stems from this simple fact.

With unlimited funds at their disposal, the problem facing Irish banks was finding people to lend to: the more they lent, the larger the bonuses they earned. While mortgages were growing fast, they were not growing fast enough for Irish bankers, but salvation appeared in the form of property developers. Back in 2000, Irish banks, remembering the banking dictum that you should never lend more to a developer than you would like to lose, lent almost nothing for property speculation. By 2008, following the lead of Anglo Irish which had used lending to developers to transform itself from a hole in the wall operation to become the joint-second largest Irish financial institution by market value (for the record, Paddy Power bookmakers is now the largest), Irish banks were lending €115 billion to developers alone, 40 per cent more than they were lending to everyone in Ireland in 2000. By 2007, Irish banks had the same exposure to property development loans as Japanese banks had before they imploded in 1989.

The early 2000s were wonderful for Irish banks: the more they lent, the more property prices rose, and the more property prices rose, the more eager people became to borrow. And the building boom, as far as Irish politicians were concerned, seemed sent from heaven. Just as their foot soldiers were deserting them to stay at home and watch TV instead of handing out election flyers, politicians found a new sugar daddy in the form of property developers. Property development everywhere is a highly politicized activity, centring as it does on obtaining planning permission for new projects. However, in few places was the bond between politicians and developers closer than in Ireland where zoning regulations existed, not as a means of ensuring the optimal and rational use of land, but as a means of generating baksheesh for politicians. You could build anything anywhere so long as you paid the right amount to the right people.

With developers flush with money and more projects needing planning approval than ever before, the dream marriage with Fianna Fáil was consummated. While most people remember the Ballybrit Tent as the symbol of Fianna Fáil's transformation from the party of rugged self-reliance under Dev to the party of boundless self-indulgence under Bertie, I think the transformation of Fianna Fáil from a mass movement to the political clients of property developers is better shown during the election before last when all the election posters, which previously had been hung by the party-faithful, tottering precariously on ladders, were put up instead by builders in hard hats with the names of leading property companies on their reflective vests.

The building boom suited everyone that mattered. The more bankers lent, the larger the bonuses they received, while developers looked after Fianna Fáil and provided jobs in rural areas that had been bypassed by the Celtic Tiger of the 1990s.

The only snag in this perfect scheme was that it required more and more people to take out larger and larger mortgages. Once the flow of new lending slowed, prices would fall. This is the one thing you need to understand about the property boom, and that clever people like Central Bank Governor Honohan failed, and still probably fail, to understand: Irish property prices were driven by new lending. Once lending stops, as it effectively has now, prices will eventually collapse.

Things started to unravel a lot earlier than most people imagine. In the summer of 2006 the number and average value of new mortgages (to all borrowers: first time, movers, and investors) both peaked and started to fall rapidly as ordinary house buyers became afraid that property was dangerously overvalued.

I first became interested in house prices after seeing so many self-described economists paid by various banks appear on TV and assure everyone that there would be a "soft landing" in the property market. They said it so often that I became curious, and started to look at what had happened in other economies after big house price booms – the Netherlands in the late 1970s, and Finland in the late 1980s – and found that their landings were anything but soft.

For a long time I had wondered how these less than perceptive people had come to realize that there was something wrong in the property market, and it was only when I saw the numbers on new mortgages that I saw that banks were afraid that mortgage demand was falling and pushed their economists on TV to try and drum up business.

Once mortgage demand started to fall in the middle of 2006 – five years ago now – the game was up for Ireland. Unsold houses began to accumulate and developers were unable to repay loans. At first banks were able to disguise the situation, but by the summer of 2007 the Central Bank was sufficiently worried about Anglo to contact the ECB (European Central Bank) about it (the ECB's response, as always, was that it was our problem, not theirs); and in February 2008 the Department of Finance produced a memo detailing how to wind up Anglo and inflict the costs on its bondholders.

However, Irish banks were still able to go on borrowing happily in international markets and make new loans to developers who could not repay their existing loans (shades of Greece and Ireland right now), until the general market panic following the collapse of Lehman in the autumn of 2008.

Looking at what happened between 2000 and 2008 we can see that, underlying the boom and subsequent bust in house prices and construction, lay a bubble in bank lending; and that the blame for what happened lies overwhelmingly with the senior management of banks who authorized this lending, and in particular with the management of AIB and Bank of Ireland. At any stage in the early 2000s they could have approached the government and Central Bank and pointed out that Anglo had gone dangerously out of control and needed to be stopped. Instead, they set out to imitate Anglo, setting up switch-over teams to try and entice developers from Anglo.

Certainly there were serious lapses of regulation, but even in places like the US, where the regulators were anything but morons, banks went out of control. It is ultimately the task of senior bank management – not regulators, not auditors, not ratings agencies – to ensure that their companies do not adopt suicidal strategies; and in this the management of AIB and Bank of Ireland signally failed.

This view is at odds with the Honohan and, more nauseating still, Nyberg reports where the general conclusion is that mistakes were made, but not by anyone in particular: a style of writing that Americans call the "past-exonerative" tense. Everyone is to blame, which means that no one is to blame.

As you all know, the first stage of the crisis came to a head in September 2008 when Anglo suffered a run in wholesale funding markets. At a late night meeting, the details of which are still far from clear, the government guaranteed, not only all public deposits in banks, but most existing bonds issued to other financial institutions. This was an astonishingly stupid move: these bonds had been bought by sophisticated investors who knew that they stood to lose if the banks did badly, and charged a rate of interest accordingly.

What lay behind the guarantee? My guess is that a mixture of bravado and desperation led Cowen and Lenihan to have a go at *shock and awe*: by putting the entire majesty and resources of the Irish state behind the banks, the hope was to end the funding crisis for Irish banks at one stroke. The probable view was that Anglo might have lost about €10 billion and that it was easiest for the government to go ahead and pay off its creditors rather than to force a restructuring – where the bonds would be turned into shares – which would frighten investors in the other banks.

Unfortunately, this effort at shock and awe turned out to be shocking and awful, but not in the way its architects anticipated: it started to emerge, as some people had warned, that the losses of the Irish banks were very large indeed, and that the Irish taxpayer was on the hook for them.

However, the real mistake was not making the guarantee: it was continuing to honour it long after it had become clear that the bank losses were beyond the financial resources of the Irish State. Governments do not obey laws, they make them, and the real mistake was not revoking the guarantee and forcing a resolution on the banks where their debt was turned into shares: immediately ending the crisis at virtually no cost to the Irish taxpayer.

Instead, after hiring international consultants to carry out a so-called "stress test" of the Irish banks, the new Central Bank Governor Patrick Honohan confidently announced that the bank losses were "manageable": of the order of €40 billion.

Honohan claimed that Anglo and Nationwide would cost about €35 billion, with €5 billion for the others. This estimate was patently ridiculous: AIB and Bank of Ireland between them had the same exposure to developer loans as Anglo (and to even worse developers), so we were looking at losses of roughly €70 billion before even starting to think about mortgages. At the time, I set up a simple spreadsheet showing, under pretty optimistic assumptions about loan losses, that the Irish taxpayer could easily lose €80 billion.

With Honohan's reassurance that the bank losses were manageable, the government went ahead and repaid all the outstanding bank bonds, even the ones that were not guaranteed, culminating in the payment of over €50 billion last September. This was followed within weeks, as a direct consequence, by international markets stopping lending to Ireland, forcing us to accept an EU-IMF bailout, and joining Greece among the deadbeats of Europe. Ireland is now effectively run by a European vice-consul, a Hungarian economics lecturer called Istvan Szekely, to whom the Irish government ministers are answerable. What started as a banking crisis has now become part of the general Eurozone debt crisis.

Ireland is now insolvent: the debts it has and will accumulate exceed any plausible means of repaying them. The current official estimate guesstimates are that Irish debt will peak at €200 billion by 2015 (€40 billion of which will have gone into the banks, plus another €20 billion from the national pension reserve fund) with another €30 billion owed by the National Asset Management Agency (NAMA). Under some pretty optimistic assumptions about GDP growth, this will leave Ireland not much worse than where Italy is now.

However, I think the total debt will be larger because of bank losses and because, even when fully recapitalized, the banks will have zero market value. I think the bank losses will eventually cost the state €90–100 billion (effectively absorbing all of its investment so far, including NAMA), and the banks will then require further capital of at least €15 billion, leaving Ireland with a debt of over €240 billion, even after netting out the NAMA assets and the value of the state's investment in the banks.

As I said, back in May 2010 when Honohan was confidently forecasting a bank loss of €40 billion, I put up a spreadsheet showing a hit to taxpayers of €80 billion. Just as the Central Bank has become more pessimistic as it has learnt more in the last year, so have I.

In particular, on developer loans, I estimated a loss of 75 per cent, based on rental yields rising from their bubble level of two per cent, to the international average of eight per cent. This will probably be true of the better developer assets – basically offices in central Dublin with sitting tenants on long leases – that can be sold to international vulture funds; but for the ghost estates, empty hotels, unopened retail parks, and land banks around small rural towns, the losses will be close to 100 per cent.

Secondly, there are mortgage losses. I guessed that of the €80 billion of mortgages on Irish property (there are another €40 billion lent abroad, largely in the UK, that I assumed would be fully repaid), 20 per cent would default and, as in America, banks would recover half of what they lent.

But that was before I estimated that the largest 11,000 mortgages given out at the peak of the boom, largely for buy-to-let investment, are worth €9 billion. The losses on these will be substantial.

In addition, banks will be hard put to recover half of their loans on defaulting mortgages. It seems, fortunately, hard for banks to evict people from their family homes, and even when stuff will eventually be sold, the price is likely to be a small fraction of the original loan.

Transaction prices are now about half their peak level, and the same people who assured us three years ago that house prices would have a soft landing are now starting to show their faces in public again to tell us that prices have bottomed out. That is patently false.

If prices had fallen to an equilibrium level, we would see the stock of unsold properties staying constant, instead of rising constantly, as it is. What we need to remember, once again, is that house prices are determined by the mortgages that banks give. You might be wondering why banks are still giving out a handful of 30-year mortgages at 3.5 per cent, when their market funding cost, as part of the Irish state, if they could even get into the markets, is over 10 per cent. The reason is to keep some kind of illusory floor on the market, to limit defaults on existing mortgages: the further people fall into negative equity, the more readily they default.

Eventually banks will be forced to stop mortgage lending more or less completely (and this could happen sooner rather than later as the Eurozone crisis escalates) leading to a cash market, which is already reappearing in rural Ireland. The nature of housing markets is that they can easily end up as undervalued as they were overvalued, and it is easy to envisage prices halving from their current levels.

Apart from mega-interest-only loans, and low recovery rates on defaulted mortgages, the banks face the potential of organized opposition to mortgage payment, from groups who believe that people were misled into taking out mortgages that they could not afford. Already I have had three emails from separate *don't repay your mortgage* groups. These are small and inchoate groups but at some stage a Michael Davitt figure may emerge to organize and energize them into a large national movement.

Given our national traditions of paramilitary violence, there is the threat that opposition to property repossession can turn violent. There has been at least one incident already, where an incendiary device was left at the office of an estate agent selling some land repossessed from a border-area businessman; and some Robin Hood mayhem aimed at our European oppressors is likely to appeal to resurgent dissident republicans.

In total, I would now estimate the likely cost of the bank bailout to be closer to €90–100 billion than the €70 billion the government estimates.

On top of this, the banks will need new capital put in, which can then, it is assumed, be recovered when they are re-privatized. The problem is that Irish banks expanded enormously during the boom, and are roughly three times the size they should be, in staff and operating expenses. When the Irish banking system shrinks back to the size it should be for an economy of our size, to earn ordinary international profits it would need to have operating expenses of under €1.5 billion a year, whereas AIB and Bank of Ireland between them currently cost €4.5 billion.

In other words, the Irish State is likely to see exactly the same return on its capital investment of €20 or so billion into the banks that it has seen on its €3 billion capital investment in CIE: precisely zero.

The Irish banks will settle down to life as gold-plated, permanently loss-making semi-state companies. The possibilities that this opens up have not yet dawned on our politicians. We know that, by the nature of the PR system, Irish politics is driven by patronage. The demise of property developers has left a patronage vacuum that will be filled by control of the banking system. This opens vistas of patronage on a scale that Charles Haughey could only dream of.

Politically-appointed bank boards will get to decide who gets a loan and on what terms. More importantly, they will get to decide who gets their mortgages partially or wholly written off, and who gets their houses repossessed.

For anyone in difficulties with their mortgage (or who would simply like it reduced) the best bet right now is to join Fine Gael (and, if you want to hedge your bets long-term, Sinn Féin). A party card with a low number may turn out to be an invaluable financial asset in years to come.

Between bank losses of €90–100 billion, and capital invested in worthless (financially but not politically) banks, Irish national debt is likely to rise closer to €240–250 billion than €200 billion. The chance that such sums can be repaid by a nation with 1.8 million (and falling) employed people is zero.

So Ireland joins Greece as the two unquestionably insolvent members of the Eurozone. In other words, the Irish economic crisis has passed entirely out of the hands of the Irish government, and become part of the larger European peripheral crisis.

This crisis has been allowed to spread from Greece and Ireland, to Portugal, and now threatens to engulf Italy and Spain, with yields also rising on Belgian and French bonds. Economists call this spread of fear in financial markets *contagion*. Unlike most metaphors in economics, contagion is exact: just as infectious disease spreads if the first few cases are not swiftly treated, so the inaction of the EU and ECB allowed fears about the creditworthiness of European economies to spread from small ones, which could have been treated easily, to Spain and Italy which will involve a huge effort to reverse.

The most interesting thing about the peripheral crisis is that it was allowed to happen at all. Twenty-five years ago, the first hint that one of the smaller peripherals was in crisis would have been followed by immediate German action to resolve the problem. That the German reaction was to punish the peripherals instead of seeking to solve their problems points to a fundamental shift in German attitudes to the European project.

The EU emerged to reverse 300 years of the growth of increasingly assertive and aggressive nation states in Europe, culminating in the disaster of the Second World War, followed by the Cold War. In effect, after destroying and dismembering much of Europe, and then being destroyed and dismembered in their turn, the Second World War left the Germans afraid of two things: of themselves, and of the Russians. The solution to both was to become acquiescent members of the EU, and being nice to poorer peripherals was a good way to show to themselves, and particularly to the East Europeans still under Soviet rule, how much they had changed for the better.

All this changed in the 1990s: the Soviet Union collapsed, and the generation of German leaders with direct experience of the war died off. Germany became just another ordinary, democratic Western country, able to act selfishly and stupidly in its own interests, without anyone finding anything sinister about it.

With the introduction of the Euro at the start of the decade, things changed further as highly competitive German firms destroyed the manufacturing sector of Mediterranean Europe: much of the social unrest in Spain and Greece reflects the lack of jobs for young people in these economies that failed to maintain their competitiveness. While individual Germans hate the Euro, their export driven economic growth of the past decade has come entirely from it.

With political paralysis in the EU, management of the crisis was taken over by the ECB. The ECB is an extraordinary institution. When it was set up in the 1990s in Frankfurt as the European Monetary Institute, nobody expected it ever to amount to anything and it had difficulty attracting high-quality staff. Those staffers it did attract, however, rose by seniority, and are now unfortunately in charge of running the crisis.

The result has been that nobody in Europe will publicly accept that Greece and Ireland have debts that they never can repay, and that these need to be dealt with. Instead, the belief is still that all of Ireland's debt, and most of Greece's, will eventually be repaid.

The Irish and Greek crises could have been stopped immediately, and prevented from spreading further, had the Irish been lent €100 billion, and the Greeks €150 billion for 50 years, or in perpetuity, at one per cent interest. All creditors could have been repaid and the Irish and Greek finances returned to sustainable levels, for a small share of Eurozone annual GDP.

Instead, European delay and denial has allowed the crisis to spread to Spain and Italy and the eventual cost of sorting it out will be far higher. At this stage, expanding the European Stability Fund, which has to be approved by all 17 Eurozone parliaments when they return after their summer holidays, is too little, too slowly, too late, and the only way to prevent panic from spreading involves large-scale ECB support for European debt markets.

Assuming then that the crisis gets cleared up eventually, with the Eurozone intact and Ireland's debt reduced – through some EU or ECB mechanism, or some amount of default – where does this leave Ireland?

National debt aside, our position is still extremely difficult. The banking and sovereign debt crises have drawn attention from the deep problems caused by the collapse of an internationally unprecedented credit bubble. We have tens of thousands of households with mortgages that they cannot afford; and with bankrupt banks, and a bankrupt state, it is not straightforward to think of any way to help these people. Eventually we will probably come up with some mechanism for reducing the amount owed by some, while allowing others to give up their houses and not be pursued for the outstanding amount. But, as I said earlier, I fear that this will be turned into an exercise in political patronage and taking care of pals at the expense of ordinary taxpayers.

The second big problem is unemployment, particularly of young men. The construction boom was a bonanza for young men with little schooling, but the employment rate for 20–24 year old males has now fallen below 50 per cent.

Ultimately, as in the past, Ireland's future economic success and recovery from its current crisis will come down to the education level of our workforce. So it was dismaying but not surprising last December, when the results of the latest PISA international standardized test for 15-year-olds came out, that in mathematics Ireland came bottom of the OECD. Despite all the banking and political disasters of the last year, this was the single statistic that depressed me most, and even more depressing was the fact that it was more or less ignored.

This collapse in secondary school achievement has been amplified at university level. The Irish universities were never great but at least they produced a large number of well-trained graduates at very low cost. Now we give out B grades to students we would have hesitated to pass a few years ago, which is nice except that the material is so dumbed down that bright students learn almost nothing. Our top students no longer go on to do PhDs in Ivy League universities: they are just not good enough. We have, all the rhetoric on "smart economy" notwithstanding, in effect, given up the education race; but the rest of the world, unfortunately, has not.

So, we have talked about the causes of our national collapse in the last three years: the greed, incompetence, arrogance, and simple stupidity which led to our credit boom, and to the fatal decision to meet the losses of foreign investors in private banks out of the pockets of Irish taxpayers.

However, the most significant thing about our current economic crisis is that it is not the first time that we have inflicted disaster on ourselves. If we step back and look at Ireland since the Second World War, we have managed three crises, at 30-year intervals: the 1950s, the 1980s, and the 2010s. What underlies this relentless appetite for self-destruction?

Part of it may be that we are such a tiny place: the problems that the Irish insurance regulator faces are not a whole lot less complex than those faced by his German counterpart, but the resources available and the pool of talent, in particular, is much smaller. Small societies, besides, are more prone to cronyism and groupthink.

However, not all small economies in the modern world are failures: look at the Nordics, Singapore, and New Zealand. What distinguishes them from us is a rigorous idea that the world owes them nothing: if they are not better than everyone else, they will fail; and if they permit any lapses from the highest ethical standards in the public service, they will fail.

For a brief shining moment in the 1990s, it seemed that we had become like them. Instead of a society based on patronage, cronyism and family contacts, it looked as if ordinary people could get ahead through education and hard work. We fondly imagined that the gombeens and pals by whom and for whom Ireland had been always been run had disappeared; only to see them re-emerge richer and more influential than ever during the bubble.

What is interesting is how little outrage this has provoked among ordinary people. Bankers, the government, and the Central Bank, in plain sight, have looted this country, and left it at the mercy of foreign creditors, an international laughing-stock with its prosperity destroyed for the next decade at least. And nobody seems to care less.

At the root of Ireland's problems there seems to be, not so much a tolerance of corruption, as an understanding and acceptance of human frailty. *If we were in Sean FitzPatrick's situation, maybe we would have done the same.* This unwillingness to cast the first stone, even at the most outrageous chancers, means that white collar criminals know that they will never be punished, and act accordingly.

The economic crisis for Ireland continues to deepen. Employment continues to fall, and insolvencies of Irish firms are running at record levels. Even if the international economy pulls back from the brink, Ireland faces a difficult task of restoring competitiveness and repairing public services, which often came to serve only their employees during the bubble. As the situation continues to worsen we will find ourselves at a crossroads as a society. Either we choose to do nothing, with those of us in jobs continuing to enjoy the good life, and poorly educated young people emigrating, or facing low paid temporary work: the Mediterranean model. Or we can decide that to survive as a small society we must be better educated, more transparent and more efficient than the rest of world, even if that means that public servants have to work hard, and bankers and politicians face prison. I have a sinking feeling about which we will choose.

This lecture was delivered on 6 August, 2011 at the Kilkenny Arts Festival.

Currently Professor of Economics at University College, Dublin (where he specializes in macroeconomics and economic networks), Morgan Kelly grew up in Dublin and attended Templeogue College. He holds a BA from Trinity College, Dublin, and a PhD from Yale University. His recent controversial articles in The Irish Times *on the catastrophic Irish banking crisis have drawn widespread attention at home and abroad.*

THE YEARS OF FORGETTING, 2006–2011

Thomas McCarthy

Accidents from elsewhere.

I am waiting at the gate at the top of our road with my new friends, Bashik and Stephane. It is a cold day in the South, unnatural cold of June made even more miserable by the persistence of Cork rain. Rain has settled in pools on plastic bags that are full of old newspapers and school notes going back to 1967. Bashik and Stephane came with a van after two or three weeks of our tidying, clearing out, trimming down, recycling, downsizing. *Letting go.* Not that we're leaving the house after 26 years. No, we are not going away. *There is nowhere to go.* But, after four years of recession, of salary cutbacks and a general sense of failure in that very special political weather created by our Irish Catholic realm, we are doing the next best thing: we are shedding what we have hoarded. We have convinced ourselves that what we've hoarded now has no meaning. It seems to be a shared feeling in these parts. Most of the neighbours and relatives have had a skip parked on their streets since 2009. There really is a frenzy of lightening, a newfound disgust at accumulations of any kind. Soon all our homes will be so empty they'll be full of echoes. There won't be a spare chair in the house of Éire. It's as if all those blunt warnings so harshly annunciated by William Carson in his *Ulster and The Irish Republic* or by Paul Blanshard in his *The Irish and Catholic Power* of 1953 have come true: Hugh Montgomery Hyde, in his foreword to the latter book, could claim:

> I have already touched on some of the proven facts which show that the bishops in the hierarchy are the real rulers in the South. Mr Blanshard examines all the available evidence in detail, and in doing so he has rendered a signal service to the English-speaking peoples. He has also demonstrated that, though it may possess some imperfections, the Government in the North is fundamentally democratic, whereas that of the South is only superficially democratic.

Maybe he was right, despite all the earlier talk of gerrymandering and B-Specials. How scary is that? *Maybe he was right.* Nowadays when we look up to

Ulster with its post-Good Friday Stormont it begins to look more and more like a commonwealth assembly of old New England, where the spoils of power are shared openly and equally among the accrued interests of reconciled old enemies. And it still looks that way, despite recent midsummer excitement about flags. It's beginning to look like the little late-eighteenth-century Presbyterian village of Villierstown in County Waterford; Presbyterians were imported South by Lord Grandison, who dreamed of a Munster linen industry. The landlord gave each Presbyterian a field but told him he couldn't till it, that he'd have to rent it to a Catholic in the hinterland. The Catholics needed the grazing, so the two communities were locked in perpetual interdependence. It's as good a model as any for a successful society. It could be the road that Ulster has embarked upon, a future that will unlock value for every citizen. This was also the promise of the earliest Dáil. When Seán Lemass, upon assuming office as minister for justice in 1932, told the head of the Special Branch to burn the file containing the names of the men who'd tortured and murdered his brother in the Dublin Mountains he added, "We might have to do business with them yet for the sake of Ireland". In those days they knew nothing about the psychology of "closure".

So, these mounds of black bags awaiting collection at the top of the steps are a kind of closure. They say farewell to my mother's *Messenger of the Sacred Heart*, to *The Fold*, to *Reality*, to *Far East* (where I learned that Edson Erantes do Nascimento was nicknamed "Pelé" by his Christian Brother teachers who always saw him "ag imirt peile" like a good Kerryman in the school yard). But here's one I'd better hold on to, a copy I bought in the Lee Bookstore in 1977: *The Capuchin Annual* for 1976, with its pious cover drawn by Sean O'Sullivan RHA and its more than 40 pages on the life and death of Mr de Valera. Ah, there it is, on page 285: T. Ryle Dwyer's essay, "Canada and David Gray's Attempts to Discredit de Valera During World War II". And there it is, that full-page portrait of Prince Rainier and the still-glamorous Princess Grace at Áras an Uachtaráin in 1962. Here are the ads for Dubtex slacks and Tal-Kraft suits for boys, the Commodore Hotel in Cobh, the EBS Building Society ("Give Yourself Everything to Look Forward To") and pictures of a young Padraic Fiacc, Dermot Keogh, Kevin Faller and Conleth Ellis; all of our kind of Irish life placed reassuringly between Lisavaird Co-Op Creamery and the Convoy Woollen Co. of Donegal. Better hang on to it; better temper this frenzy of wanting to forget.

This wanting to forget began a few years ago. It was an economist quoted in the *Irish Independent* in 2007 who first put a name to our feeling of anxiety. This was a few months before the banking crisis. He said we should stop having these feelings of guilt about our success. He mentioned the expression "benign paradigm" to explain the great success of the Celtic Tiger. "Get over your Catholic guilt", he said. "Accept your success." That's when we first began to yearn for an elsewhere. We found an elsewhere at the seashore, the seashore of West Kerry preferably. We were extravagant in the boom; we bought a second two-person tent and a battery-lamp and a waterproof radio and coloured markers so that we could write even in the rain. I sit in the tent at night and listen to the distant wave sounds, the wind in the bushes, the rustling of animals. Now as we walk to work through the crowded streets we are either at the seashore or dreaming of the seashore. There is no property between high-water mark and low-water mark, and no rich man can be given permission to build within this sandy realm. Now I can write only about inanimate things: stones, sand, water, cliffs, seaweed, the wind off the Atlantic. The anchorite poets are my constant companions – the ones who sought a solitude of stone and water: Michael Longley in his Connemara retreat, Richard Murphy braving the storms of High Island, troubled Theodore Roethke who walked to the far field. These are the poets who camp outdoors with me. In them is a companionship of the tested ordinary. They are the very antithesis of politics. Politics has saturated and ruined our brains and it needs a salty cleansing. Well, OK, I relent. I carry *The Capuchin Annual* back indoors, but I wonder, while descending the wet steps: is there anyone out there who might start a new conversation?

Let me explain.

No matter how hard we try, a country will always be more than the sum of all its poems; even more than the sum of all its poets. And when it comes to Ireland, including all of Ulster, we are in disputed parliaments of responsibility. Much of Ulster was elsewhere while Catholic Ireland became its all-singing, all-house-building self. While Northern Ireland made itself into a rose-growing, golf-coaching, Fenian-excluding Liechtenstein of the Moyle Water, Saorstát Eireann became something else entirely. What the South became now looks like a marvellous, cattle-rancher and priest-ridden Delia Murphy land. The entrenched bourgeoisie grabbed a little country with the only power structure that it could recognize. Now, it all looks like a dreadful conspiracy, a Catholic Nineteenth Century that lasted nearly two hundred years, from the victory of Daniel O'Connell to the defeat of Taoiseach Cowen. This era of power is neatly bookended by the Irish Protestant banking crisis of the early nineteenth century and the very

Catholic private-school banking crisis of the early twenty-first century. Both crises left us with an excess of vain building projects, both utterly unsustainable within local economic activity: Georgian house and contemporary ghost-estate. We have lived in that twilight zone of time, as Conor Cruise O'Brien put it in his essay on Seán Ó Faoláin, that zone of time that never quite belongs to the rest of history. Certainly, our elders have talked their memories into our memories – not that we might learn from the past, but that we might not notice the breach of planning regulations. So, 27 black bags of everything irrelevant – old diaries, old calendars, old concert tickets, old newspapers (oh, except this other publication: a copy of *Hibernia* for 24 June 1977: "Jack Swings Back!" with its picture of Jack Lynch swinging a hurley in front of a crowd of party-enthusiasts after the famous victory that brought down the Cosgrave/Conor Cruise O'Brien coalition of the mid-seventies. The same *Hibernia* carries an advertisement for "Macrobiotic Weekends" in Kilkenny and offers 16 per cent on your funds, "tax not deducted", from the Leinster Investment Society).

As heroes, time has undone us. So now, in exchange for a reasonable fee and over one and a half thousand jettisoned books, Bashik and Stephane, citizens of lands between the Danube and the Dnieper, are ready to clear the detritus of over 20 years of Irish family reading. When I thank the two men for lightening my load they are not sure what I'm talking about. For Bashik, these are his last weeks in Ireland – he's been head-hunted by a California games company who spotted his online game-development work, uploaded from his bedsit on Blarney Road onto YouTube. He is a highly qualified programmer, but in a different programming language from that used by game designers in Ireland. Stephane and I will miss him when he goes. We've had a thousand conversations over the last eight years about corruption in both Solidarity and Fianna Fáil. It has left us both wondering if there's a peculiar kind of *Catholic* corruption, a teeming form of old-world life that is passing away in our own era; that both our native lands have had to work out of their systems. Like Bashik, I sometimes feel I use the wrong programming language in my poems. The games of national life must be the same in any language, but I am still using the old Commodore-64 basic of Austin Clarke or Patrick Kavanagh while the others have rushed ahead using Beckett-Flash, or is it Leontia-Flash? The human heart, though, is still the same human heart in every kind of poem. In any poetic playground there are several generations at play together. Sometimes there is a conversation, but most of the time they have nothing to do with each other. As David Thompson wrote in his marvellous book on Hollywood films, "Here is proof that the most special effect in the movies is always the human face when its mind is being changed". That is also the camera angle at which the nation's grief becomes etched upon a poem's lines. It is the poet's duty to map those changes in the face of our nation(s) in each generation. The wonderful thing about the coming generations is that they haven't had our experiences, including our national failures of nerve. Anxiety about the Republic, for example (if you are only 24 years old and emerging into daylight from a poetry workshop) may be as academic as anxiety about the lost GDR.

Before I consigned all the black bags and recycling boxes to Stephane's white van I typed up some of the notes I'd made years ago, at the very beginning of thinking. What these notes were for, or who they were written for, is irrelevant now. I must have imagined an audience, an engaged audience that I now believe has faded away as imperceptibly as the subscribers' list of *The Capuchin Annual*. Thirty years ago I was an assiduous reader of diaries: poets, statesmen, artists, actors, reviewers – all life was reduced to the naked witness of the personal journal. I bored colleagues at the City Library with pithy quotes from Stendhal, Gide, Camus, Harold Nicolson, Richard Crossman, Evelyn Waugh, Arnold Bennett, Yeats and Gemma Hussey. *Make a note*, I used to say to myself. Keep the habit of the pen. *Survive*. At the time, they were my scrawls on the wall as I passed through the Free State cave. The people we meet day-by-day are like the politicians we get; as far as art is concerned, they are a series of accidents. Here are some of the pages I've thrown away. They are accidents from elsewhere.

See page 26 for extracts from the McCarthy Diaries.

So, here we are, at the narrow gate of 2011. As they say, the rest is recycled. We wait at the top of the steps while the white van is parked awkwardly. The black bags with their contents are placed hurriedly along the double yellow lines. It is good to lighten one's life, to go away mentally from the things that oppress the spirit. There has been an unbearable weight in these last four years. Last week, I could even feel twitches of kidney pain: the ghost of half a kidney I lost in 1986 crying, "come back, come back!" The pain reminds me how intensely personal poetry is; how it has its seed in one's tissue. As tissue and pain are to humans, so humans must be to the landscape – we map Ireland with a renewing *dinnseanchas* arising from the fragments of what we know. We have this foolish belief that others have suffered less for their success, for their landscape. How foolish can you get?

Our country has been undone. The national purpose is in a heap of fragments. We are living at the heart of a national catastrophe: the result of one or two key miscalculations by a brilliantly educated but very ill minister. If Ulster had been in charge, like the Great Earl of Kildare, decisions would have been different. I'm sure of this. Ulster would have been able to hold all of Ireland steady. The citizens of the Dáil are now the indentured servants of European capital. We must all work like dogs to pay for our passage through this great night of the Irish nationalist soul. Scholars worry. Theatre directors fret and form "citizen assemblies". Poets worry. Yes, the poets of my generation really worry. Was it some single process of national thinking that brought this catastrophe to pass? Was it our careless way with words? The misjudgements of Brian Lenihan have undone our South, a minister fooled by bank directors and economic risk analysts; the poor, hoodwinked, dying creature. Thank God the executives would never want to tamper with poetry. Auden was right: poets live in a parallel universe, a state where policy lives through the changing expressions of a human face. Yesterday, I was full of rage with him, the dead minister. But I was full of pity too, a raw and howling pity, because he was a very attractive and charismatic man. I tried to make a poem for him, for his memory, because there is something Parnell-like about his passing. He brought down a country, but death, the final speaker, removed him from the house before he had time to recover his composure. I shake hands with my Polish friend who will make a happier life in a sunnier country, the silicon valleys of Robert Duncan and Denise Levertov. The rain doesn't ease off as I fold back into myself the fragment of this unfinished poem. For the next decade, let us be pleased merely to be still alive. When everything is undone, let us be happy to live on fragments:

I can see more wreckage far out to sea;
And receding still. The pilot boat,
With all its unused life-belts,
Has the mark on its prow where you
Were pushed, Brian. Black gulls return
To their feeding grounds: Paris, Berlin.

ACCIDENTS FROM ELSEWHERE
(*from* THE McCARTHY DIARIES)

(Editor's Note: these diary entries are a continuation of the previous essay. See page 24, paragraph three.)

4 January 1974

At Glenshelane House, Cappoquin. This post-Christmas winter midnight darkness envelops me as I sit at the kitchen table. Tonight a westerly wind rattles the shutters, specks of rain skimming across the windowpanes and our rampant Superstar rose moving across the light from the window – a spectral survivor of 1973, another dreadful year in our land. I am alone in the house in the woods and delighted with my solitude. DHF has gone to Château de la Garoupe, near Antibes, for Christmas. Here in Ireland, a sinister time, security forces everywhere. Even in west Waterford. I was detained by *gardaí* at Lismore Bridge on Christmas Eve. They insisted on opening the carrier-box of my motorbike. They found two books within, Lady Anson's memoirs and *A Book about Roses* by Canon Reynolds Hole of Lincoln. Neither publication was banned by Liam Cosgrave or Conor Cruise O'Brien, so I was waved on without comment. Some good things in the last year, I admit, like Heaney's *Wintering Out* and the Sean Keating painting *Economic Pressure* that I saw in the Crawford Gallery.

6 January 1974

Petrol shortages. The Minister for Education has ordered secondary schools to stay shut for another week. I went to the Post Office in Cappoquin to ask for an application form for a petrol allocation for Glenshelane, but the P.O. has run out of forms. A letter from Mr Hallamore in Bermuda – because of the oil crisis and the Middle East situation, he thinks the world is coming to an end. Yet he and Mrs Hallamore are planning to go on a visit to Mexico – a funny way to prepare for the end of the world. He says that when the lease of their Cappoquin house is expired they intend to spend their summers in New England. I'll miss them, with their *International Herald Tribunes* on special order from Fraher's shop and their *New Yorkers* coming all the way from America every summer. Mr Hallamore warns me not to become too involved with poetry to the detriment of my livelihood. His warning comes too late.

27 January 1974

Terrible storms during the week: the worst continuous winds since the Big Wind of seventy years ago. Wind gusts of up to 110 miles an hour were recorded at Cork Airport. At Glenshelane the eucalyptus fell down, damaging the electricity wires. The huge rhododendron fell across the path to the garden. At least five other major trees fell. The telephone link was cut. On top of this storm, the government has announced that it is going to introduce new taxes. Dolores Price, the IRA bomber, has gone on hunger strike. The British are force-feeding her.

20 July 1974

DHF came home today. Full of London stories and Conservative Party gossip from all the business luncheons and projects he's involved in. He had no useful literary news. It occurs to me that the circle he moves in is the wrong circle for me. I have no business being interested in them. He spends his time with capitalists, directors and shareholders of publishing houses, rather than with the humble and impoverished editors. It is the salaried and depressed editor sweating on the afternoon Tube rather than the grandee proprietor at Ascot who will determine whether I succeed or fail. He mentioned again the possibility of an office job in Sidgwick and Jackson (he met Lord Longford). At least, that would be the beginning of a real literary life in London. I could live on bread and soup in a bedsit in Holborn or Camden Town, yet another aspirant to fame like all the London Irish before me. There is already a huge contingent of UCC people in London.

Rereading the 40 pages of my play, "Local Election". Pubs and meetings and grocers' shops; the thing disgusts me. Too much Fianna Fáil, but my character Edward says, "We have had too much talk. We've had too many lies and too much silence". I suppose that will always be the story with FF. I must stay away from it now. I must stay away from them for my imagination's sake. I saw Jackie Fahy TD and his Cappoquin "fixer" John Fraher outside Mescall's shop in the Square. Must stay away from them. I like John, though. He was one of the heroes of my childhood. I spent more of my childhood with the Frahers, with Paddy, Eddie and John, than I did with my own family. John introduced me to my Bray cousins who were in the Mount Melleray Fianna Fáil Cumann. It was John who got me into FF. He said I must join the party of my grandparents and Mount Melleray cousins. Now I'm trying to put him into a play. John is my FF father-figure because my own father is more a Labour man, a socialist, an idle, complaining intellectual. I will never be able to separate John Fraher from his Mercedes, his love of gadgets, his telephone, his minibuses. Whenever I sat into John's Merc I was rejecting my father's asceticism. I reject it still. It doesn't put bread on a child's table.

5 August 1974

Molly Keane, relaxed in the summer heat of the patio, read my poems for about twenty minutes. She likes the Protestant Church poem as well as "Shattered Frost". Again, she pointed out a fault in "Shattered Frost" – the totally unsatisfactory closing couplet. Pat Crotty in UCC pointed out the same weakness. I will have to take advice. It's the only way to improve. AE remains a minor poet because he refused to change his verses, even when Yeats pointed out mistakes. In order to be great one must be ruthless with the structure and flow of the words. The poem should not be the poet's spoilt child. Great art form must have its basis in great craftsmanship and deliberate craftsmanship, not in a doting parentage.

10 August 1974

Michael Hartnett has decided to write exclusively in Irish. He shouldn't have gone to live in Dublin in the first place; he should have stayed in London or Limerick. Now his head has been turned. Perhaps the Irish language will be like a second wife to him:

> As gold-green moss
> close to the bark
> when the winds toss
> my limbs to tragedy and dark.

But it is sad to lose such a good poet in English. Almost like Ledwidge, but very primary and raw. It's amazing how much poets are like each other in their lofty ideals and ideas: at first all poets react in the same way – that primary movement away from convention. Then they go their own unique way according to their backgrounds, education, personal possibilities, etc. But we all suffer this primary break with the stream of social unconsciousness, the unconsciousness of conventional living. Like all poets, Hartnett is just finding a new way to escape. It's not just a language question; I mean a question of Irish or English language. We must expect a looser kind of Irishness. Each one of us has to work towards a much wider definition of what it means to be Irish. We have to break away from Corkery's *Prefaces*: Irish life just isn't that simple. To hear Sir Richard Keane of Cappoquin House proclaim in a voice and accent like the Duke of Edinburgh or Sir Anthony Eden that he feels completely Irish is to have one's views of nationality severely challenged. Politically, I don't quite accept Sir Richard's proclamation, but socially and historically he is completely entitled to his own Irishness. This is where complications always begin in any Irish discussion: I'm convinced that only literature and art can reconcile these impossible tensions of identity. Only literature has that capacity for *stretch*. And, as poets, it is literature we proclaim.

12 October 1974

Good lecture from John Montague today about Dryden and Pope. He delighted in talking about the Restoration of the Stuart king. And Dryden's political timing – when the king was brought back from France, Dryden tried to bring back French theatre as well. Also, the echoes of Milton in Dryden, especially in "Absalom and Achitophel". Later, I could see JM identifying himself with Alexander Pope; with Pope's Catholicism, with his "Essay on Criticism". John spoke very well about the "Rape of the Lock" and the whole mock-epic tradition, especially as a narrative of a feud between two English Catholic families. JM quotes Hobbes approvingly: "Imagination is nothing else but sense decaying or weakened by the absence of the object" and then he quoted Blake on "the object" – "natural objects deaden and weaken the imagination in me". Montague told us we should read Ian Jack's *Augustan Satire* and F.R. Leavis's *Revaluation*. When his lecture was over there was a mad scramble of ambitious scholars. They couldn't wait to get to the library to take the drug of a Leavis essay. Had JM mentioned a Margaret Drabble essay there would probably have been a fist-fight at the exit between those same creatures. This mad scramble to ingest received opinion, all to be regurgitated in the vomitorium of the exam hall: it disgusts me. It is an act of deepest humiliation: it would disgust any true poet. I am more and more convinced that poets are people who refuse to submit to learning. We are creatures beyond reform, and revel in the freedom that is conferred by ignorance.

19 February 1975

Charles Haughey has been recalled to the front bench of Fianna Fáil. The party was forced into accepting him back. He has a brilliantly calculating mind. He has become the Fianna Fáil spokesman on health. Of course he is a man who can never again be trusted, and – in the long term – his reappearance will do untold damage to the party. However, I doubt if I will be a member of FF for very long more. I shall find it very difficult to break away, for most of the local people I know and like are supporters of Fianna Fáil. There are also dangerous people, like JX and DX. When I think that they are vociferous, opportunistic supporters of Charles Haughey I realize what a dreadful future has just opened for the Soldiers of Destiny: as long as it's only FF and not the country that suffers. I live in the hope that Haughey will end up in jail soon, otherwise every honest and respectable person will leave FF.

5 May 1975

Robert Graves came to visit us at UCC. I sat beside him and Mrs Graves at the Oyster Tavern dinner. He said to me that Rupert Brooke was the finest of the Georgians. He also said that "of that lot" Winston Churchill was the only gentleman. He said that poetry is no longer being written in England but that he got "the sense of poetry" when he landed in Ireland. At the reception afterwards he was besieged by people; very fatigued with a face the colour of aluminium. He looked at the crush of students, then looked at me, the Auditor of the English Lit., and seemed very frightened. I went over and talked to him for a while. Montague was there; in absolutely great form. At one point in the evening, Graves at dinner turned to me and said, "You know, Thomas, I have been to Heaven". I thought he had taken too much drink, until he showed me his box (silver with what looked like an emerald set into the lid), a little box of hallucinogenic mushrooms that had been a gift from Carlos Castenada. I doubt if Professor Lucy would have approved. Graves's wife slapped him on the wrist and said, "You mustn't ruin that young boy with your dirty mushrooms!" He returned his magic mushrooms to his pocket very sheepishly. What an old devil he is, what a pure, irresponsible lyricist of the mid-century. Still, his sanity is recovered every ten years with every new version of his *Collected Poems*.

Later, at the not-very-successful seminar in the English Department, Graves was asked if he had any advice for budding poets. He answered, "Poets! If you are budding come into bloom!"

28 July 1975

DHF gave a terrific picnic today by the river under the old Lyre Bridge. Brilliant sunshine. Mrs Merrill of Villierstown Rectory and Mrs Phyllis

Mitchell, an old friend of Dean Acheson, of Fortwilliam House, Ballyduff, as well as the DHF and the Stevensons of Castle Dodard on the high road from Lismore. The Stevensons used to live in North-East India, and they still have an imperial aura, an aura of the Raj. Pam Stevenson, a woman in her mid-forties, is spectacularly beautiful, absolutely ravishing. She is like the beautiful Sylvia Syms in *Ice-Cold in Alex*. She is the most beautiful woman in County Waterford, certainly. I find it difficult not to stare at her. When she catches my eye she stares back, laughing sweetly because she knows the effect her looks have on a very young man. Her husband is a real colonial gentleman of the old school, self-possessed, self-satisfied as a man who sleeps with a Kimberley diamond on his pillow. Whenever they visit Glenshelane House the atmosphere becomes charged with a sexual energy. All the men in the company form a kind of unconscious choreography of Martinis, snacks, cushions offered, coats taken, seats vacated closer to the fire in the drawing-room beneath the portrait of the equally beautiful Lady Inez FitzGerald. DHF is always trying to seat Pam where he can have both his mother and Pam in his line of sight as he speaks. It is graceful and interesting behaviour, but it is charged sexually, even if all the people involved are over 40: sex must be beyond them all at this stage.

6 October 1975

Montague and Ó Corráin had a poem in *The Irish Times* on Saturday.

21 January 1976

Poems in *The Irish Times* and in the *Examiner*'s "New Poetry" page. "Grandmother" was broadcast on RTÉ. Up at Montague's last night. John was upset by the review of *A Slow Dance* in *The Irish Times*. Edna Longley's praise comes only at the end of the review, within which she calls him a "fussy" writer. I said, "John, isn't it better to be called fussy than fuzzy?" I see that William Peskett's book got a review in *The Irish Press*, but not Gregory O'Donoghue's book. Why? Why is everything from the South ignored?

20 May 1976

Was it Yeats or Joyce said that a writer knows everything he needs to know at the age of 20? A writer's life is the search for a method, a style. We are given the world as a proposition, as a problem to be solved. A literary life is not the accumulation of ideas, but a reconciliation with the proposition that is the writer's life. To answer this proposition Yeats placed the poet as a special being before the world; on the other hand traditional Romantics place the poet in the world as a suffering being. In all great art the world is a problem in the process of being solved. Like Pascal's father, the poet resists the temptation of "information gathering". It is through poetry that we find ourselves; that is, we shed information and get to the core of something.

Yeats never believed in a little poetry of little people. For him the act of making was a mighty act. All poets should continue to honour Yeats for that belief alone.

15 September 1976

Molly Keane came to stay at Glenshelane tonight. We gave her a heated room, nice new blankets and an electric fire. "Anything else?" DHF asked her as he left her bedroom. "Oh, yes please. A hot water bottle, dear." She brought two volumes of Proust for me: "A little light reading. Thomas, you must read all of Proust, all of him, I tell you". We spoilt Molly by giving her breakfast in bed. She wanted to talk about Proust again. I had tried the two early volumes of "The Guermantes Way" in the DHF's library. But I need to read more Beckett than Proust. And Strindberg: Beckett had seen Strindberg's *Ghost Factory* [*sic*] twice before sitting down to write *Waiting for Godot*.

I spoke to Molly for a long time about her book *Conversation Piece*, especially the long story "Pullinstown". –

> Inside the archway I paused. I love stables and horses and grooms, the cheerful sound of buckets, the heady smell of straw, the orderly fussiness of a saddle-room; always the same and ever different. The mind halts, feeling its way into gear with a new brave set of values at the moment when one sets foot within a stable-yard.

Molly was delighted that I had been reading her work very carefully. Nobody reads her now, except for Ascendancy friends along the Blackwater. My questions were unexpected, so much so that when she rose from her bed she was in terrific form. Also, today, an American lawyer called Tyler recommended a book by Leon Uris called *Trinity*. She promised to send me this book which is, according to Molly Keane's arch-enemy, Lady Keane, very "pro-IRA". At lunch there was a woman who is divorced from a director of Covent Garden. This woman promised to send me something else. Glenshelane is too busy at the moment. I can't get any bloody writing done.

26 February 1977
I now have 36 publishable poems.

St Patrick's Day 1977
Spent the day with Dervla Murphy in Lismore. She lives in an atmosphere of scholarship and travel: there's a very British nineteenth-century atmosphere in her library, even more than in the old Carton Library at Glenshelane House. She has really picked up the journey of discovery where her mentor, W.E.D. Allen of Belfast, and St John Philby and Freya Stark and people like them left off. But she has a less imperial view of the world. She understands though – like Wilfred Scawen Blunt and T.E. Lawrence and Laurens van der Post – that the Islamic world between Istanbul and Kashmir is an entirely different place, a charged kingdom as strange and unrelated to us as the planet Mars. One of the great disruptive horrors she fears is the creeping Westernization of these lands. To Westernize the Arab world would be a disaster of astronomical proportions. Not only would it ruin an entire central Asian civilisation, but, thinks Dervla, it would bring about the ruin of the West. (Like Fidel Castro, she looks forward to the latter event with great relish).

She hates war, seeing it as encouraged and funded by the arms industry of the world, and the main purpose of the arms industry is to create regional victories that smooth out cultural-legal differences for international capital. In a sense, Dervla is a classical Marxist without the Communism. The fact is it is not the West, but Islam, that would survive such a political and military Armageddon. She said that, irony of ironies, it is the Cold War that keeps the irreconcilable forces of Christianity and Islam apart. She says that if the pernicious espionage activities of the American and Russian security priesthood (with their nuclear bombs as tabernacles) fell away then international diplomacy would revert once more to the assassin's knife and the guerrilla's bullet of the Steppe. The world would return to political first principles as outlined in our beloved Mr Allen's *Problems of Turkish Power in the Sixteenth Century* – it would return to a conflict of continental versus oceanic powers, a long war between the Steppe and the Atlantic West.

As I motorcycled back from Lismore, a damp roadway, a dangerous wind, I thought how in this world murder is just waiting to become an intimate and personal activity once more. We move relentlessly from wars on the plains of Europe to a more intimate, opportunistic assassination and counter-strike. In terms of war, the world will become more like Ireland.

30 April 1977
The Old Days of the Party or Last Days of the Party: it is the party of old men, of tobacco-blocks and medallioned watches. Old men who tell the same stories framed by Guinness and Smithwicks. Saturdays, after the last meetings they held in the small room:

> You planned to leave with dignity: after
> Years of election committees and country
> Meetings you had hoped for an after-glow
> Of respect, a friendly exchange of roles:
> Instead, you discovered a packed meeting,
> Delegates like matadors waiting for blood.

The father of course isn't my poor father, but John, our FF neighbour. With me, it will always be the father-figure and not the father. This is one thing I've learned after a year of studying Roethke under Montague.

17 June 1977
I go blindly through the days. I feel so sorrowful. My father dead at the age of 55: his entire life a terrible struggle, a series of deep humiliations. Life was beyond him. Why didn't my father go away to England, to America? He would have thrived in Queens, NY or South Boston. He was absolutely brilliant, a sharp, methodical mathematical mind, a bundle of nerves, yes, but so intelligent and so admiring of displays of intelligence. He would have prospered elsewhere, but something was missing: will-power, a necessary aggression.

25 September 1977
Today I applied for a job in Cork City Library. It would mean finally leaving Glenshelane House, my poetry nest since I was seventeen. But I need to get away from the parish where my father died. A poem is not a political document. There is a loss suffered; a father or father-figure, and a growing

into grief. There is witness and anger at such loss; the voice in the poem is the witness. But at the end of the day a poem is its own father. I must write without the slightest fear. Right now I am in the embrace of truth, but that is cold comfort. I feel a complete absence of warmth. FF's pact with the Gaullists was a complete sell-out. God almighty, Fianna Fáil is gone to the dogs. Literally. Dogs now run the party. Dogs probably win elections.

27 September 1977

Still working on the poem on the party; the witness to failure, the father-figure who collapses in the party. Still too unclear, too unsure. Reading Anne Sexton's "45 Mercy Street". Jesus Christ, what a woman. I'd like to put her in a sleeping-compartment on a long Russian train-journey with my tormenter, Sr Una Nelly of University College, Cork.

20 November 1977

President Sadat of Egypt has gone to Israel. God bless him. He is a noble person, as noble and gentlemanly as all Egyptians. I hope there will be an historic compromise; the return of pre-1967 Arab lands, a homeland for Palestinians, but a guarantee of security for the state of Israel so that Ben-Gurion's own proud people can live in peace. It's now 30 years since Israel became independent.

7 March 1978

Fever went down this morning. 103 degrees. Kidney pain. If I die soon I'll surely die in March. The worst possible time for a gardener to die; and inconvenient for any poet with new potatoes to sow.

15 March 1978

Reading César Vallejo today. A peculiar obsession with numbers, dice, luck and ill-luck. Not as good, certainly not as monumental, as Neruda. But some of the rhythms are the same; the nuances and that peculiar soft-whoosh wordplay. Poetry to the Latins seems a lush exuberance. Even in Ungaretti – the thin phrases don't hide the exuberance. Wish we could bring some of that exuberance into Irish poetry; the softness of wordplay especially, a sensuous South. Even in sorrow, exploring it and exploring the outward-unwinding-growing as sorrow recedes and life filters through again. One should try to use the sensuous wordplay, the Latin richness of sound and the physicality of grief. Letter from Seán Dunne. He is much happier now; sounds much happier as well. Said he saw "Greatrakes" in *The Irish Press* and liked it. John Ennis praised it too, as did Liam Murphy. I thought it too traditional for those Liverpool-sound Waterford City muses. John Ennis has had another child, a daughter. God bless his balls, wrote Seán.

22 March 1978

Cearbhall Ó Dálaigh died. A most ill-used, exploited and brilliant scholar-patriot. Life has treated him badly and unfairly. He had just moved into a new house at Sneem, County Kerry. What a beautiful man he was, and talented. He had just begun working on his books after coming out of hospital. As far as I'm concerned, all of the best are gone now. He was certainly one of the best of this miserable nation of ours.

23 March 1978

Busy cleaning out my room. I put my books together – the ones I need in Cork. Over three Gouldings fertilizer bags full of books! Incredible, the number of books I accumulate. The three bags I'm taking away in my leaking Renault 4 hardly make any difference to my library here at Glenshelane House.

29 April 1978

Hitched a ride from an Englishman all the way from Cappoquin to Cork. He was fascinated by Cork, the port and the city centre. He thought that Cork city had great unused commercial potential. The conversation oscillated between the unused commercial and consumer, rather than industrial, capacity of the Irish economy and the fiction of Sir Charles Lever. A shrewd Englishman with a great sense of being the citizen of a free world – one gets that sense from almost all the senior ex-military and wealthy Englishmen who rebuilt Europe after the war (the friends of DHF). And, as usual, great affection for Germany and the Germans.

27 May 1978

Saturday at Glenshelane. Dolmen Press sent me the completed copies of my book. Publication date is 22 June, officially. Exquisite production. If only I could get some hard covers. Reading Gide's journals again. I love Gide, his intelligence and good manners. His comfortable wealth attracts me too, an aristocratic ease that spreads to everything in his nature and renders his opinions sanguine and cosmopolitan. There's no doubt that the lack of a need to earn a living has given him a tendency to repeat himself, to be spendthrift and repetitive with ideas. As in all aristocratic, habitual life there is an overwhelming capacity for repetition and self-parody. Even his Mozart exercises, the undoubtedly homosexual night prowls, the train journeys, all become a form of self-parody in his journals. Sometimes he's aware of this tendency in his daily life. In an entry for 23 September 1917 he writes: "I should like now a more abrupt, less obliging way of speaking". He was so much a master of his own daily life that the abruptness of things to which ordinary mortals are exposed did seem like luxurious moments, or epiphanies.

29 May 1978

Nancy McCarthy, Frank O'Connor's old love, rang me at the library the other day. She wanted to know if I knew of any letters from Frank O'Connor to Corkery or Dermot Foley still existing in our files. Macmillan and Harriet Sheehy, O'Connor's widow, are planning to publish a selection of his letters. Good old Michael O'Donovan. The well-to-do McCarthy "Moll" still working for him – it seems to me that Nancy defines her life now through the validation of having been loved by Frank O'Connor. That's sad; yet on the other hand it keeps the memory of O'Connor alive in Cork. Met John Montague in the Long Valley. He said I should go barefoot throughout the summer to increase my sensuous perceptions. I think this is what he would want to do, he is such a sensuous creature. I showed *The First Convention* to him. He liked it very much, but thought that Dolmen should have kept the price down. John had had lunch with the singer Mary O'Hara. She has asked him to write a song for her. If he does write it maybe he'll make some real money. Poets never make any real money. Poets are like curates in the Church of England. We must abandon all hope of property and think only of finding a decent living in an obscure parish.

I found this in Gide's journals, an entry for 3 January 1892:

Our whole life is spent in sketching an in-eradicable portrait of ourselves … We recount our lives and lie to ourselves, but our life will not lie; it will recount our soul, which will stand before God in its usual posture.

(Editor's Note: "DHF" is Denis Henry FitzGerald, born in 1911, son of Lord Henry FitzGerald and grandson of the Duke of Leinster. He was educated at Eton and Sandhurst after childhoods spent at the family homes of Carton House, Johnstown Castle and Kilkea Castle. He fought in the Normandy Campaign and crossed the Rhine as Colonel of the Irish Guards regiment in 1945. He was a partner in Panmure Gordon, a London stockbroker, and restored an abandoned garden at Glenshelane House, Cappoquin, Co Waterford with the help of Thomas McCarthy between 1973 and 1987. He died in 2006.)

Thomas McCarthy was born at Cappoquin, Co Waterford, in 1954. A public librarian in Cork for over 30 years, he was a writing fellow at the International Writing Programme, University of Iowa, in 1978–79 and a Visiting Professor at Macalester College, Minnesota, in 1994–95. He is the author of eight collections of poems, including The First Convention *(The Dolmen Press, 1978),* Mr Dineen's Careful Parade *(Anvil, 1999),* Merchant Prince *(Anvil, 2005) and* The Last Geraldine Officer *(Anvil, 2009). He is a member of Aosdána.*

POEM

Gerard Smyth

SOUTH OF THE BORDER

We have seen it at the head of the march,
seen it dance, seen it dangle:
the Easter flag that the south wind catches.
It is part of the pomp, pageant fodder –
the billowy Tricolour hoisted in honour
of the seven back from Purdah:
Plunkett, Clarke, McDermott, Ceannt,
Connolly, Pearse, McDonagh.

It is the flag they carry when the State
pays homage with drums, salutes and rhetoric
less honest than the men it praises –
Tone and Davis and whoever else
is still remembered when they lay a wreath
for all the dead beside the monument,
under the epitaph for those
who if they reappeared to form a circle
would see a time of yearning –
the consequence of sorry days:
our Aegean stables but no Hercules to clean them,
and the harvest of *savage indignation.*

Gerard Smyth worked for over 30 years as a journalist with The Irish Times. *He is the author of seven collections of poems, most recently* The Fullness of Time: New and Selected Poems *(Dedalus Press, 2007). He lives in Dublin.*

CLAY PIGEONS
(memoir)

Harry Clifton

In our secular Eden.

On the morning of Easter Monday, Al Hocevar phones. He ought to be in Oregon, thousands of miles away, finishing his semester, in a linoleum-floored classroom with a circle of acolytes, a pile of mimeographed drafts. Instead he is passing through to Ljubljana on a Spring break, to check things there for his going back in July. The house, the Australians renting it, the present situation. Am I aware George Bush will be meeting Vladimir Putin there in June for their first summit? He is ambivalent about this, having a foot in both camps, but old-world nostalgia has gripped him for the moment. He is only stopping over in Paris to make sure his wife is still on board.

"I have a great student", he says excitedly, "better than the professors, those idiots. A thoroughbred. Multilingual. Needs to rein herself in, out of respect for the others. Maybe a bit heavy intellectually, a bit scholarly. For this kind of thing you need levity too …"

"When are you coming back?"

"In May. We'll talk about it then, over a coffee. John is doing readings everywhere …"

And then he is gone, and Chatillon on its Bank Holiday flows back in. Since the start of April, the new rhythm has taken over the city. Communal indolence, strings of public holidays, and departures that will go on now until the *rentrée* in September. Shoutings upstairs, parties on balconies at night, as working life breaks up. But the wild, windy weather that drenched March lingers into April, the greatest Paris rainfall since 1873. In Brittany, Picardy, Normandy, villages and fields are under water. In Paris, the Seine roars greenly through its arches, the *bateaux mouches* are cancelled, the trees stand starkly out of flooded riverside walks. But Spring has arrived, in spite of everything – the weightless moment of yellow and pink blossom in the gardens of Clamart and Meudon, of flowers in the concrete tubs, and workers turning the clay in the public parks under a scudding grey sky.

"After the twentieth century", the priest at Easter Mass said yesterday, "it's hard to believe in Resurrection …" Paris, in the local elections, has swung Left. But here, the Gaullist mayor has won again, without the need for a run-off. The yellow apartment buildings between the stilled cranes tell their own story, of a new middle class moved in, a new generation, on the Right. In the real elections, that is the direction the whole country will go – against Paris, against the intellectuals, the *bien pensants* of race integration. Back to the values of Aveyron, *France Profonde*.

"You're not on holidays?" I ask the North African arranging tomatoes outside his *alimentaire*.

"For us", he says with restrained bitterness, "there are no holidays."

I have gone there times out of mind, in the depths of summer and winter, in the emptiness of public holidays, through the twilit streets, to the only light still on. Spirits, wine, at double the price. And the little Algerian boy between the aisles, forever keeping watch for the robbers, the break-ins.

"Pauvre France!" a war veteran sighs, as a coloured woman screams for the release of her shoe at the cash register. He looks around for support, but everyone is suddenly staring, embarrassed, at the ground.

Where does Danielle, whose flat I am to visit this afternoon, stand in all this? As I carry groceries back, the day has freshened and brightened. There is yellow broom on the divide in the Versailles dual carriageway. Apple-blossoms cling to the wet, black trees of condemned gardens. A limp arm of wisteria trails over a wall. The nest-smell of thrushes and blackbirds hangs in the air. After the dead months, time-awareness blooms again, a season of transformations.

Meanwhile, in Doran's Ireland, Easter Monday is as complicated as it has ever been.

———

"So did you take part in the public process?" I ask her that afternoon, in the tiny flat she shares with her boyfriend in the eleventh arrondissement. "Did you vote for a person or a party?"

For a moment, I feel like her father, interrogating her. I have not come all this way across town to talk politics, but to live for a moment in the energy, the electric force-field, of a young French woman dedicated to poetry. An exception. Even getting here I met with the other energy, the blind untrammelled energy of the disaffected young, cannoning, ricocheting in and out of metro carriages, living out their underground afternoons. Boys with military haircuts but no orders, waiting for someone to beat the drum they will march to. But not the drum of politics, of votes and elections in the understood sense. Another drum.

"I posted my vote home", she says, "I couldn't afford to travel to Poitiers just to put an X on the paper. But if I didn't use my vote, how could I complain if things in this society are wrong?"

She has not demonstrated in Paris yet, not in the year she has been up from Poitiers. Only in passing has she come upon the marches, the one against the Debret immigration law for example, where you have to declare if a foreigner is living in your flat or employed by you. There was a stand-off at the Pont Saint Michel that time, with the Le Pen supporters on the other side, who had already drowned an Algerian in the Seine. She was walking back from a class in the Sorbonne and felt the tension.

"Many of our friends don't vote at all", her boyfriend Christof says as he places a tray of weak tea and three mugs between us.

"They put blank votes in the ballot box", she says impatiently, "as a kind of protest. They make no difference, no matter how many there are."

"Do you take sugar?" Christof asks, as he hands me the clear green tea. From a compact disc machine on the bookshelf, modern jazz describes its aural arabesques on the air. Two gentle people, the apartment they share is behind a construction yard, up a flight of wooden stairs, the windows of its two rooms overlooking another yard. Hot sun streams through now, in the clearing afternoon, and the rooms are uncomfortable.

"It was someone from Poitiers who already had the studio", she says, "so I just took it over."

"We are very lucky students", Christof says self-consciously, "and we know it."

The second room also is plain and lino-floored. On two desks, against opposite walls, are word-processing terminals, ganglia, wires, the paraphernalia of contemporary information retrieval. On the wall is a nude study in charcoal of a young woman in a bed. An inbuilt mezzanine, piled with white duvets, is where they sleep. That and the sprawling nude are the only concessions to sensuality in the austere mindscape of thesis preparation. He stays at his desk while she and I adjourn to the living-room to continue our discussion of the Irish poet who is the subject of her *maîtresse*. Next year she will live in Ireland, and after that who knows? She speaks of Paris as somewhere exciting but temporary. We come to a poem in the Irish poet's second collection where love meets biology, and her face darkens.

"Soon I will be ready for children", she says, with implicit reference to the young fellow next door, "but *he* isn't – yet. I tell him – one day you will change ..."

Unlike him, she seems to have a life behind her already – boyfriends lived with, on and off, for years, in the near presence of her ever-loving family of New Age Catholics at Poitiers who wait for the closing of the circle. Meanwhile, there is this city of intellect and sensation, with the riptide of biology flowing beneath it. The heat, the afternoon, the dried flowers in a glass on the coffee-table – all seem already like a way-station, part of a trajectory that will bring her, a flower-child in leather bellbottoms, back again to the oldest convention.

"Do you mind if I smoke?" she asks, rolling a thin twist of tobacco and paper between her fingers, puffing fastidiously at this little indulgence, dabbing the ashes into a glass receptacle. I remember Al saying, they have nothing, you know, to rebel with now, not like our own generation. Sex, for them, is unsafe. The hard drugs are dangerous. And they are apolitical, too afraid for their careers and examinations. All they have left is cigarettes.

"On the stairs", she says, "the junkies sleep if the door to the construction yard has been left open at night. In the mornings we trip over them there, or their syringes and needles. It's not very pleasant ..."

The eleventh, east of the fashionable Bastille area, is a *quartier populaire*, a pocket of common humanity at the heart of affluent Paris. The yard below, she says, is where shell-cases were brought in the First World War, to be melted down. Jewish artisans lived in these very rooms, and the streets all around, till the days of deportation. Now it is the rich, the trendy who invade, spreading in like dry rot from the wealthier areas, turning the old workshops inside out for sterile, modern living-space, alienation. We don't go out much at night, she says, it is too costly. Maybe now and then, to the flats of student friends.

My jacket has been hung, reverently, on a hanger behind the door. I am, after all, a *professeur*, in a system that respects professional distance. Even in shirtsleeves, though, it feels hot. I imagine how intolerable it will be here once the real summer arrives. It is five-thirty, and we have worked for nearly two hours. Christof puts his head round the door and listens in.

"What are you reading?" I ask her, putting aside the tasks of the afternoon.

"Rimbaud", she answers, "Apollinaire. Christof is obsessed with Mallarmé. Recently we visited his house outside Paris, at Ivry."

The latest French poetry, she says, is too hermetic, too much a thing of special editions on handmade paper, sold to bibliophiles, read by *cénacles*. But there is no social reality in it, none of the buzz and squalor and ephemeral beauty of Paris in its passing hours. For that you have to go back to the nineteenth century. Except perhaps for Bonnefoy, although he is not a poet of the city, but of forms and archetypes. He read his poems recently, she says, to a respectable crowd in Poitiers. She was there.

"It is the fault of the publishers too", she adds. "They only publish poets who are already old. They give no encouragement, they are too conservative. Christof sent some of his writings to Gallimard and they replied that they only wanted a conventional story."

I too had been given Christof's writings, a slice of the life of rue Saint Denis, the *rue des prostitutes*. The medieval slum quarter behind the streetfronts, the fetid wooden stairs with their endless coming and going of women and clients, the pimps and strong-arm men on stools at every landing, and the sad little attic rooms, the bargaining, the hysteria. He had crossed over, it seemed, into that dream – or nightmare – world where clothes fall soundlessly, money changes hands and bodies meet or do not meet, and afterwards all is forgotten. He had brought something back, a fugitive snatched reality, through whatever door he had passed. A Paris reality, old as Villon or Baudelaire. About the feelings of Danielle – *if you cannot be good, be careful* – I did not ask.

"There are those of us", says Christof, returning to an earlier topic, "who gave up on life by the age of 20. They will never vote."

"Except", she says, "for the party that wants to protect the city pigeons from being killed."

Outside, the dry flutter of wings in the courtyard gives an odd depth to the hollow space between buildings. South of the city, on the hill street of Chatillon, pigeons from Paris roost in their thousands on the roofs of the new apartments, spattering the tiles with bird-lime, vanishing at night through the needle's eye of a top-floor window in the Society for the Protection of Birds and settling there in a noise of cages, a smell of Franciscan squalor, till the demolition squads move in and the wrecking ball does its work.

"Do you ever travel?" I ask Danielle.

"My grandparents did", she says, as if that suffices for three generations. "They met in Vietnam, in an internment camp. My mother was born there, but she left at the age of five, when Ho Chi Minh drove the French out. She went back recently, when it opened up again."

"The French travel badly", Christof says, "they can't adapt to other societies. They think they have given Justice and Reason to everyone else."

"*Auto-satisfaction française*", Danielle says contemptuously, as she gets me my coat off the hanger.

The street beyond the construction yard is hot and empty at this hour. Plane-trees dapple the pavements with fresh green shade. There is an air of lightness and delicacy, of the dancing shadows of translucent leaves at my feet. I would like to come back here sometime, maybe in another life, and live it as they are living it, unburdened by history or memory. A bookshop spills its second-hand wares onto trestle-tables outside. Two Vietnamese eat noodles at the front table of a tiny food-shop. An Algerian looks out of his *alimentaire*, checks his tomatoes and oranges. At the corner of Saint Antoine, a woman sits at a café window, pekingese at her feet, waiting for passing trade. I have to stop and tell myself that this bird-haunted evening street is democracy, is the West, is perhaps as good as things can get on the face of the earth, and if it is not loved as perhaps only two young lovers in their early twenties can love it, then poetry, beauty are nothing but empty words.

———

At the *periphérique*, between Paris and Malakoff, two East European women stand. A car draws up, one gets in. Away they drive to a neighbouring street. The other preens herself in a powder-puff mirror. Another car draws up. Suddenly, the traffic island is empty.

Men circling, for diversion from their lonely selves on a Bank Holiday, at the afternoon hour of aimlessness, faithlessness. The hour of lowest self-image in a secular society.

Harry Clifton was born in Dublin in 1952 and has travelled widely in Africa, Asia and Europe. He is the author of seven collections of poems, most recently Secular Eden: Paris Notebooks 1994–2004 *(Wake Forest University Press, 2007), and two prose publications. The above chapter is from a forthcoming memoir. He is the current Ireland Chair of Poetry, and lives in Dublin.*

RIGGING THE RISKS

Janet Dine

Why commercial law kills.

I

Poverty is not only endemic in poor nations,
but equally real in "developed" countries

We estimate that 1.75 billion people in developing countries experience
multidimensional poverty, meaning that they suffer from deprivations in
health, education and their standards of living. More than half of these
individuals live in South Asia, though national rates are highest in Sub-
Saharan Africa.
(United Nations Development Programmes, 2010)

The following UN figures represent an underestimate of the deaths and
suffering caused by global poverty. Very much an underestimate – as they
omit problems caused by over-exploitation of natural resources, for example
mudslides caused by excessive logging and deforestation in the Philippines.
Nor do they include disasters caused by climate change. But even using these
conservative figures we certainly know that the problem of world poverty is
catastrophic. Of 6133 million human beings in 2009–10, some

- 799 million are undernourished.
- 50,000 humans die daily of poverty-related causes.
- 884 million people in the world do not have access to safe
  water, roughly one in eight of the world's population.
- 2.6 billion people in the world do not have access to adequate
  sanitation, almost two fifths of the world's population.
- 1.4 million children die every year from diarrhoea caused by
  unclean water and poor sanitation – 4,000 child deaths a day,
  or one child every 20 seconds – which equates to 160 infant
  school classrooms lost every single day to an entirely
  preventable public health crisis.

All this means the global poverty death toll over the 15 years since the end of the
Cold War was around 270 million, roughly equal to the population of the US.

So this is a subject of the utmost seriousness. And like all such subjects it attracts a particular brand of black humour. My favourite story is that of Bono when trying to get his rock-and-roll mates to perform at a charity concert for the Third World. Clapping his hands he says, "Every time I clap my hands a child in Africa dies". Mick Jagger replies: "Well for fuck sake, stop clapping then".

Poverty is also becoming endemic in "developed" countries because of the global financial crisis which started in 2008 and continues. Perhaps the Crisis should be redefined as a *debt* crisis rather than a *financial* crisis. In 2008 when I wrote my professorship's inaugural lecture I did not expect that the powerful countries of the rich Western bloc, including Europe and America, would be susceptible to the same problems that bedevilled the poor nations, particularly the debt burden. However, it has happened and the theory behind the economics is exactly the same.

Commercial law is predicated on a capitalistic market system in many countries, particularly since the great collapse of the Soviet empire. China and some other Asian countries have different varieties of economic system. However, the aggressive neo-liberal capitalism which overtook American and European economies has left those societies weakened and broken. Capitalism is simple in essence: goods are traded by humans to try to alleviate their needs or wants. The tool to grease the interplay of commerce is a simple concept: the humble contract. This is a brilliant concept, not only because it works, but also because it is ethically sound. Contract is supposed to be a way of distributing goods equally. But like any other human institution it can be corrupted. This essay is about the corruption of several institutions based on a contractual model: *multinational companies* (including banks) and *international financial institutions* (IFIs), particularly the International Monetary Fund (IMF).

However, my thesis must start at the beginning. Humans are frightened. For Christians this is the real moral of the *Genesis* story; God is all-benevolent but since the time of Adam and Eve understood freedom, all people are doomed to live in fear. Of course, other religions have similar doctrines and myths. What does this mean in modern society? How can our economic model cope with the fear factor? Since human beings are social animals, we banded into groups for organizing our needs. Each individual fears risk, however; each person has different things that she is frightened about. Clearly basic needs are paramount: they are water, food, warmth and shelter, including the shelter of each other.

What does this mean in contemporary society? One way that human beings have used to lessen their fear is to cooperate in organized groups. However, this immediately means that there is another risk, which is that each individual person fears other human beings. This is the paradox of the human condition; and it is crudely illustrated by two ways of organising economic concerns, the polar opposites of capitalism and communism. The risk for people is lessened by these two diverging concepts. Capitalism fears domination by other people, which means that society is individually based; communism prefers to ameliorate the risk by banding together, thus meeting society's needs that way. There are paradoxes within paradoxes, because the tension is exacerbated by the way that the opposing societies organize their concerns, leading to strains and tensions. The communist bloc tried to organize their affairs in an egalitarian way and this led to dictatorship, since humans have an entrepreneurial streak which cannot be easily blocked, and which had to be stopped by harsh measures – a wonderful paradox itself, since the whole idea was to have a system predicated on equality and freedom rather than fear. On the other hand, capitalism wanted freedom but found that the risk was inequality, often leading to poverty, which constrains freedom anyway: again there are paradoxes, and they are fundamental, often leaving the "common people" in distress. Each system of course went too far: in the communist system, not enough individual autonomy was allowed, so that democracy shrivelled; in capitalism, poverty means the very poor have no freedom, for if people do not have their basic needs satisfied, their political aspirations are largely thwarted. Both systems were/are *extreme* – meaning that some individuals were/are killed by the regime, and human rights violations were/are rife.

The role of commercial law in a market economy is to allocate risk. Controlled economies attempted to eliminate the risks of commercial transactions to individuals, transferring the risk of failure to the whole community. The move to a market economy from a controlled economy thus entails complex political questions about which market participants shall bear the risk of market transactions.

II

The role of commercial law in a "free-market" system

The thesis of this essay is that international and national commercial laws – written mostly by wealthy élites – bear significant blame for the appalling statistics of poverty cited above. In order to discover why, we have to consider the role of commercial law in a market economy. Its role is to allocate risk …

I first began to understand this connection when involved in a commercial law project in Russia (and I have subsequently been drafting laws in transition economies). In Russia I was with a team with lawyers from France, Germany, Spain and England. It became clear to us that we were not communicating with our Russian counterparts and that this non-communication was more than just language-based. The Russians were approaching the law from a perspective that understood commercial law as a series of regulations which attributed certain roles to individuals within the system. The Western Europeans, however, realised that a move to a market economy meant making choices about which participants in market transactions would bear greater risks. It eventually became clear to all of us that the move to a market economy from a controlled economy entails complex political questions not only about which market participants shall bear the risk of market transactions but, because of that, the likely distribution of power and wealth within society. Drafting laws was no longer an apolitical regulatory exercise, but became fundamental to determining the shape of society.

An example illustrates this fundamental role of commercial organization in society and the crucial responsibility of the law of contract. At first sight agreement between two individuals to buy and sell might seem a politically neutral transaction and the decision by the state to provide enforcement mechanisms to back such a transaction (such as sanctions for non-performance) might similarly appear to be politically uncontroversial. However, immediately any disparity of bargaining power is taken into consideration, a state decision to provide enforcement mechanisms will clearly benefit the party who started in the more powerful position, since that bargaining power will have been used to gain a more beneficial bargain. Only if safeguards such as Unfair Contract Terms legislation are enacted to re-balance the equation can neutrality be regained. Let me illustrate this …

On a cold day I once had half an hour to kill before meeting my daughters from school. I went to buy a minor electrical item in one of the big electrical superstores. As I had some time, I read (for the first time ever) the small print of terms and conditions of the sale. And I found a term which I considered to be outrageous. I can't remember what it was now so maybe it wasn't so bad after all. Anyway, I presented the item to the young person at the till announcing that I would like to buy the item but mentioning that I had crossed out this particular term as I didn't agree with it. This caused a delightful chaos. Of course, the person at the till couldn't accept the changed bargain so he called the supervisor, the supervisor called the store manager, the store manager called the area manager. At this point I ran out of time and left without the item. But what it made clear is that these large companies are used only to dictating the terms on which they will deal. It is not a contract between equals. Consider how important such misbalance is in a contract of employment; or when states are signing financial treaties between themselves, or with the International Monetary Fund.

For lawyers contract is one of the most crucial implements of economic management in a market-based economy. The theory is that each individual has freedom to trade and this leads to each person getting their needs and desires satisfied. However, a contractual system has some significant flaws – one risk has been already identified, and that is the difficulty of inequality. So contract law is able to be an instrument of equality, simultaneously benign and also fundamental to the building blocks of a market economic system. Equally important, however, is that when a benign instrument is mishandled, all sorts of consequences flow from it. Thus contract can be a malign construct if you believe in equality; and the paradox lies in the way that freedom can devalue freedom via the freedom to allow trade, although the whole idea of contract was to enhance freedom.

Therefore, if the fundamental principles of a capitalistic system can be easily debased by inequality, it is not surprising that power bases like multinational companies of enormous reach are rife, and that poverty and degradation are so common. One of the most powerful blocks against equality is the implementation of huge economic empires built on contract. Companies using the Anglo-American model are based on contract. Most multinational companies are based on a structure which predicates a contractual model. Shareholders of the company are the sole stakeholders in the enterprise. This allows them enormous power, particularly if the next significant part of the equation is also understood: the limited liability of companies, that is, the creation of companies granting limited liability to shareholders. This means that shareholders only ever put the price of their shares at risk: they will never need to pay more, even if creditors cannot be paid from the company's money. In other words, this represents a clear transference of risk from shareholders to creditors. These "creditors" include people who have been injured by corporate activity, for example employees injured by companies producing dangerous substances such as asbestos. Thus the state makes profound choices when crafting its commercial law. And the same is true on the international stage, where commercial law regulates the economic relations between states.

One of the most fundamental roles of commercial law is to set out rules defining and protecting property. This is what it is doing when it crafts laws about contracts. A claim to "own" something will often be the result of transference of that property by contract. And the law has also to define what can be owned and the strength of those property rights. Commercial law, then, regulates the way in which people acquire and dispose of property. The rules may choose to favour the already powerful or they may seek to regulate that power to protect the weak.

We must always remember that property rights are not rights over *things* but, on the contrary, rights against other people. Thus the statement "I own this computer" tells the world that I may prevent others from selling or using this computer. It is a right to *exclude* others. Inevitably, then, if you wish to favour those who already own property, you will define property in the widest terms, you will argue against regulations limiting the use of that property, even a use that might be said to be for the benefit of society. In other words, you will argue for the widest concept of property and freedom to trade, trade free of regulatory control. Your commercial law will be constructed to give nearly absolute protection to individual rights to property against any claims that might be made in favour of use of property "for the common good". Commercial law will therefore permit and encourage accumulations of property without imposing countervailing responsibilities to use that property in any particular way. In corporate terms, we will have companies but no corporate social responsibility. If, on the other hand, property rights are understood as exercisable only subject to significant responsibilities, an opposing model of companies and commercial law will be constructed within which *the accumulation of property brings responsibility*.

III
Expansionary property rights

Let us look at how "talking up" property rights may change the way in which law is viewed. Harris talks about "expansive" definitions of property (Harris, *Property and Justice*, 1996). This is where an attempt is made to change the rules by claiming that something should be protected "because it is a property right".

"Property rights" are a rhetoric which will resonate with the reader according to the "meaning" of property in a particular society. Put simply, if you claim that something is a "property right", it will assume greater importance than a more careful analysis might accord to it.

Imagine the following dialogue.

Egalitarian: "For reasons of a, b and c, I maintain that everyone ought to have an enforceable right to work."

Conservative: "For reasons of X, Y and Z, I disagree with you."

Egalitarian: "But you believe that property should be protected, don't you?"

Conservative: "I do."

Egalitarian: "Well, the right to work is property."

Conservative response 1: "No, it isn't."

Conservative response 2: "Why didn't you say that before? Of course, I now change my view to yours."

In this dialogue the right to work is put forward as a "property right" which should only be interfered with carefully, and probably with compensation following. This is likely to have the effect of a redistribution of wealth to poorer communities. As we shall see, a common understanding of companies is that they are "owned" by shareholders. In this case, the claim of shareholders-as-owners is making an expansive property claim about shareholder rights and is an attempt to persuade lawmakers to "rig the risks" in favour of shareholders, to the detriment of others on whose life the company may have an impact, especially employees. In this case, the redistributive effect is likely to be reversed. It will be the shareholders in whose favour "the risks are rigged" and the employees whose right to work will be downgraded. So strengthening the shareholders' rights excludes from consideration the interests of others and assumes, in particular, that shareholders may profit at the expense of employees. The enhanced protection by representation of these rights as "property rights" is likely to have the effect of redistribution of wealth from employees to wealthy shareholders.

IV

A "free-trade" society

Now let us take a look at one historical "free-trade society" and how it designed and protected its "property rights".

It is not easy to find explicit statements by those who favoured the slave trade and fought hard to retain it. But note that abolition was widely viewed as an attack on the "right to free trade". Clearly, here, only the freedom of the powerful counted, not the freedom of those defined as "property" … And, of course, it was because the slaves were defined by the commercial law at the time as "property" that they could be treated in the horrific ways that we condemn so readily today. Remembering this episode of history should remind us how powerful commercial law is. When researching the sugar trade I was grateful to the British Academy for funding a trip to Barbados. (I had great difficulty persuading my colleagues that it was an absolute *necessity* to do research in Barbados in January!). In one year (1650), the slave-sugar plantations of Barbados were worth the modern equivalent of £15 million to the English economy. This, despite the fact that as early as 1569, the courts had declared that "England was too pure an air for slaves to breathe". This is probably the most extreme form of NIMBYism ever. Consider, for further example, *Gregson vs Gilbert* where the captain had thrown 132 slaves overboard because the ship *Zong* was short of water. The issue calmly decided by the court was whether the cost of the slaves came within the relevant clause of the marine insurance policy. Lord Mansfield held "the case of the slaves was the same as if horses were thrown overboard". Thus commercial law, by defining the slaves as property, by permitting contracts to buy and sell this property, and by failing to regulate the gross exercise of power relating to this ownership, was at the heart of this horrible trade, causing the death of countless and the suffering of millions.

What we need to avoid is repeating a similar system by profiting from the net transfer of wealth from the poor world to the rich by allowing companies to operate unregulated in the poor world (including the world of poor people in Europe and America), and exploiting workers in appalling conditions – so that we will have cheap T-shirts made in export-processing zones and high profits fattening our pension funds. In short, is contemporary commercial law beginning to look like a replica of that regulating the slave trade?

On the international stage, commercial law, constructed by treaties, has been drafted in accordance with the economic tenets espoused by the large international financial institutions: that is, "the Washington consensus". This holds that the only way that countries will develop their economies is to become entirely open to market forces. Thus there must be no protection of local industries, the state must not meddle in commercial matters, and money must be allowed to flow freely around the world. The last of these we will return to later. The first two require "free trade" and privatisation of state-owned assets. But there is confusion about the meaning of the concept of "free trade". The General Agreement on Tariffs and Trade (GATT) was established after the Second World War, and tried until 1995 and the establishment of the World Trade Organisation to reduce tariff barriers which levied charges on goods entering a foreign country. This was a particular and restricted concept of "free trade". It is controversial as it means that local industries must compete with the world's giant companies, a practice which often leads to local unemployment in poor countries since the large companies have economies of scale on their side. However, it is nothing like as controversial as an emerging understanding of "free trade" as "trade free of regulation". And this latter understanding is very dangerous because, as we have already seen, it is the powerful who call for freedom. The poor would very much prefer regulation to reign in the operation of freedom.

What role do companies play in this system of commercial law? Let us look at how companies are constructed to take maximum advantage of national and international laws. We will need a whistle-stop tour of company law.

V

Companies as property

You will often hear or read that "shareholders are the owners" of companies. Despite valiant attempts, Paddy Ireland has failed to dispel this "myth" (Ireland, "Company Law and the Myth of Shareholder Ownership", *Modern Law Review*, 1999). But myth it certainly is. My students ask, "Do you mean that if I own 20% of the company's shares and the company own an office block that I don't own 20% of the office block?" And the answer is, "No, you certainly do not". In fact shareholders have very limited rights: in the UK, they do not even have the right to force the directors to pay a return on their money, i.e., a "dividend". That is entirely at the discretion of the directors. So it is clear that this discourse of "ownership" is an "expansive" property claim aimed at rigging the risks in favour of the shareholders and to the detriment of others affected by the company's operations, including employees and the environment (so therefore all of us).

The way in which company law has chosen to "rig the risks" is by translating the expansive property claim into the idea that because shareholders are owners, the company must be run in their interests. And this is somehow translated into the concept that companies must "profit maximize". And that means that they must minimize protections and pay for workers and minimize their care for the environment. It is a curious perception. Every year I challenge my students to find a company law, anywhere in the world, which requires companies to maximize their profits. I offer a prize. But none has ever been brought to my attention. It is another instance of the power of discourse. And it is powerful. One of the consequences of our prioritization of shareholders and profit maximization is that states, governments and courts are extremely reluctant to interfere with and regulate the activities of companies which are guarding the interests of the powerful. Indeed, the interests of companies drive the negotiations at the national and international levels. Drahos and Braithwaite in *Global Business Regulation* (2000) note that US trade representatives ask the large corporations what they want from a trade negotiation and then negotiate accordingly. So companies themselves become more and more powerful ...

The immense power of corporations is indicated by a comparison between the economic wealth generated by corporations, measured by sales, compared with a country's gross domestic product (GDP). On this basis, the combined revenues of just General Motors and Ford exceed the combined GDP for all of Sub-Saharan Africa; and fifty-one of the largest one hundred economies are corporations (Anderson and Cavanagh, *The Rise of Global Corporate Power*, 1996). It is also the case that 75% of world trade is trade between different parts of corporate groups, thus making it even more difficult to regulate even if the will to do so was there. But why?

I teach a course with my colleague, Professor Peter Muchlinski, entitled, "Multinational Enterprises and the Law". And I always start with a particular slide and suggest that we can all now go home. Because, legally, multinational enterprises do not exist. A multinational company is made up of legal entities which owe their existence solely to the commercial laws of different nation states. They are connected in a multitude of ways, by contract, by franchising agreements, by cross-shareholding – but there is no corporate regulation of the whole commercial entity. This has the following regulatory consequences.

Let us imagine the simplest possible model of a multinational company: *Cheap Clothes Plc*, an English holding company holding shares in three subsidiaries in Mauritius, India and Nigeria. Suppose that one of the employees in India is injured in the course of employment. That employee will have no claim whatsoever against the English company. The English courts have made it absolutely clear that they will not look beyond a narrow legal understanding of these companies as separate from each other "even if the interests of justice" would be served by them doing so. In *Adams vs Cape Industries*, Lord Justice Slade said, "If a company chooses to arrange the affairs of its group in such a way that the business carried on in a particular foreign country is the business of the subsidiary and not its own, it is, in our judgment, entitled to do so. Neither in this class of case nor in any other class of case is it open to this court to disregard the principle of *Salomon vs Salomon* [1897] AC 22 [principle of separate corporate personality] merely because it considers it just so to do." It should be noted that this was a case concerning employees who were seriously injured, some dying because of unsafe practices in the asbestosis business managed by an English parent company through various foreign subsidiaries. The English Court of Appeal allowed the English parent to walk away.

So multinational companies can play "regulatory arbitrage", by finding the jurisdiction with the least protections in order to profit maximize. This is the well-known "race to the bottom", encouraged and protected by our commercial laws, just as the law protected the slave trade in earlier times.

VI
Capital account liberalization

When I was researching for *Companies, International Trade and Human Rights*, I encountered a particular difficulty of presentation. The subjects covered were so complex that it was extremely difficult to present the large picture without being dismissed as naïve and lacking understanding of the complexities of the relevant commercial law context. Conversely, a presentation which included all the complexities would be immensely long and technical. In order to counter this difficulty, I chose to study a number of issues in depth. One of them was the Asian financial crisis of 1997. And I found that this was a particularly good example of "risk-rigging", so much so that I called the relevant part of the book "Risk-free Banking". We are experiencing something very similar today in the ramifications of the financial crisis which started in 2007. The frightening similarities between the Asian crisis in 1997 and the recent continuing catastrophe are fascinating. Let me share with you how this research began.

When I was growing up in the late 1950s, there were two sorts of comics: girls' comics and boys' comics. Because I was a girl I was assigned *Bunty*, which had a curious desire to turn all girls either into ballet dancers or nurses. There must be thousands of people who should be grateful that I took neither course. But the boy's comics were much more exciting. My brother got *Eagle* and the best part was the adventures of Dan Dare. Dan Dare's sworn enemy was the Mekon. Dan Dare had to spend a great deal of time saving the world from the Mekon. As I remember it, one of the Mekon's tactics was to cover the world in green slime.

Some 40 years later, running on a treadmill in the gym, I noticed on the big screen an advertisement for HSBC bank. The final frame was supposed to prove that this was a bank with connections all over the world, so a map of the world was gradually covered with little red triangles (the HSBC logo). Immediately I was reminded of the Mekon taking over the world, only this time the takeover was with red triangles, not green slime. More seriously, I realized that much attention has been lavished on multinational companies which produce goods such as garments or footballs but little attention had been paid to the activities of banks which are some of the largest and most powerful companies on the planet. Research has shown that, in Jagdish Bhagwhati's words, "There is a dense network of like-minded luminaries among the powerful institutions – Wall Street, the Treasury Department, the State Department, the IMF, the World Bank, most prominent amongst them – which have hijacked the argument in favour of free trade markets and applied to promote free capital mobility everywhere".

The Nobel Laureate Joseph Stiglitz explains the way in which the IMF has changed its objectives to assisting the multinational banks:

> The IMF is pursuing not just the objectives set out in its original mandate of enhancing global stability and ensuring that there are funds for countries facing a threat of recession to pursue expansionary policies. It is also pursuing the interests of the financial community ... Simplistic free market ideology provided the curtain behind which the real business of the "new" mandate could be transacted. The change in mandate and objectives, while it may have been quiet, was hardly subtle: from serving global *economic* interests to serving the interests of global *finance*. Capital market liberalisation may not have contributed to global economic

stability, but it did open up vast new markets for Wall Street. (*Globalization and Its Discontents*, 2002)

This reassessment of the IMF turns partly on the "bail-out" policies it has pursued. The allegation is that loans to risky areas are encouraged and underpriced because it is known that the IMF will support the country's currency when a crisis threatens. Eichengreen and Ruhl describe the "moral hazard" thus: "Investors, it is argued, have been able to escape the financial costs of crises through the extension of international rescue loans. These 'bailouts' (as they are described by their critics) give governments the funds they require to pay off their creditors, who are then able to exit the country free of losses. Not being subject to the cost of crises, investors disregard the risks of lending, and the consequent lack of market discipline allows feckless governments to set themselves up for a painful fall" ("The Bail-in Problem: Systematic Goals, Ad Hoc Means").

The allegation that the IMF is in the service of international finance essentially flows from the insistence by the IMF on liberalization, in particular capital account liberalization. The intended result is to permit capital flows to take place freely across the world. However, while this may be good for the financial community, it is not necessarily good for developing countries. "The cocktail of free capital flows, floating exchange rates, domestic financial liberalisation in G3 countries, and unregulated innovations in financial instruments and institutions such as derivatives and hedge funds has dramatically increased financial instability after the collapse of the Gold-Dollar standard" (Eatwell and Taylor, *Global Finance at Risk*, 2000).

Consequent instability is a result of a system of liberalization based on neo-classical assumptions, including perfect information flows. "If one asks which of the neo-classical assumptions fail in a way that permits [financial] crises to develop, it is the information structure on the basis of which lending decisions are made. Rather than each investor deciding individually his or her expectations on the basis of their estimate of the fundamentals, investors make their decisions on the basis of what others are expected to do, resulting in herd behaviour" (Underhill and Zhang, *International Financial Governance*, 2003). We know now that this situation has now been replicated in Europe and America. The casino bankers are now playing with sovereign debts, with chaotic consequences for the poor in the First World.

Just as in 1997, in 2007–08, investors were blissfully unaware of the exact risks they were running. In all markets this is likely to lead to increased instability, as Keynes explained by reference to a beauty contest run by a British tabloid in the 1930s, in which readers were asked to assess from pictures which women would be judged as the most beautiful by the entire readership:

> In other words, readers would not win by giving their own opinion about the women's beauty, not even by assessing what others' personal opinions would be, but by guessing what people would, on average, believe average opinion to be. In financial markets, a trader will not bid a price according to what he or she believes an asset's fundamental value to be, but according to what he or she assesses average opinion to be about average opinion of the asset's value. The beauty contest analogy helps understand why market participants tend to engage in "momentous trading" (i.e., herd behaviour) and why market valuations are subject to sudden shifts in "market sentiment". (Oxfam, *Global Finance*)

Underhill and Zhang point out that "more than seventy financial and monetary crises of different proportions and characteristics have occurred in both developed and developing countries over the past two decades". They see as "a common background to these developments ... the intensifying process of global financial liberalization and integration ... As financial crises have become more frequent and more severe over the past two decades, this has raised the question of whether the growing frequency and severity of crises correlate with the emergence of this liberal and transnational financial order" (*International Financial Governance*, 2003).

My research showed that before the Asian crisis the big banks had money to invest and that "safe" investments were giving poor returns because of low interest rates. The money was therefore "pushed" into the Asian markets. These were riskier but the returns were higher. Note the parallels with "pushing" money at the sub-prime market in the current credit crunch. In the Asian crisis the banks demanded repayment of their short-term high-interest loans as soon as the currencies began to collapse in a herd-behaviour stampede. When the countries ran out of money, in came the IMF with taxpayer funds, which then lent money to the affected countries, which were then able to pay the money out to the banks. The losers? The taxpayers whose contributions make up the funds administered by the IMF and the people of the Asian nations who must repay the debt. And evidence shows that the repayment burden falls disproportionately on the poor. It is too early to have had significant research results about the now unfolding financial crisis but there are some recent indications about the gap between the rich and the poor in several debt-ridden countries.

So for the banks this is "risk-free" banking. Can you think of any modern equivalent involving Northern Rock, and/or government funds to bail out banks recently, in Ireland, Greece, et cetera?

VII
Moral deflection devices

Doing this research led me to conclude that we use companies in a way described by Professor Thomas Pogge as "moral deflection devices"(*World Poverty and Human Rights*, 2002). "Does that mean as scapegoats?" enquired a student. "No", I said, "It's more than that". The example Pogge uses to first illustrate this notion is that of the example of a lawyer hired to manage an apartment block. The most efficient use of the block would be to convert the flats into luxury accommodation and so double the rent. Some of the flats are occupied by poor elderly tenants who would be forced to leave and would have difficulty finding accommodation elsewhere. The lawyer is appointed to manage the block "efficiently", thus saving the owner from himself evicting the elderly residents. Pogge argues that this solution cannot absolve the owner of his moral responsibility. Companies are used by rich societies in an exactly equivalent way, to be the agents carrying out reprehensible moral acts from which rich societies benefit.

Building on this insight I came to the conclusion that there are three ways in which companies are moral deflection devices. First we get them to act in reprehensible ways from which we benefit. Then we make a great show of blaming them, without taking effective measures to control them. And thirdly, we talk up corporate social responsibility and human rights as control mechanisms knowing they are ineffective.

VIII
Just one rebuttal

I am aware, of course, of many differing views, often directly contradicting the ideas presented here. I hope I have dealt with many in my written work.

I would like to deal here with just one of the most commonly argued. That is, that corruption is to blame for much of the poverty and suffering in developing countries. I agree with this but also believe, again with Pogge, that blaming corruption is itself a moral deflection device concealing the underlying mechanisms at work within the international commercial and financial order, which provide huge incentives to those who would favour corruption and despotism, and huge disadvantages and disincentives for struggling democratic regimes. Take one of Pogge's examples again. A gang of thieves breaks into a warehouse and steals jewellery. In domestic law they do not own the jewellery and cannot either sell or borrow against it. Now if the same gang take over a country, they are immediately endowed by the international community with ownership of all the country's resources and the ability to borrow money from the international financial institutions. However, if after doing so, they are deposed and a democratic regime replaces them hoping to spend money on making the lives of citizens better, the international financial regime demands that the debts run up by the despots should be repaid before money can be spent on hospitals or education. The citizens see no improvement brought about by democracy and the scene is set for another gang of despots to exploit the country.

IX
What remedies?

One thing that has become abundantly clear is that there is no one solution and there are no easy answers. Future research to which I am looking forward will try to bring together a whole raft of different initiatives which have been proposed, many of which are small local initiatives that get away from the "everything-must-be-big" form of development (the "penis-extension" version of development theory). There are also less-explored areas such as the role which taxation can play. We also need also to ensure that commercial lawyers think always of how the laws which they draft will impact on populations in the real world, and to explain (in ways that are easy to understand) the rules and the assumptions which lie behind them; there is too much refuge taken behind technical complexity. I believe that the following questions should be asked when drafting commercial laws: 1) *Who is at risk and what is their moral claim to protection?*; 2) *What is the degree and nature of the risk?*; and 3) *What are the mechanisms and institutions available to manage the risk?*

X
The free-trade contribution of Fair Trade

One current focus of my research is the Fair Trade and Ethical Trading movements, especially the Fair Trade labelling system.

Trade in Fair Trade goods alone topped $2 billion in 2006, and trade in both Fair Trade and ethical goods has been rising at an amazing 20 per cent per year over the past few years. The Fair Trade movement has recently entered into mainstream trade. The global sales of all Fair Trade products amounted to approximately £500 million in 2003. Since then annual growth rates have been about 30 per cent; total sales were $1 billion in 2005. In 2006 the figure was over $2 billion. In 2007 there were 2,000 companies selling Fair Trade products and 569 producer organizations representing 7 million farmers, workers and their families in 57 countries. Since 2008 there has been an estimated 700 million retail sales in the UK.

I lead a team with Professor Brigitte Granville and funded by the Arts and Humanities Research Council researching the "mainstreaming" of Fair Trade. That is the movement away from control of Fair Trade by the charitable organizations and the involvement of major multinational companies in retailing Fair Trade goods. We have some anxieties about whether this poses dangers for the movement – for although the movement when small was less effective in its reach, it could be wholly trusted, since the goods were always in the hands of the charitable organisations. People may be more cynical when they see Fair Trade goods on the shelves of major supermarkets which have a less than squeaky-clean reputation, especially in their dealings with suppliers. What is clearly heartening is that the growth has happened purely because consumers have chosen to look for value in ways other than in monetary terms and are demanding an "ethical value" built into their purchases. There are no government regulations or price controls involved. All the regulations are developed by consensus and adhered to by choice. The whole system works entirely on choices freely taken. It is truly a free-trade system and rests entirely on the consumers' choice to turn away from using "the system" as a moral deflection device and to act to take responsibility for their actions. Whether a fair-trade system can ever displace the current mainstream international "free-trade" system is not at all clear. We could still do with a Dan Dare to assist us with saving the world …

One of the foremost scholars of the interface between commercial law and global poverty, *Janet Dine is Professor of International Economic Development Law at Queen Mary,* *University of London and a Senior Fellow of the Institute of Advanced Legal Studies.* Her *recent books include* Company Law *(Palgrave MacMillan, 2005) and* Companies, International Trade and Human Rights *(Cambridge University Press, 2005). She has also edited* Human Rights and Capitalism *(Edward Elgar, 2006), in which she contributed an essay,* "Using Companies to Oppress the Poor".

POEM

Tom Mac Intyre

A PURE, UNCLOUDED BLAZE

for T.R.

Brink of the one-strand river, mate,
is where it's all happenin', damn
the hate much elsewhere, commend it
to your slew of children, *Manannán*
Mac Lir does exist, *Pan* is dead,
not he; we met on the lower shore,
life full of meetings undeserved,
radiant white, head to toe, before
me stands yer boyo, jacket of shells,
culottes likewise, in his hand a trumpet
made of *shells*. We looked at
each other, then he smiles, caress
for the trumpet, artful messenger bow,
spoke – "like to hear it, would you, now?"

A poet, dramatist and fiction-writer in both English and Irish, Tom Mac Intyre was born in Cavan in 1931. His most recent collections of poetry are Stories of the Wandering Moon *(The Lilliput Press, 2000),* ABC *(New Island, 2006) and* The Final Mother-Fuck *(Perhaps) (New Island, 2010). His plays for the Abbey Theatre include* The Great Hunger *(1983),* Good Evening, Mr Collins *(1997), and his version of Brian Merriman's* Cúirt An Mheán Oíche/The Midnight Court *(1999). A collection of short fiction,* The Word for Yes: New and Selected Stories, *was published by The Gallery Press in 1991. He is a member of Aosdána, and lives in Co Cavan.*

THE LAST THING WE NEED

Mike McCormack

Let us pity the Guards.

Using the edge of his hand the sergeant swept to one side the little bits and pieces which littered the top of his desk – a spool of thread, a little coil of silver wire, a neat little pliers, and what looked at first glance like a small mound of hair and feathers. Then, with a large space cleared in the centre of the desk, he laid down a sheet of blotting paper and placed an unusually hairy-looking insect in its centre. Only then, stark against the white background, was the hook concealed within the coloured hair and feathers visible.

"The Olive Gold Invicta", the sergeant announced happily. "What think ye of it?"

The question fell to the young guard who stood on the other side of the desk. At this moment he looked particularly nervous, giving the giddy impression that he might bolt from the room at any moment. After a long pause and with the cautious tone of a man taking a considerable gamble he said, "It's lovely".

The sergeant smiled indulgently. "It's more than lovely young fella, it's downright irresistible." He turned the fly over so that now it presented an iridescent green belly to the light. "You're not looking at it properly. If you were a small brown trout now, about two and a half to three pounds say and this lad lit on the surface over your head, you'd be beside yourself with happiness. One lep out of you and you have him." He looked up brightly. "Of course then I'd have you and that's when we'd have some sport." And for a few moments then the sergeant was lost in such a happy, heedless reverie that the young guard thought it best to remain silent. When he came back to the present the sergeant's tone was fond. "I started tying flies shortly after I came here – learned it from a man by the name of Billy Phelan. You wouldn't know him – he's dead now this good while. Billy would come into town of a Tuesday to draw his pension. He'd buy two plugs of tobacco and that would do him till after second Mass on Sunday. But he'd break your heart, the same Billy. Trying to get him into a hackney at night to take him out home ... many's the night he slept in one of the cells. But for all his faults though there was no one to tie flies like him." And with that the sergeant sat back and looked up at the young guard. "So tell me, what do you have?"

Startled by the sudden change of subject the young guard's head jerked from side to side. "Nothing", he blurted, "not a thing."

The sergeant squinted at him. "There can't be nothing, there has to be something."

The young guard looked down at the fly on the desk and repeated. "There's nothing, we've looked everywhere."

"There must be something, some few pages, a document of some sort or other."

The young guard swallowed thickly but said nothing.

"There must be some sort of a sketchy outline or a synopsis of some sort."

The young guard remained silent. The sergeant leaned forward onto the desk.

"What about the obvious – a short account of his inability to get on with a silent and sullen father?"

"None whatsoever."

"No tender account of loving regard for his sainted mother?"

"No."

"A disturbing account of clerical abuse?"

The young guard shook his head, his misery now deepening as the note of incredulity thickened in the sergeant's voice.

"We were poor but what we had was clean – something along those lines?"

"No."

"Any description of him wearing a sleeveless *geansaí* or of his head hopping with lice?"

"No."

"Short trousers?"

"No."

"No account of him going shoeless through the fields and developing a thick, protective callus on the soles of his feet?"

"No."

"A harrowing account of his struggle with the *modh coinníoleach?*"

"No."

"Any character sketch of him looking up with fright and bemusement at the adult world, an account possibly offset in the third person?"

"No."

The sergeant considered a moment. His face was now furrowed with anxiety. "A small parish publication, it'd be easy to miss?" he ventured quietly.

"None."

"A vanity publication, badly edited on poor quality paper, loads of typos?"

"No."

"No sign of a tattered manuscript anywhere? Possibly in a small box that might have fallen down the back of the dresser?"

"Nothing, we did a full search, the house and outhouses, all clean."

"The fridge, did you check the icebox?"

"A block of ice cream, nothing else."

"Suffering Christ", the sergeant breathed, now visibly awed and beyond caring who saw it. "And how did he account for himself?"

"He shrugged his shoulders."

"He shrugged his shoulders?"

"He shrugged his shoulders and produced a birth certificate from a coarse bag under the bed; that's all."

The sergeant finally snapped and surged to his feet. He threw his hands wide. "Fuck the birth certificate", he roared, "where's his ISBN?"

Had he taken the moment to look, he would have seen that the young guard was now trembling on the verge of tears.

———

"It's no one's fault", the sergeant amended an hour later, his fit of temper now evidently behind him. "He might be one of those anomalies the system throws up from time to time. He might be, but I doubt it. I have a feeling … Either way, the thing is, what are we going to do about it? Tell me again what we know about him."

The young guard turned a page on his notebook hurriedly, visibly relieved to be able to finally contribute something positive. "We have his name, date of birth, educational records, and invoices from his place of work."

"Which is?"

"He owns a small breakers yard beyond the quarry. We also have several bank statements and electricity bills. He has a wife and two grown-up sons, all of them fully compliant; they were severely embarrassed. "

The sergeant snorted dismissively. "None of that's worth a damn. How did he justify himself?"

"He said it slipped his mind."

"Slipped his mind! How the hell … you'd swear to Jesus we were talking about a dog licence."

The sergeant opened a drawer and pulled out a glass and a small bottle. Ignoring the young guard he poured himself a generous measure and drank. He looked off into the distance then, his gaze lost in the white walls of the barracks. Then, turning the glass in his hand, he asked the young guard, "How long are you here now – two, three months?"

"This is my eighth week", the young guard said, wanly.

"Eight weeks", the sergeant sighed, "and this is what you come up with – the only man in this jurisdiction not to have written a childhood memoir." He pursed his lips and shook his head in disbelief. "That's some start to a career in law enforcement." He sipped from the glass and thought for a moment; then he motioned to the chair by the wall. "Pull it over and sit down. I'm going to tell you something."

The young guard swung in the chair, embarrassing himself again by clattering it awkwardly off the front of the desk. When he was seated the sergeant began by sweeping his hand across the room.

"I come in here every morning and I sit at this desk and the first thing I do is study all overnight intelligence and activity. I analyse and interpret and then I collate my conclusions with the Threat Matrix for this jurisdiction, chapter and verse, all twenty seven pages of it. Then, in light of my analysis, I reprioritise anything that needs reprioritising and I finish up by submitting my final report. That done and God in his heaven and all other things being equal, I put the whole lot back in the vault and I open my paper and drink my mug of tea. I've been doing that for nearly 40 years now and I have never had a security breach like we're looking at here. Now, I'm two months away from retirement, two months away from a civic reception with a lot of nice speeches and a small gold watch with the force's crest inscribed on the back of it. But now … ," he motioned towards the young guard's notebook, "this lad crops up." He gazed off into the middle distance, a gloomy expression swelling his features. The effort it took to control his frustration made it necessary for him to place both hands on the desk. "Is there anything to be gained by bringing him in for questioning I wonder?"

"It's standard procedure", the young guard reminded him.

The sergeant nodded. "So it is. OK, let's bring him in for questioning.

Let's get a full account from him, names, dates, a complete timeline. Bring him in."

The young guard nodded and turned for the door. With the room now empty the sergeant leaned back in his chair and stared up at the ceiling. His tone was low with aggravation and fatigue, imploring. "The self as the first object of suspicion – each man responsible for his own surveillance. What, exactly, is so difficult about that?"

———

Later that evening the young guard's expression was one of open wonderment. In the dim light of the barracks his eyes fairly sparkled with disbelief.

"One man, one dole form", he breathed, "I never knew you invented that."

Behind the desk the sergeant trimmed some loose hairs from the end of a golden fly. He spoke without looking up from his work. "You couldn't keep track of them", he said, his face expressionless. "Whatever chance you had in winter when things were quiet you had none at all in summer when there was work to do. You'd have lads off building bits of houses, and lads cutting silage and other lads off to the bog. One of them would round up all the dole forms in the parish and drop them in here. I had to put a stop to it, I didn't know down from Adam who was coming or going. It got so bad I couldn't put a face to half the names coming across the desk to me. I couldn't tell whether there were hundreds of men out there on the dole or whether there were only a handful of men drawing benefits for hundreds of spouses and dependents. I had to put a stop to it."

"I answered a question on it in my final exam", the young guard said happily. "*The origin of voluntary compliance has its roots in the doctrine of one man, one dole form. Discuss.* It's still part of the core curriculum."

The sergeant nodded. "I was asked up to the college to give a lecture on it but I got out of it some way or other. There are better men than me standing in front of an audience speechifying. How did you score on it?"

"I got a B plus."

"You were happy enough with it?"

"Yes."

"Good."

The sergeant blew twice on the fly and held it up to the light. Satisfied, he laid it to one side of the desk and then drew a thin sheaf of papers towards him. He eyed the documents with distaste. "So, this gent, what did he give us?"

"Twenty-two pages, about seven thousand words."

"Give me the gist of it."

"It's the usual story. A poor upbringing at the heart of a large family dominated by an unsympathetic father; a saintly mother who intervenes from time to time on his behalf but who is largely left drifting around to no effect in the background. There is a poignant account of sharing a small truckle bed with two brothers and two sisters. It's the standard account."

"In summary."

"In summary, a plucky and ultimately forgiving account of a marginal victory over poverty and adverse parenting." The young guard sat back.

"Nothing subversive."

"No, nothing we have not heard a million times before."

"And what the hell was so difficult about that", the sergeant wondered aloud. "Are there any internal inconsistencies or contradictions in it? Is he indexed in the other contemporary accounts?"

"Yes."

"And in the revised and expanded editions?"

"Yes, several times and they all tally with his account. He flew through the polygraph as well."

"What did the Profilers say?"

"They concur with his account; they can find nothing in it which points to a pathology of evasion or non-disclosure."

"Nothing political?"

"No."

"Did they give a recommendation?"

"No."

The sergeant snorted scornfully. "I'll bet they didn't, the fuckers, say nothing that might hang them. See what they're doing there, washing their hands of it, disclaiming any responsibility. You want to watch out for that."

The sergeant now considered. Evidently things had come to a crucial juncture. By way of gathering his thoughts he swept some imaginary pieces from the surface of the desk, using a rhythmic sweeping motion as he considered. When he finally spoke it was clear he did not wish to clutter an already complex situation with further possibilities. "The way I see it this gent presents three options. Firstly, and however unlikely it may seem, it might be an honest omission on his part – he may indeed have forgot in which case it means nothing in security terms; that's the first option. The second option is that the omission is intentional, that it is part of a plan and that this man presents a direct if as yet unspecified security threat. Or the third – and this is the worrying one – such an omission and the questions which arise from it may in fact be a decoy, something to draw the eye and resources from wherever it is the real threat is being developed."

The young guard could not help but notice how the sergeant had been transformed by his own thoughts. There was a lightness and sharpness about him now, a swiftness and directness about his speech and reasoning which flourished under its own impetus. For all his bulk there was nothing faltering or sluggish about him now. "How far did you have to go with him? You showed him the machines?"

"Yes, I showed him, gave him the full tour."

"And you showed him how they worked, the damage they can do?"

"Yes."

"And?"

"It didn't knock a stir out of him."

"No!" The sergeant grimaced and swore. "That's not good. That's all we need now, cranking up those machines." The sergeant pursed his lips and sat looking into space for a long moment. Then he let his gaze drift to the edge of the table. He picked up the fly and turned it over in his hand. The young guard watched him give himself over fully to the fly. "Hacklers Muddler", he said, "one of Billy's finest. He claimed to have invented this one himself. The same Billy claimed a lot of things though; you couldn't believe the Lord's Prayer from him." He laid the fly on the desk and continued. "There's a great story about Billy, about the time he came up in front of Judge Hanlon … Billy got caught red-handed with half a dozen salmon in the boot of the car. The bailiff came upon him one morning on the bank of the river, the boot of the car thrown open and six fine salmon lying in it but no licence. So up he comes in front of Hanlon and whatever was on Hanlon that day he took a liking to Billy. Now Billy had no notion of pleading guilty so he starts off some rigmarole story about how he was out checking stock that morning and had come upon these salmon lying there on the bank of the river. Then Billy starts playing the part of the upright citizen to the hilt. 'I put them into the boot of the car your honour and I was just about to turn them over to the bailiff when he comes along. It was very comical Your Honour.' 'You were doing your civic duty as you saw it?' Hanlon says. 'Yes Your Honour, because there is nothing more abhorrent to me as salmon poaching.' I'll always remember that phrase. Hanlon almost fed him a complete defence that day. But he didn't swallow it completely; he let Billy off with a fine, something like a hundred pound in the court poor box. But it took the full morning spinning out that story between the two of them, Hanlon prompting him along when he got stuck. And if you were to listen to it you'd think Billy was the most upright citizen who ever pulled on a trouser. I'd have given a lot to have seen him that day in the witness stand with the stick and the hat. I read about it afterwards in *The Sentinel*, two whole pages of it – there was great reading in it. And you tell me you've never done any fly fishing." The sergeant shook his head wonderingly. "You don't know what you're missing. Up there on the river, the sun shining, a flask of tea and a few sandwiches ..."

"It's skilful work?"

"Oh it's a lot more than that", he chided. "Time stands still when you're fishing. *God will not subtract from man's allotted span the hours he has spent fishing.* A Babylonian proverb. Those lads knew what they were talking about. They gave us the first calendar and astrology. I'll bet you didn't know that."

The young guard shook his head. "No, I did not know that."

———

"I didn't know you were a teacher", the young guard said as he stirred two spoons of sugar into his mug of tea.

"Three years", the sergeant said, putting the lid back on his lunchbox and shoving it into the drawer. "The longest three years of my life."

"You weren't happy at it?"

"No, I wouldn't say that. It's not that I wasn't happy at it or that I didn't enjoy it. It was more that I wasn't suited to it." Now he gazed querulously at the young guard. "You're a man of broad enquiry. I see you there at your desk every day with your head stuck in some book or other. Answer me this. You look at a child and what do you see, a five- or six-year-old child, what do you see when you look in their face?"

The young guard shrugged his shoulders and looked down at the floor. He hadn't anticipated a question. He sensed a trap. "A small adult", he ventured carefully, "a solid, compliant citizen in the making."

The sergeant nodded approvingly. "That's what I thought too, once upon a time. Farmers, firemen, dental hygienists, long jump invigilators at community games – these are the sort of things you should see in a child's face. But I never saw any of that. I saw something completely different. They'd come in the school gate with their little faces aglow with excitement and all I could see were things like … *possession with intent to supply … conspiracy to defraud … public order offences … breaking and entering … ID theft* … awful stuff like that. Plain as day those were the things I saw written across their faces. It took a toll on me. In the middle of my third year I went to the principal and told him about it. He was a kind man but he had no sympathy for me that day. 'Those are the things you see', he said, 'now let me tell you what I see, the things I see before they're even born. I see their parents, young couples out walking hand in hand and all I see between them are things like … *mandatory sentencing … life plus ten years … both sentences running concurrently …* if I'm lucky I might see something like … *community sanction.*' That startled me I'm telling you, that put me in my place. Imagine living with that, seeing that sort of thing day in, day out. It broke his health in the end, the poor man. He slumped onto his desk one afternoon and was carted off to hospital: a stroke. He lost all feeling down his left side and it was six months before he could walk again. A fine fresh-faced man, he had a daughter doing the Leaving Cert the same year … Anyway, I didn't need twice telling. I threw my hat at it towards the end of that year and joined the force and I wasn't one bit sorry. You wouldn't believe how dangerous children can be. You can't turn your back on them …"

———

They closed the door behind them and stood out into the early night. The sergeant turned and gazed up at the lintel over the door.

"We need to replace that bulb tomorrow. One of us will split ourselves coming out of here some night. That's all we'd need."

They made their way across the gravel towards the sergeant's car. The young guard opened the passenger door and was about to lower himself into the car. The sergeant placed his flask and lunchbox on the roof of the car and stared across at him.

"Eight weeks you said, that's how long you've been here."

"Yes, eight weeks just gone."

The sergeant considered a moment and then went round the front of the car. He leaned back against the bonnet and folded his arms across his chest and appeared to stare out into the dark night beyond the road for a long moment.

"I'll tell you what we'll do", the sergeant said softly. "We'll release this gent tomorrow morning and we'll put him under 24-hour surveillance – bugs, taps, intercepts, visual, audio, the whole shebang. And when we've done that we'll open a file with his name on it and backdate the first entry to three months ago ... that's what we'll do tomorrow." He turned to gaze at the young guard who now stood with one foot already in the car. The young guard blanched and stood back from the car. Callow and all as he was he recognised the deception immediately and saw clearly its full consequences. His first instinct was to protest. The word was out of his mouth before he could check it.

"But ..."

"No buts", the sergeant said shortly, "you're young; you don't know the half of it. Take if from me, you don't want drawing attention to yourself with something like this. You'll get no thanks for it, mark my words. And I'm only two months away from retirement so I don't want this hanging over me either. This could go on for years – there will be an investigation, hearings, adjournments, appeals ..." Now a thin note of apprehension undercut his speech. "Up and down on that train three or four times a week." He grimaced at the prospect and shook his head ruefully. "No ..."

And now the young guard truly saw the gamble, what was wagered on it and what its full consequences might well be. And the prospect humbled him. He now saw that in backdating the discovery of the anomaly to three months ago the sergeant was taking full responsibility for it. And in the event that it turned out to be something more dangerous than an anomaly the sergeant was gambling on the authorities letting sleeping dogs lie, not seeing the point of persecuting a retired man. And now ... and now the issue ... the whole moment was hopelessly blurred – there were too many options, things had been suggested, things proposed, and the young guard was no longer sure what he had agreed to or what he was complicit in. He gulped and raised a hand, then dropped it onto the roof of the car. "But someone like that, he might be capable of anything." The sergeant nodded. "Yes, he might, and then again he might only be a glitch in the system." The sergeant studied the young guard. The lad had shown genuine acuteness throughout the investigation, a degree of thoroughness and clear reasoning he would never have credited him with. Now he made a mental note to stress all this in whatever report he may have to write. Also, despite a bookish nature which kept him unusually quiet, the young guard had proved to be easy company in the small barracks. But now the sergeant saw that he really was on the verge of tears and he was embarrassed for him. He could well sympathize. It had been a tough few days, certainly not the sort of thing he would have wished for someone at the beginning of their career. He turned and looked out into the gloom.

"How far would you say from here to the other side of the road?"

The young guard bent forward and squinted. The sharp night air had drawn the nervous flush from his face. He straightened up. "About 40 yards, give or take a few."

The sergeant nodded. "About that I'd say, 40 yards. You know, if you were to leave your cap over there now, I'd drop a fly into it from here." And with that he stepped away from the car and planted his feet. He drew his forearms back across his chest and with his imaginary rod he cast out over the road. He spoke to himself.

"I mightn't do it the first time, but I'd do it the second."

And he drew his wrists once more behind his right shoulder and cast out across the road. And as he stood there watching him the young guard was as certain as he would ever be that he was seeing someone lost in a moment of contentment. He watched him cast out again into the darkness while above them the night sky closed over the earth, a night sky crossed with planes, satellites, unmanned drones …

Born in 1965, Mike McCormack is the author of one collection of short stories, Getting it in the Head *(Henry Holt & Company, 1998), and two novels,* Crowe's Requiem *(Henry Holt & Company, 1999), and* Notes *from a Coma (Vintage, 2006). He currently lives in Galway, where he is working on his next novel.*

BEING HERE

Eamon Grennan

A loophole for the soul.

DATA, RENVYLE

Midday
Gleam of two mute swans at ease, raising a lake-
family among the rushes. Through the pathos of
their weak cheeping, robins resist the rain that
clings, a wet dishcloth, to rose-hips and hedges.
No wrong in the throng of sand-fleas leaping
around a sea-green bone. Sea a sleepy tide lap-
slapping at the brief three-pointed feet of plovers,
hysterical oystercatchers, indifferent gulls. Wind
whispers idiot mantras in the chimney; cat
contemplates a black-out grate; hills give up their
ghost to a cloud of rain. Small birds huddle on
branches, untempted by breadcrumbs among the
stones. Caught in this matter-dance, your eyes
impale themselves where a hawthorn bristles into
the invisible. But no *jade-gold world* hereabouts,
only anointed sky, bone-white sand, sea roiling
on black, buddha-patient rocks.

Early evening
Lake-circle of shine: a cormorant shadows a half-
submerged rock. One sudden fish: glitter-rings
blinking in water. One red-eyed dove catches
light: doveshape, pink air, white body vanishing.
Wait in a fit of hope, so, for the next messenger
to slake your nameless thirst: like a bee desiring
the blue and green it glimpses beyond glass. A
few last wisps of dead grass quiver, stand still, as
if something light as a tongue of air had finished
its journey.

FAMILY VALUES

1.

Because as a child you lay alone in the dark
waiting, counting, aching till you'd hear the hall
door pushed open, your father safe home again no
matter the hopeless state of him, it's impossible not
to think of your youngest daughter abroad alone in
the dark on unknown roads when you see the
straggle of homing crows overhead under slate-grey
broken cloud, scattered but knowing their way:
impossible not to feel the heart-ice in your chest
while the anything that could happen steals your
breath, and nothing to smooth away the thorn-
spiked edge of anxiety till you hear the door pushed
open and there – safe home like your saved father –
she is.

2.

A world of black branches, blue sky, cloud scraps
head over heels in puddles after rain. No words to
reach the wild anxiety of things any ordinary
Saturday: families tumbled tooth and claw into their
own nest and bosom. Nerves go electric, blood
seeps drop by drop, staining the frayed foot-of-the-
bed Karaman, bringing its muted allegories to light.
Air remains radiant, a mask of gold we shiver into,
feeling the fall in Fall, the smell of vallied apples,
small signs of this-world absolutes, though still no
hint of absolution. Cross your fingers, so, into
hope's own plaintive, dream-lit cipher.

LEAVING THE GARDEN

Head bent, ready to address the garden gate
and the pot-holed road to the village, you're
taken out of yourself a moment by the
flurry of midges shimmying in noonlight,
and the minute-splitting shimmer of
leafshadow on gravel – parcel upon parcel
of quiver making its presence felt, flinging
forth its robust little anthem of revolution, a
dance tune to which the blood in its own
radical hope keeps turning and turning,
journeying heart to head, heel to toe
through a sort of sabbath of the will in
which the whirl of action resolves into two
people sitting silent on a sea-rock in
sunshine and passing between them the one
cup brim-full with steaming tea, or settles
into the speckled young robin inspecting its
universe of possibility among the loose
stones of the wall of the world – pecking
wet moss, making the most of these hacked
and fallen fuchsia branches, till an older
bird evicts it, its pinhead eyes shining as it
snaps a fly, a vagrant seed, anything in
eyeshot, travelling through the moment as
if the moment were a place, the place to be
right now, as you clang closed the metal
gate behind you.

VASSAR FARM WALK, AUTUMN EVENING

We were walking away from the light when you put your hand in mine
and clasped like that slid both into the warmth of my duffle's woollen
pocket while we went on walking. Walking, we take in the fading
sights of the Farm, the late autumn twilight thickening with every step
through spent goldenrod, phalanx after upright phalanx of funereal
browns that stood either side of the dirt path lit at intervals by the sheer
patina the remaining rain puddles were still glazed by, brief beacons
soon to be quenched by night's descent in silence. Silent as the owl we
saw as a solid shadow, an icon of patience on a bare branch, skull shape
among the black bones of the ash-tree he'd abandon on the hush of a
single wingbeat, to take whatever ground-hugging scuttler whose eye's
tiniest light pool gleamed a giveaway then went out, the whole saga
over before we'd made it back. Back to the car in darkness still talking
of how the smell of the rotting vegetables from the spent garden plots
brought back your grandmother's English farm, the cabbage leaves
mashed and cast into the big pig-sty, the thick rich stew of smells off
abrasive air that followed and filtered into the girl you were growing
into there, gathering yourself for the next stage of the journey. The
journey that has you here and now stopping in the dark and sniffing the
scents it offers before taking your warm hand from mine, opening the
car door, and noting the one star, evening's star, starting to shine in a
clear sky over which a black scatter of crows goes homing.

HERE

You wonder if *Anywhere ... but somewhere else*
could be a morning offering you'd cling to here
where trees are passing gleams of gold and
silver, of lemon, orange, auburn, shades of
leather, amber, burgundy and rose until, in a
week or so, they'll pale, dry out, give up the
ghost of their green selves and let what happens
happen? Or better on reflection – is it? – to be
here in the churn of change and all this turning,
here where how you've lived has landed you
without a compass, just in time to see the sun dip
under the pitch of rooftops on the other side of
this wet street and tip the still-leaved trees with
platinum, so they glitter an instant like Sheffield
steel then all's a wall of shifting grey through
which a mockingbird vanishes among flowers
you have no name for: lush, phallic-stemmed
blood-red heads in their native grave, nodding
sagely at the way whatever made them left them
to their own endangered devices and left (is this
how to put it?) *a loophole for the soul*, that we've
no reason not to – against the odds, just being
here – look into.

*Eamon Grennan was born in 1941 in Dublin and was educated at University College,
Dublin, and Harvard. He is the author of eight collections of poetry, most recently* Out of
Breath *(The Gallery Press, 2007). His* Out of Sight: New and Selected Poems *was
published by Graywolf Press in 2010. He was the Dexter M. Ferry Professor of English at
Vassar College until his retirement in 2004, and now divides his time between the United
States and the West of Ireland.*

IN THE LONG RUN
(on Samuel Ferguson)

Patricia Craig

Not a colony of Great Britain.

There's a famous image of High Street, Belfast, as it looked in 1810, engraved from a drawing by T.M. Baynes, and showing a ship unloading its cargo at the bottom end of the street, a soldier in tunic and pantaloons engaged in conversation with a man wearing a top hat and carrying a sack slung over his shoulder, a water-seller with a barrel on a cart, various passers-by, a child with a bundle accompanied by a small black-and-white dog about to step across the street, and, in the background, rows of stately three- and four-storey houses fading away into the distance. These were the homes of up-and-coming, professional, mainly Presbyterian people; and in one of them, at this time, a future poet, antiquarian, man of letters, barrister and pre-Yeats Yeatsian, was just emerging into the light of day – or into the darkness of riotous, sect-ridden, volatile, ramshackle, nineteenth-century Belfast.

When the youthful Yeats described Samuel Ferguson as the greatest of Irish poets, because "the most Irish", he was, either consciously or unconsciously, opening the door to all kinds of ironies and complexities. It was a tricky business, classifying Ferguson in this way. This was a Belfast Protestant of Scottish ancestry and East Antrim parentage. The home his father apparently lost through fecklessness was in Antrim's Parkgate. A covenanting strain was strong among his forebears. None of these is exactly in tune with romantic ideas pertaining to the country. Add the daunting Victorian respectability which overtook Ferguson in his Dublin years, and you get, indeed, an unexpected contender for the "ultimate Irishness" accolade. But Yeats wasn't altogether talking through his hat. Ferguson's eventual political conservatism was not incompatible with the strongest form of Irish cultural nationalism, as many commentators have pointed out.

Before Yeats came on the scene at all, a lot of ground had to be traversed by Samuel Ferguson. Some of this ground was in Belfast (not yet a city), in High Street itself and in Hill Street, where he attended Irish classes to supplement the Irish taught at his school, Inst (the Royal Belfast Academical Institution, founded in 1810 and housed in a building designed by John Soane). But it seems clear that rural Antrim, Parkgate near Donegore, and Glenwhirry, where he spent long holidays with his grandmother Ellen Gillilan, was Ferguson's chosen home territory. Its remoteness and crepuscular possibilities fired his poetic imagination, even if the latter proved expansive enough to accommodate elements of the North's industrial advancement into the bargain.

Praise for Ferguson sometimes comes with a faintly sardonic undertone, as in the comment of the critic Malcolm Brown, who designated him "laureate of Belfast shipbuilding and inventor of the Celtic Twilight" – an unlikely combination on the face of it. The first refers, of course, to his poem "The Forging of the Anchor", in which

> The windlass strains the tackle chains, the black mound heaves
> below;
> And red and deep a hundred veins burst out at every throe …

and further feats of the shipbuilding industry are extolled. Ferguson was only 21 when he wrote this exercise in industrial euphoria, but even more extraordinary was the piece of full-fledged lyricism that flashed into his mind one evening, a couple of years later, at his lodgings in London where he was reading for the bar. It was, indeed, Ferguson's "The Fairy Thorn" that lay behind Yeats's somewhat tongue-in-cheek aspiration when he wrote:

> Nor may I less be counted one
> With Davis, Mangan, Ferguson …

pursuing a form of Irishness congruent with the utmost romanticism and supernatural stirrings. But if "The Fairy Thorn" was a precursor of the Twilight mode, with its "dreamier the gloaming grows" and so on, it was none the less grounded in a piece of plain Antrim lore, a story recalled by Ferguson from the heady days of his adolescence. Four young country girls, from irrepressible *joie de vivre*, trespass on fairy ground to dance a reel, and unwittingly unleash unearthly forces.

> For, from the air above and the grassy mound beneath,
> And from the mountain-ashes and the old white-thorn between,
> A power of faint enchantment doth through their beings breathe,
> And they sink down together on the green.

The end of the story is the fairy abduction of one, Anna Grace, "the fairest of the four", and the slow decline of the other three: "They pined away and died within the year and day, / And ne'er was Anna Grace seen again".

One would like to know if Samuel Ferguson was aware of the strong erotic charge carried by this poem, augmenting its eldritch delicacy of tone: did he invoke it deliberately, or was it unconscious, simply pervading his narrative as an element of its indigenous picturesqueness? We don't know, but it's easy enough to envisage the exiled 23-year-old author in his London lodgings, succumbing to an impulse of pungent romanticism. What seems less plausible is the idea, mooted by several critics of the present, that Ferguson composed "The Fairy Thorn" as a political allegory, with the "fairest" Anna Grace standing for his native Ulster, and the point of the poem being her separation from her slightly less fair friends, i.e., the other three provinces. What would the author have said to this interpretation?

"Nonsense", one imagines, "it's just a small local legend, current in Antrim when I was a boy, dressed up in clothing as decorative and fanciful as the red rose-bordered hem of Mr Yeats, or the purple cloaks and ankle-length tunics with red embroidery worn by the third division of the army of Queen Maeve of Connacht." The allegory doesn't stand up, he might go on; no one can claim that Ulster was spirited off the face of the earth, or that Munster, Leinster and Connacht thereafter went into a terminal decline.

If "The Fairy Thorn" was the highlight of Ferguson's early literary career, he didn't for long remain fairy-led. His Belfast outlook asserted itself, with some of the traits that outlook implies. He was not temperamentally attuned to Catholicism, or, politically, to a separatist ideology. His dislike of the former came out in a skit entitled "Father Tom and the Pope", published anonymously in *Blackwood's Magazine* in 1838, and targeting the Church's policy of imposing ignorance on its adherents in the interests of fostering piety. Malcolm Brown calls this work "the solitary literary masterpiece of Orangeism as such" – however, if he was occasionally impelled to speak for "Orangeism", like the good Ulster Tory he was, Ferguson undertook nothing (he claimed) other than with the fullest consciousness of being "an Irishman before I was a Protestant". And being a Protestant was not, in Ferguson's book, an impediment to Gaelic cultural attainment, not excluding proficiency in the Irish language.

Ferguson must have picked up a fair amount of Irish from one source or another, but we don't know how fluent he was – that's another of the questions one would like to ask. The class he attended in Hill Street, Belfast, was probably taught by a Padraig Ó Loingsigh – Patrick Lynch – whose name crops up in the opening line of the first of Ferguson's translations from the Irish. It is now generally accepted that Ferguson had at least a hand in translating "The County Mayo", though for years it appeared solely under the name of his friend and collaborator George Fox. "On the deck of Patrick Lynch's boat I sit in woeful plight", the poem begins. ("Ar an luing seo Phaidi Loingse do ghnimse an dobron.") Perhaps it was just the coincidence of the names that got the two young men, in a spirit of merriment, working away at their English version. But Ferguson was already developing strong ideas on the subject of translation, ideas he expressed emphatically in a review for the *Dublin University Magazine* of James Hardiman's *Irish Minstrelsy*. His onslaught on Hardiman's pusillanimity and po-faced Catholicism had a tremendous impact on future adaptations from the Irish.

Ferguson at 24, and *not* (at least, one assumes not) an adept Gaelic speaker, had the temerity to present examples of how it should be done. Hardiman's two-volume collection, he thought, distorted the tone of its original Gaelic songs and poems by rendering them into an excessively decorous and high-flown English. His own more robust approach immediately strikes a far more modern note. If he could be resurrected for an afternoon, or if time travelling were an option, one would like to congratulate him on this, on his evasion of archaisms and outspoken repudiation of a method he judged "spurious, puerile, unclassical – lamentably bad". That was the verdict he delivered, in the aesthetic sphere. When it came to the political, or sectarian, implications of Hardiman's rationale, the young Belfastman came out inveighing against the notion that Irishness and Catholicism were inextricably linked. An Irish identity was an altogether more flexible concept, a matter of choice and inclination as much as ancestry (even if ancestry could be shown to be untainted, which was unlikely). But it was never exactly an easy or an uncomplicated matter. In his "Dialogue Between the Head and Heart of an Irish Protestant" (also published in the *Dublin University Magazine*, in 1833), Ferguson sets out a few of the contradictions between pragmatic, clear-sighted Head and responsive Heart, with its romantic attachment to colourful Ireland, popery, peasantry and all. Indeed, Heart thinks, if the Irish populace is lovable despite its papist proclivities, how much more so it would be if the whole epidemic of "superstition" were replaced by a rational Protestant ethic. Head pours cold water on any such prosletysing imperative: the country is too far gone in priestly veneration, Head says, for wholesale conversion to be a possibility. This is true, indeed – though one would like to chime in with a word about the opprobrium attaching to the "turncoat" mentality, something ignored by Ferguson's "Heart" in its well-meaning urge to make good happy Protestants of his deluded fellow-countrymen. (This was in the wake of Catholic Emancipation, achieved in 1829.) One might have looked for a more even-handed "plague on both their houses" outburst. But of course it's only with the benefit of hindsight that one can equate the overthrow of sectarianism with a universal Irish secularism (even more of a chimera then than now). What would Ferguson have made of that? He'd hardly have agreed that nineteenth-century Ireland was clergy-ridden, not just priest-ridden – or that one man's superstition was another's revelation.

Another of the ways in which "Heart" claims Irishness is in its alignment with Ascendancy outrage at *England's* betrayal of "the loyal Protestant gentry of Ireland", leaving them at the mercy of an alien church and seditionist elements in the country. At the time Ferguson's essay was published, Repeal of the Union looked set to follow hard on the heels of Catholic Emancipation – and with Papist objectives on the upsurge, as it seemed, the Irish Protestant nation had reason to succumb to qualms. As with the Hardiman review, Ferguson's ire is aroused by any attempt to exclude him and his fellow Protestants from the fullest participation in Irish nationhood. "Neither Whig tyranny nor Popish malice can deprive us of our birthright, which is the love of Ireland", declares beleaguered, patriotic Head. It's a sensible enough stance, anticipating by three-quarters of a century his fellow Instonian Robert Lynd's assertion that an Irishman (or woman) is simply a person "who has had the good or bad fortune to be born in Ireland ... and who is interested in Ireland more than in any other country in the world".

Every aspect of Irishness fascinated Ferguson, from the Orangeism of Belfast to Catholic chicanery and the idealism of the Young Ireland movement of the 1840s. None of his allegiances was monolithic, though; he was subject, like most of us, to contradictory ameliorative impulses and complexities and changes of heart. His elegy for one of the architects of Young Ireland, Thomas Davis (dead at 31) – "Young husbandman of Erin's fruitful seed-time / In the fresh track of danger's plough!" – this elegy was followed by a kind of repudiation:

I do not care a button for Young Ireland, or Old Ireland;
But as between the two, I rather like old Dan ...

"old Dan" of course being Daniel O'Connell, who stood for everything
Ferguson was opposed to: bourgeois advancement, the Catholic sectarian
state, a disparaging attitude to the Irish language. What brought on this
mood of tolerance on Ferguson's part, we don't know (though he shared
with the old "Liberator" an aversion to physical force). As for the language
– O'Connell viewed Irish, which he spoke himself, as a barrier to the social
betterment of the masses; while Ferguson, though it's unlikely that he ever
mastered it completely, was wholly in favour of its survival.

In the interests of preserving the riches contained in the storehouse of
mediaeval Irish literature, of which he was well aware, he worked hard on
his translations of certain bardic tales (with help from his friend John
O'Donovan, who provided the basic translations). He worked hard, and he
made the result hard work for readers of the future, who were apt to baulk
at lines like the following (from "The Death of Dermid"):

"Ah me", said Dermid, "hast thou then forgot
Thy warrior-art that oft, when helms were split,
And buckler-bosses shatter'd by the spear,
Has satisfied the thirst of wounded men?"

So it plods on. "Intolerably boring" was the majority verdict. But
Ferguson by this stage (the 1860s) was in a position to please himself as far
as his writing projects were concerned, without reference to any potential
readership. He had secured a niche among the intellectual Ascendancy elite
of Dublin, partly as a consequence of his marriage (at 38) to an heiress,
Mary Catherine Guinness of the brewing dynasty, and partly to do with his
enhanced status as Deputy Keeper of the Public Records of Ireland (not to
mention the knighthood conferred on him in 1878, eight years before his
death).

The rather dashing, clever and opinionated Belfast youth had become a
man of substance and correctitude, immersed in antiquarian pursuits, living
in a gentlemanly fashion with his wife at 20, North Great George's Street in
Dublin. Did he take at all an ironical attitude to his aggrandizement? One
would like to think so, to dismiss the stuffed-shirt figure that emerges from
Lady Ferguson's two-volume biography of her husband as merely a figment

of wifely piety. If only one could go back to 1880 or thereabouts and form an opinion for oneself … What did his friends make of him? One friend, the aforementioned John O'Donovan, appealed to Ferguson for help in resolving a fraught situation with his next-door neighbour, "the mad poet" Thomas Caulfield Irwin (actually, an accomplished and much underrated poet). "He says I am his enemy", O'Donovan wrote. "… One of us must leave. I have a houseful of books; he has an umbrella and a revolver." The tone of this plea is not altogether serious: we don't know if Ferguson intervened in the matter, or to what effect if he did; but poor Irwin, driven mad by the death of his young son, was not really a danger to anyone, revolver notwithstanding. The incident just makes an intriguing footnote to Dublin literary goings-on of the period, and Ferguson's part in them.

It's also a tiny antidote to the blandness of Lady Ferguson's book. In the end, the greatest service *Sir Samuel Ferguson and the Ireland of His Day* performs for its subject is to publish, for the first time, those late Browningesque monologues, "At the Polo-Ground" and "In Carey's Footsteps", which show their author shaking off his antiquarianism and becoming, for the moment, thoroughly modern and psychologically astute. The occasion was a dramatic instance of Victorian-Irish terrorism, the "Phoenix Park" murders of Lord Frederick Cavendish and his colleague Thomas Burke, by a group affiliated to the Irish Republican Brotherhood calling itself the Invincibles. The year was 1882. Ferguson, now in his seventies, must have shuddered to think that any work of his might have seemed to sanction so drastic and distorted a form of "nationalism" – just as Yeats, later, would ask himself, "did that play of mine send out / Certain men the English shot?" – but, with these monologues, and for all his revulsion, Ferguson gets inside the minds of James Carey, who gave the signal to the Phoenix Park assassins, and of a priest who might have acted to stop the atrocity, but didn't. His failure to

> Express some detestation – say at least,
> Such crimes are cowardly, and Irishmen,
> Having the true faith, should be bold to act
> The manlier part

bothers the priest, but perhaps not unduly. The end – the establishment of a Catholic nation – is the main thing, and whatever it takes to get the Viceregal Lodge made over as an archbishop's residence will be justified in the eyes of God. Or so thinks Ferguson's priest, in the wake of Carey.

With these impersonations – a far cry from bardic turgidity – Ferguson displays yet another side to his many-sided expertise. The political commentator and the poet are finally fused. Or, looking at Ferguson's life in another way – with benefit of hindsight – you could say the youthful lampooner, translator, inspired balladeer, Ulster pragmatist and Tory, the tentative Young Irelander, Dublin barrister and grandee, antiquary and Irish revivalist, all separate into their proper contexts, giving a coherent structure to Ferguson's prodigious gifts. His protean quality, though, never worked greatly to his advantage as a literary figure; and after his death it left him in a kind of limbo, unclaimed by any powerful literary or political faction in the country. (Yeats had long outgrown his mentor.) Many people had cause, or thought they had, to be sniffy about this or that aspect of Ferguson's outlook or his output. Would-be admirers soon found something to curb their enthusiasm. "The Fairy Thorn" was one thing, if you relished an indigenous grace and otherworldliness, but what about "Father Tom and the Pope"? "Father Tom", as we've seen, is a stricture on clerical – Catholic – ignorance and bigotry, which certainly existed in the 1830s when Ferguson pilloried them. But this exercise in satire wasn't geared to win over the Catholic nation, any more than Ferguson's immersion in Celtic culture would have struck a chord with the general run of Unionists. Too Protestant for the Popeheads – and Northern Protestant at that – and too Irish-orientated for the Billy-boys, he was relegated to a spot on the periphery of Irish letters – from which, occasionally, he's ushered up towards the centre, whenever someone recognizes a prescient moment in his work, an exciting innovation or an insight felicitously expressed.

Too much going on in Ferguson's working life, then, to consolidate his achievement? Not a bit of it. I would like to suggest that his multiplicity of styles actually works as a source of energy and independence of thought, as well as setting him up as a representative Irishman, full of mixed elements and contradictory affiliations … As far as the latter are concerned: we can only admire the aplomb with which he ended a speech to the Repeal Union in 1848, even if we remain mystified by his final joint assertions, "Rule, Britannia" and "We are not a colony of Great Britain". However, if the enticing concept of time-travelling were to become an actuality, and one might find oneself knocking on the door of an imposing Georgian house in Victorian Dublin, redolent of a bygone elegance and formality – and if one were then brought face-to-face with the poet and antiquary with his pince-nez, frock coat and spruce cravat, looking a bit bemused at encountering a visitor from the twenty-first century but politely waiting for whatever communication was about to be vouchsafed to him … rather than seeking any kind of explanation, the first utterance one would come out with might take the form of an apology.

We need to apologize for the eclipse of his reputation, particularly in his native North: mention the name Ferguson in philistine Ulster, and everyone thinks you're referring to the inventor of the tractor. *Our* Ferguson's house in Dublin has sported a memorial plaque for years, but his birthplace – or what is left of it – in High Street, Belfast, has only acquired one in this, his bicentennial year. I cannot explain the city's tardiness in commemorating the laureate of its once-great shipbuilding industry. The sad decline of the High Street Ferguson house from Georgian handsomeness and prosperity can be traced through its existence as a hat shop in the early twentieth century, then as part of the site for a branch of Woolworth's once the original terrace had been cleared away; now, an undistinguished Dunne's Stores stands right next to the spot.

Even with that item of dereliction out of the way, we might continue to feel abashed at having to explain to Ferguson that the only full-length biography of him, a hundred and twenty-two years after his death, is written in Irish: *Samuel Ferguson: Beatha agus Saothar*, by Greagoir Ó Duill (1993). All right, it's appropriate in one sense, given Ferguson's contribution to a cultural climate conducive to the revival of the Irish language; but it's not exactly geared to raise awareness of his predominance, or his impact, outside a limited circle of Irish-speakers. Between his wife's hagiography of 1886, which tells us very little about Ferguson himself *or* the Ireland of his day, and Ó Duill's account which is necessarily a closed book to the English-speaking world, very little of Ferguson's intriguing personality or day-to-day activities emerges. Why is this, we might ask, when hundreds less noteworthy or exemplary have had the minutiae of their existences obsessively re-created? It can't be solely because Ferguson's high Toryism doesn't chime with ideologies of the present, or because no one can face having to plough their way through the whole of *Congal* or *Conary*. ("*Congal*", says the critic Patrick Power in the tone of a put-upon schoolboy, "is seldom read nowadays except by those who must do so.") No, there must be some reason I'm overlooking for this bewildering *lacuna* in the field of Irish biography.

It's a circumstance which no apology can possibly mitigate. But one might, without impertinence, express a measure of regret for the tendency of nearly every critic who considers his oeuvre, to poke mild fun at Ferguson's antiquarian exercises, his failure to render his versions of the sagas into an English sufficiently lithe and vernacular to withstand obsolescence – disregarding the valuable breakthrough his excavations were in their day. My apology here might be a little tongue-in-cheek, as I have, myself, quite a bit of sympathy with that putative badgered schoolboy mentioned above. I have not read my way through the whole of *Congal*. But I hope I can appreciate Ferguson's reasons for tackling the task, and the immense scholarship he brought to it.

What I'd be unequivocally apologetic about, in those imaginary circumstances, is the dismal condition of Ferguson's grave, which somehow stands as an image of all the neglect and undue disparagement surrounding the poet and his work. Offered a resting-place in St Patrick's Cathedral, (Dublin's answer to Westminster Abbey), Ferguson chose instead to be buried near his ancestors in the tiny Anglican churchyard perched on the side of Donegore, a haunting and mysterious hill on the outskirts of Antrim town. (I'd like to think it was this setting Ferguson had in mind when he wrote "The Fairy Thorn".) It wasn't a wise decision, in terms of his ultimate prestige. Since a ceremony was held on the spot, in 1910, to celebrate the centenary of Ferguson's birth, no group of admirers has gathered there to do honour to this key figure of nineteenth-century Ireland. It was left to the Belfast poet John Hewitt – one of Ferguson's spiritual descendants, despite his socialism and egalitarianism and the earlier poet's Unionist hauteur – it was left to John Hewitt and his wife Roberta, coming in the 1940s and 50s from their holiday cottage in the Antrim Glens, to keep the grave of Ferguson and Mary Catherine Guinness looking as tidy and cherished as possible. Up the steep side of Donegore they would trek, carrying flowers and trowels to smooth the earth and make the tomb pristine. Now they are dead too, and their charming act of homage has gone unrepeated. Rusted railings, overgrown grass, flourishing weeds, a barely legible inscription, cracked and falling-in gravestone mark the Ferguson burial plot. Actually, the single grave within the small enclosure, with its stone slab broken in pieces, isn't Samuel Ferguson's at all. A Godfrey William Ferguson and his wife are buried there, where they've lain since the 1930s. Our Ferguson's solitary memorial is a plaque attached to the back wall of the plot, "Sacred to the Beloved Memory of ...", of fairly recent date. One would infer that the original wall collapsed at some point, taking the grave – mausoleum? – with it, and that the whole lot, instead of being restored, was simply covered over with clay. Well! This evidence of penny-pinching and disrepair is a testament to Antrim's indifference to the most distinguished person laid to rest within its environs. It's doubtful if many people know the grave is there – now buried itself? – or would take the trouble to excavate it if they did. It can only be that its significance is not appreciated ... And how would Ferguson respond to that? With a shrug, no doubt; an urbane acknowledgement of the fickleness of human attitudes, of decline carrying with it the possibility of rehabilitation, of the wheels of fame perhaps coming full circle – or perhaps not – and the fact that it doesn't matter a great deal in the long run. He might then quote four lines from his poem "Aideen's Grave":

Let change as may the face of earth,
  Let alter all the social frame,
For mortal man the ways of birth
  And death are still the same.

A critic, essayist and anthologist, Patricia Craig was born in Belfast and lived for many years in London before returning to Northern Ireland in 1999. She has written biographies of Elizabeth Bowen and Brian Moore, and edited many anthologies including The Oxford Book of Ireland, English Detective Stories, Modern Women's Stories, The Belfast Anthology *and* The Ulster Anthology. *Her memoir* Asking for Trouble *(Blackstaff Press) was published in 2007. She is a regular contributor to* The Irish Times, The Independent *and the* Times Literary Supplement.

THREE POEMS

Hugh Dunkerley

FIRST CONTACT

I
Through a haze of ultrasound
we make you out, little amphibian
curled in your amniotic pool.

You're still a long way off,
still trying to imagine limb buds,
kidneys, a central nervous system,

still wrestling with your DNA,
the fishtail that loops you
back into the Devonian.

On the monitor the nurse
picks out your infant heart
draining and filling

with new minted blood,
pulsing its tiny human code
of hope.

II
Almost unnoticed
you've slipped into our lives,
moored yourself to existence.

Even now you could slide again
into non-being, re-enter
the ceaseless, inexorable

lumber room of the world
where the dead
and the yet-to-be born

commune with glacial till,
dust from supernovas,
the mulch of a billion summers.

III
Press on little navigator,
summon the will of your ancestors:
the few hundred who left

the brown breast of Africa,
their children's children's children
finding a toehold

in the alien wilderness of the North,
the tribes clinging on somehow
through plagues and famines,

the ice age's long amnesia.

IV
With each passing month
you move through the constellations,
Gemini, Cancer, Leo,

gathering mass and light,
your heavenly body arcing
across our night,

our waiting hands spread,
ready to catch you
in the net of love.

PREMATURE

I

The anaesthetist's still joking with you,
perspiration beading his thick moustache,
when I realise it's already started

— the rummaging in your womb —
your whole slack body shifting on the table,
the heads of the surgeon and his assistant

bobbing in and out of sight
beyond the green wall of cotton
they've rigged up to hide your lower half.

Then there's a sharp tug, and it's all over
it seems, before it's really begun,
and you ask me *what's happening, what's happening?*

and I can only stand, my legs swimming below me
until I hear a long needling cry
that stitches itself into my brain.

II

What they give me to hold seems too delicate
to be exposed to the brutal air,
a small seed shucked early

from the fruit of your womb,
still matted with blood
and waxy with vernix,

a stunned survivor from some terrible accident
slowly coming round,
tiny fists uncurling like ferns.

III
Under his dome, he's swaddled
in oversized baby clothes,
rigged up with an ECG,

apnoea monitor, the machines
chirping and whinnying,
his face below the blue bobble hat

wrinkled like an old man's in sleep.
When we take him out,
he cries at the light,

grasps your finger,
watches the semaphore of our smiles
from a far-off place

where words of comfort
can't reach him, where every breath
is a stumbling foothold.

THE REFUGEE'S CHILDREN

are dark-eyed and breathless,
all talking at once so what I hear is a babble of dialects,
the older boy's almost perfect English,
the twin girls with their heavy Iraqi accents,
the two-year-old squealing in any language
she cares to make up on the spot.
"Tea, tea", their father says, disappearing into the kitchen
while the children swarm around me,
holding up pale dolls, drawings, animals,
pointing at the Arabic TV channel blaring in the corner
and laughing, always laughing
in this damp, half-forgotten seaside town
where their parents have brought them
so no one will try to kill them;
where the smallest girl dances
in the bare living room
with its peeling wallpaper
and hand-me-down sofa,
remembering nothing of war.

Hugh Dunkerley grew up in Edinburgh and Bath. After publishing two pamphlet collections,
Walking to the Fire Tower *(Redbeck Press, 1997) and* Fast *(Pighog Press, 2007), his first*
full-length collection was Hare *(Cinnamon Press, 2010). He teaches at the University of*
Chichester, and lives in Brighton, East Sussex.

PORTFOLIO

—

Mark Granier

Outcomes

Skip, Blackrock, Co Dublin
December 2010

A Dublin-based poet and photographer, Mark Granier was born in London in 1957 and attended Dún Laoghaire School of Art. He has published three collections of poems, Airborne *(Salmon, 2001),* The Sky Road *(Salmon, 2007), and* Fade Street *(Salt, 2010). His photographic work includes portraits of well-known writers and performers, such as Allen Ginsberg and Jo Brand; and he has done cover work for a number of publishers and publications, including Faber,* The O'Brien Press, Salmon, Poetry Ireland Review *and* The Stinging Fly. *This is the first publication of a suite of his photographs.*

Chairs
2009

Flooded Road, Near Gort
June 2010

Outcome
2006

New Love
2009

Tracks
January 2010

Couple
2009

Seals Near the Ice House, Coal Harbour, Dún Laoghaire
2008

Fern in Gryke, The Burren
2006

Cloud Crossing, Blackrock
February 2008

Ghost Estate, Wexford
2010

Bloomfields Shopping Centre, Dún Laoghaire
2007

Burst Balloon, Baggot Street
October 2010

Mannequins, O'Connell Street
2008

Protest
December 2010

Ringsend, Dublin
2006

PORTFOLIO
is generously supported by Nicholson & Bass Ltd, Belfast.

MUSIC OF TIME IN
REMEMBRANCE OF THINGS PAST
———

Manus Charleton

Involuntary happiness.

Proust is known to have wanted his writing to be like a cathedral. He notably places a cathedral as an image in the mind of Marcel, his narrator and alter ego in *Remembrance of Things Past*, when Marcel first foresees the novel he will be able to write. And though Marcel then modestly opts for the less grandiose image of a dress, we are left in little doubt that his ambition is to produce the literary equivalent of a cathedral. My impression of the novel on first reading it almost 40 years ago was a bit like one a boy might have of a cathedral which his parents bring him to visit while on a foreign holiday: it was too much to take in and understand. The scale of the novel's intricate and sophisticated world of many parts, expressed through rich, lengthy sentences, obscured the internal coherence of its design. My second attempt, I thought, would be like a revisit in which I would be able to appreciate a cathedral-like structure of ornate, integrated sections open to a transcendent domain of meaning.

But once I was into the novel, it seemed less like looking around a cathedral and more like listening to music. Marcel has a particular interest in music. He loves Venteuil's sonatas and septets, especially an encapsulating "little phrase" of three notes. So, it's not surprising Proust would want to try and make his prose flow in a way that enables us to hear it as music; and to hear it as music of time, for the passing of time, along with transcending time, are of course the novel's great themes. The music of time emerges from a movement of descriptive detail rising and swelling into an encapsulating reflection, a reflection whose meaning radiates and subsides through a return to further description which again gathers momentum towards another encapsulating reflection. It's a music we read in the interplay between the literary description of a person's experience of his life and philosophy as his reflection on his experience. Proust's *Remembrance of Things Past* is, among other things, an example *par excellence* of a work in which there is interplay between literary description and philosophical reflection.

By philosophy I don't mean here academic or professional philosophy. I mean the tendency inherent in all of us to try to make sense of our experiences, especially those we find difficult and troubling. We naturally struggle to understand painful experiences as a means of alleviating them. Reflection can loosen their grip and with some release comes some relief. Moreover, because our reflections can seem to apply to the very nature of particular aspects of life, they relieve us through a feeling of having gained general knowledge or truth.

We feel we inhabit Marcel's distinctive, inescapable inner life of feeling and thought in its movement from detailed description to reflection. He describes how other people appear to him in their personal and social lives, such as Swann and Gilberte; how nature appears, as in hawthorn in bloom; and how objects look, such as the twin steeples at Martinville from a horse-drawn carriage. And we follow him into his reflections on his descriptive observations, reflections which come with seamless inevitability.

In particular, we follow his descriptions of, and reflections on, his obsessive love through which we can hear the music of time sound. His antennae of feeling and imagination are highly tuned towards his suspicion that Albertine is unfaithful to him. He suspects she may have "a taste" for sexual pleasure with other women and that she regularly meets with them to satisfy it. Even a chance remark she makes arouses his fears, and he forensically probes its possible meanings for evidence that his fears may be justified. His anxiety intensifies to an unbearable degree and he finds some respite in Albertine's assurances that she is not sexually interested in women, and from observing her behaviour in their company. However, his periods of respite are always short-lived. As he reflects at one point, generalizing from his own particular experience: "Besides, we know all too well that however profound these temporary respites may be, anxiety will still prevail".

Yet his anxiety spurs him to reflect, and he realizes that it's not Albertine's lesbian practice which causes him anguish. Had she been honest with him, he says he would have been quite prepared to allow her indulge her taste in order to retain her affection. The root of his anguish lies in the fact that her lesbianism is a side to her that is cut off from him, a side he can never be part of. He realizes that, like all of us, she has more than one side to her, and that in loving her he desires to love her as a whole, which he cannot accomplish. And so he reflects that love is sustained by what it cannot attain:

Love in the pain of anxiety as in the bliss of desire, is a demand for the whole. It is born, and it survives, only if some part remains for it to conquer. We only love what we do not wholly possess.

Love is bound to "the inaccessible". And so love is inseparable from longing, which immediate circumstances beyond his control make all the more evident. He realizes his longing for a good-night kiss from Albertine (they sleep in separate rooms in his apartment during the period when she lives with him) is part of a pattern of longing which began when he was a child waiting for his mother to come to his room and kiss him good night. And when Albertine doesn't come to his room he suffers in the same way as when his mother didn't come.

We sense how his reflections enable him to rise above the hold his emotion has over him, and how it provides him with some release. However, we see, too, how the emotion continues to maintain its grip. For his efforts to persuade himself that he no longer loves Albertine ring hollow, at least while she is still alive, which is for the greater part of the book. At one stage he tells himself, "Albertine is utterly meaningless to me". Yet in the same sentence he says there is still "the chain that bound us". In the phrase, "utterly meaningless" we can hear his roused emotion which conveys the precise opposite of the phrase's literal content. Like the lady in Shakespeare's play, by protesting too much he succeeds only in revealing how deeply he is still beholden to what he is trying to deny. Even after Albertine's death he remains preoccupied by his memory of her and the effect she had on him. He tracks down some of the women with whom he suspects she had sexual relations, and when he learns from them the truth, the truth he can no longer doubt, he continues to be affected by the relation he had with her.

We can see in Marcel's anxiety, and in his reflections on it, the anxiety we suffer ourselves. If we're anxious about our job, our health or our children, it's because we don't possess any of them as a whole. No matter how we try to contain them they are always to some extent outside our control, especially insofar as our relation to them will have to be played out in the future.

Towards the end of the novel he acknowledges how he had thought it impossible that he would ever be able to get over the idea that Albertine loved women. But he now finds she is no longer even on his mind. His reflections on her hold over him helped. And he attributes the reason to our human strength to conquer our worst fears. But also time has passed, and time is of course the great healer. Also, over time we change, and he recognizes he has become a different person. The result is that we leave behind what had once held us in its emotional grip. "At every moment of our lives we are surrounded by things and people which once were endowed with a rich emotional significance that they no longer possess."

While we can, and do, overcome particular anxieties, anxiety remains as a more or less constant feature of our lives. And the repeated re-engagement with a preoccupation which affects us emotionally is the motor-force of the movement from description to reflection. There is a certain absurdity in the human condition which requires us to try and allay a preoccupation which, when we succeed, persistently returns. Proust doesn't depict it as absurd, still less humorous. Yet there is something about Marcel's anxiety over Albertine which chimes with chivalrous Don Quixote tilting his lance at the windmill he perceives of a giant foe. The Don has only to realize the futility what he is doing and stop, but of course he can't easily do this, no more than Marcel can easily stop feeling anxious. Their minds are made up by the power over them of their emotions even while they struggle to gain reflective insight into their plight. And though the Don does eventually see the folly of his combat, he has no sooner moved on when another chimera presents itself to preoccupy him, just as assuaged anxiety will return, if not from the same immediate cause then from some other.

In a similar vein, in *Waiting for Godot*, Vladimir and Estragon tramp the treadmill of one absurd, temporally engaging set of circumstances after another, circumstances as recalcitrant as they are humdrum. Beckett's characters are caught up in having to go on while knowing in their bones it is absurd. Despite periods of despair, they are still capable of rising to the bait of some interest. It is a fleeting interest for whatever might be on hand. And if, as Cervantes indicates, well-intentioned misperceptions are our human fate, or, as Beckett suggests, our fate lies in the whirligig of passing interests, both show us how we can find relief, if not transcendence, from viewing our fate as comic.

This is not to say *Remembrance of Things Past* lacks humour. Proust lampoons the superior mannerisms of the French aristocracy just as Oscar Wilde lampoons them in the English upper class. Unlike Wilde in his comedies, Proust also exposes the serious underside of people's lives, as when we see the licentious Baron de Charlus as a coarsened, sad and pathetic figure. One notable example of humour is Proust's lampooning of

Brichot, the excitable and pompous Professor of Moral Philosophy at the Sorbonne. He is shown as an academic who lives in his head, who gets carried away by his own thoughts, and whose erudite endorsement of learning from life over learning from books is more than anything intended as a reflection of his own brilliance. We see him as laughably out of touch with the real world while sounding off on its merits as a teacher. But I think there is a deeper purpose here for Proust besides humour. Brichot is commenting on the very process of interplay between life as lived and life as reflected, the very movement through which Proust makes the music of time sound. And the fact that Brichot is shown to be living an unreal or distorted version of the relation serves to throw into stronger relief Proust's attention to writing sensitive and perceptive description as a means of informing accurate reflection. It serves, too, to draw attention to both description and reflection as the recurring compositional elements of his musical prose through which he evokes the passage of time. Where Brichot distorts the relation through living too much for reflection and not enough for experience, the Baron distorts it through living too much in the moment at the expense of learning from reflection on experience. Proust sends-up the Baron's self-importance when he shows him dismissing an interest in history: "I'm not interested in history … this life is sufficient for me, it's quite interesting enough, as poor Swann used to say".

Throughout the novel Marcel continues to move towards some more compelling, rarefied release from his anxiety, move towards it through his appreciation of the arts and, in particular, through his as yet unrealized desire to write literature. He arrives at an experience of this more compelling, transcendent release when, on his way to the Guermantes's salon, he stumbles on uneven paving stones in their courtyard. The jolt transports him back in time to experience again some memories: his childhood taste of the madeleine dipped in tea, his view of the twin steeples at Martinville, and of standing again, as it happens upon two uneven stones, in the baptistery in St Mark's in Venice. He feels he is reliving these experiences from inside them, complete with all the feelings and sensations that were originally present. He has further experiences of recovered memory in the Guermantes's small sitting room used as a library while he awaits admittance to the salon at which the invited guests are listening to a performance of Venteuil's music. The butler has given him a starched napkin along with a selection of *petits fours* and a glass of orangeade, and the touch of the napkin evokes in him the same texture of stiffness he felt from a towel he used while in the holiday resort of Balbec. Through the memory of how the towel felt he relives standing at the window of his Balbec hotel room looking at "the plumage of an ocean green and blue like the tail of the peacock". He also relives ancillary details such as the smell of his room and his anticipation of lunch, details which specify the experience in its lived uniqueness in moments of passing time.

Marcel is entranced by this return of past experiences. He feels especially the happiness the experiences gave him originally, and he tells us it is *the same* happiness he is experiencing again. He is determined to try and grasp what is making the memories so different from normal before they slip away. He realizes that they have come back to him unbidden, out of a past in which their lived reality had been forgotten, and it is this that makes them different. It is precisely because they have come back involuntarily that they are alive with their original feelings and sensations. It is as though the lived reality had been frozen in time such that, on the first touch of a thaw, everything about that reality begins to melt back. Ordinary voluntary memories, in contrast, are pale shadows of these involuntary ones. They are "snapshots" which have been "made arid by intellect" whereas involuntary memories are fertile with immediate feelings and sensations.

This re-experiencing of the still-living past in the present is for Marcel an illumination. The still-living past has escaped its normal fate of oblivion. And he now has an enhanced appreciation of it compared to its first occurrence as a real time happening when his grasp of it was necessarily constrained by the then inherent ongoing press of passing moments. Re-experiencing it enables him to proclaim that he can now discern in it "the essence of things". Moreover, a still-living past exists outside the flow of time and, in experiencing it as such, Marcel also feels outside time. And this feeling sets his anxieties at rest. He has discovered in himself a person who is "an extra-temporal being and therefore unalarmed by the vicissitudes of the future".

Most of all, he finds the experience has provided him with his long sought opening into writing literature. For he now has some compelling memories with which to get underway. Then in the salon, when he observes in great detail the effects that time, like a slow-working portrait artist, has wrought on the features of people he has known over many years who are now old, he sees how he will also write about the changes people undergo. He has, too, an insight into the prose style appropriate to his task, which is one that will emulate music. For he identifies the emotional response he felt while re-living his past memories with how he feels when listening to Venteuil's last music. This music seemed to him to convey "the quintessential character" of the emotion of happiness, an emotion he had cherished in the music for its intimation of something of the highest importance about his experience of life, and which has now become clear to him through visitations from the past. And so in musical prose he can hope to convey the effect of the movement of time through which people age, and convey also, at its heart, the effect of remembering in their still-living form the experiences which had given him happiness in his journey through time. It is music, too, through which we will be able to hear the poignancy of something intimate which has been saved from being lost forever. It is music composed of pendulum-like swings between descriptive and reflective modes of engagement with experience, while centrally alive with the possibility of a transcendent experience of time regained. It's why as we read through the closing stage of the long book we can hear most clearly the music of time playing in a crescendo of descriptive and reflective writing, a crescendo infused with the strains of deeply affecting emotion.

In the interplay between the experience of life and reflection on it, in the call of each for the other, neither is adequate on its own. They are bound in a symbiosis which is our life impulse. Yet experience is primary in all its ongoing rich diversity and subtle shades and tones. It animates and sustains the interplay. While Marcel recognizes that the urge for life necessarily involves the urge for philosophical reflection, in a revealing observation about his ill health he declares his appreciation of life over his appreciation of philosophy. He finds his ill health uproots many sides of his personality, uproots the different "persons", as he calls them, of whom he is composed. Ill health reduces him to a few "hardier" selves. One of these selves is "a certain philosopher" who continues to look for ways to oversee life by thinking about it in general. It is the person "who is happy only when he has discovered between two works of art, between two sensations, a common element". Yet Marcel declares that on his death bed his hardiest of all persons will be the one that desires over again to respond to life's sensations, to experience its simple pleasures. It is "the little person closeted inside me", which he also calls "this little manikin", suggesting it is under some unknown power akin to a puppet-master. It is the one who will respond "if a ray of sunshine steals into the room while I am drawing my last breath, the little barometric manikin will feel a great relief, and I will throw back my hood and sing: 'Ah, fine weather at last!' I will ring for Francoise.

I would open the *Figaro*. I would scan its columns and ascertain that it did not contain an article, or so-called article, which I had sent to the editor ..."

Proust's instinct to place the sensations of life over the acquisition of ideas is not only touching, it is philosophically justifiable. For French Existentialist philosopher Merleau-Ponty there is the sensation of what he calls "brute being". This is existence itself, existence we experience first and foremost through our sense perceptions, but distilled in one intuition in which its physical presence takes on a metaphysical dimension. And it is the mining ground for philosophical ideas. But it is an intuition of existence which impresses on us above all its inestimable depth. It shares inestimable depth with our experience of the vastness of the universe in whose midst we have opened, still very recently in geological time, our eyesight a blinking pinprick lined with consciousness. Brute being shows up ever beyond the horizon of our attempts to grasp it fully, just as a complete, in-depth understanding of the universe continues to elude cosmologists. If we compare the sense we have of brute being's depth to any attempt to express it in philosophical language, we will realize just how inadequate our language is to capture it. This is the conclusion Merleau-Ponty came to in his last, unfinished book, published after his death, *The Visible and the Invisible*. Philosophers, he wrote, have lifted brute being into language, and they need to continue to return their language to the experience of being in "its wild state" to see if their language can still hold. And when Marcel tells us that, at the approach of death, he would continue to desire to experience life afresh, we can sense also his desire for a more satisfying understanding of what his experience has so far meant. Whatever our understanding is, consoling or otherwise, it cannot, if we are honest, fully satisfy us.

When I thought of Merleau-Ponty while re-reading Proust, I remembered my 22-year-old self in the library of University College Dublin at Earlsfort Terrace, a library which was located in The Great Hall (now the National Concert Hall). I had happened upon Merleau-Ponty's book and, as I read his account of philosophy as a necessary interplay between language and the deep silence which prevails around our sense experience of the bare presence of existence, I felt hairs prickle at the back of my neck, for here at last, after a year's search, was the subject I could write about for my Master's thesis. I felt again the emotion I had felt then, a mixture of relief and excitement. And I remembered, as if I was there again, details such as the librarian standing behind the high, three-sided counter, with the passageway through the wall behind her to where the books were kept. And I remembered watching an assistant going down the passageway to look for the book whose title and catalogue reference I had found in the card-index drawers and handed in on a paper slip. And though I wouldn't have recognized it then, there was interplay going on between the murmur of students talking at the library's long tables and the librarian's call for silence when the murmur rose beyond a certain level. For even though the silence settled for a while, the murmur would begin again to rise and spread and she would eventually call again for silence with what seemed infinite patience. And though I wouldn't have recognized it then either, there was music of a kind in that interplay, a music which presaged the music of time I would come to hear reading Proust almost 40 years later.

Manus Charleton lectures in Ethics, Politics and Morality & Social Policy at the Institute of Technology, Sligo. His book, Ethics for Social Care in Ireland: Philosophy and Practice, *was published by Gill and Macmillan in 2007.*

SHORT STORY & TWO POEMS

—

Jacqueline McCarrick

—

HELLEBORES

The untravelled earth.

"Did you say *girls*, Bobby Jean?" Jessica asked, wondering what kind of girls her friend was referring to. "I'd love to take them. I would. But this is no place for ... BJ, do you know what time it is?" Jessica held the phone away as Bobby Jean pleaded and hollered on about it being an emergency. "I can't. It's Jules. First he washed up from God knows where, and now he's gone off again. I've just about got my hands full with him and the plants."

But Bobby Jean wouldn't take no for an answer. She worked on Jessica, carefully. Knowing that Jessica couldn't resist it when she told her the girls' parents had floated off somewhere down the swollen Mississippi. That when the levees had been breached and the bridges destroyed they had never been seen again, and that the two girls had been shunted from Pineville to Baton Rouge to Atlanta. Bobby Jean knew her wards' story would chime with something deep inside Jessica. Because it had familiar themes: losing the people we love and having to carry on all alone without them. Bobby Jean knew pretty much everything there was to know about Jessica May Lawson.

The day the girls were due to arrive Jessica had a clear out of her house, which was really the living-quarters above and beside the store. She cleaned the spare bedroom upstairs, and had Guy, a landscape-designer with no physical strength at all, help her bring a double-bed and a coat-rail into the room. She put fresh sheets on the bed and brought in a bedside table from her own room and placed on it a vase of freshly cut irises. Then she went into Tina's room, stood at the threshold and looked around at the dustsheets covering the furniture. She knew that the two girls could just as easily have had this room, or even a room each, except it wouldn't have been easy for her. She closed the door. She noted how expectant the house seemed, as if it awaited the arrival of the two young girls, hungrily.

The next day, Olivia and Ashleigh T. Williams arrived at Lawson's Nurseries with Bobby Jean over two hours late. Once unpacked, and seated at the table, the girls sat quietly and had hot chocolate and lemon cake. When they were done Jessica showed them to their room.

"They barely said a word other than 'yes Ma'am, no Ma'am'", Jessica said to Bobby Jean when they were finally alone together.

"They're traumatized, and why wouldn't they be? They've just seen the earth open up and steal away their folks. And they had to navigate some deep and mean floods, too, before they got picked up."

"What did the parents do?" Jessica asked her friend, a well-respected realtor who was always doing some kind of good in the community.

"Father a preacher, mother led the Pineville choir. There are relatives in Atlanta, that's how come the girls were sent there, but Atlanta can't find them. Not yet anyway."

As the two girls slept, Jessica walked out into the warm air of the Panama City night. She went to the new delivery and brushed her fingers along the thick green shoots. She could hear the surf crashing on the sands and the sandpipers chattering; between the lull of the waves she could hear new winds gathering. After a while she went to her chair and watched darkness race through her palms and bamboos like the tide. She hauled on her cigarette, pressed her face and neck up against the clear wide sky. This was how Jessica found her unity with the world: imaginatively, and in the dark. And sometimes, cast adrift in the night air, Jessica would think of the nights on the beach with Tina and Jules, back when they were a family. Sometimes she might even hear Tina getting in or out of her car, and it would make her jump. It would never be Tina, of course, but usually Jules with some beach girl. It would never be Tina because Tina had been gone a long time. Jessica's thoughts were just about to slip back to the days of Jules and Tina on the beach when she heard a noise out front. She was ready to chastise her son but turned and saw the taller of the two girls, shaking and crying.

"Are you alright, Ashleigh?" Jessica asked.

"It's Olivia, Ma'am, my sister", the girl replied.

"What's wrong with her?"

"She's sick and we ain't got no medication with us." Jessica stood up. She could hear thrashing noises coming from the room upstairs.

"What's wrong with her, Ashleigh? You needn't be afraid to tell me. In fact it's best you do."

"Olivia, Ma'am, she's, well, sometimes she has these fits." Jessica ran faster than she had done in an age. On reaching the room she restrained the crazed motions of the child, who was lying half out of the bed soaked to the skin in sweat and spit, by holding down a tight and twisted-up cloth between her teeth. When the shaking stopped, Olivia passed out, bone-rattled and exhausted, like the entire State of Louisiana in the weeks after Katrina.

———

"Jessica, I did not know. There was no time, and believe me I'm gonna give Atlanta shit on a stick for this." Bobby Jean sounded furious. And Jessica believed her friend would indeed give the Atlanta authorities shit on a stick. Nonetheless, when she had agreed to Bobby Jean's requests for shelter, Jessica had not planned on offering the two girls anything more than that.

"How come she didn't have a seizure until now, is what I want to know?" Jessica asked.

"Well, you know how it is. I guess her body thought if anywhere was a good place to have a fit, yours was it."

Jessica sat in the waiting room with Ashleigh beside her. She was beginning to regret letting Bobby Jean get the better of her.

"Are you gonna give us back to Atlanta now, Mrs Lawson?" Ashleigh asked.

"Well, of course I won't be doing that", Jessica replied, and looked furtively at the pale, willowy child sitting beside her. There was something odd and overly mature about her. She reminded Jessica of a hothouse flower, as if she'd gone from bud to bloom without much flowering in between.

Olivia was led out by a male nurse. The name on his badge said Eric.

"Sometimes it happens like this with children", Eric said. "They sort of tailor their suffering to the situation. They can just up and decide to feel it later." Eric urged Jessica to get both girls seen by the hospital psychiatrist in the coming weeks. "Standard procedure for Katrina victims. If they lost their parents the way they say, these kids are gonna hurt."

The girls were quiet on the way home. Olivia curled herself up against her sister's shoulder in the back of the car. In the mirror Jessica could see Ashleigh peering out at every blown-away door, broken window or house-frame, as if they were all signs she alone seemed able to read.

"You alright back there, Ashleigh?" Jessica asked.

"Sure", Ashleigh replied.

"When the hurricane made landfall here, it wasn't so bad, as you can see. It got worse towards Alabama. Panama City was pretty much prepared for what it got. You see my bamboos in the nursery?" Ashleigh nodded.

"Saved the whole place. Bamboo bends with the wind, see. Better than stone. And it protected everything inside. All the plants and flowers. All my stock."

"Bamboo wouldn't have stopped the water though, Mrs Lawson. Coz nothing stops water. Water is real patient. I seen what water can do. I only beat it coz …" Ashleigh stopped short, flung herself back against the seat and sighed.

"Because what, child?"

"Well, because I got in touch with my own strength. I pulled it out of me. I had to."

Once again Jessica was struck by Ashleigh's grievous words and gravity of tone.

"What does the T stand for in your name?" Jessica asked, as if might offer up some kind of vital clue to the child's severity.

"I don't rightly know. Troy, I think. I guess they wanted a boy", Ashleigh replied.

———

Night fell on Panama City in late-September around six. After the store closed, Jessica would usually make a light supper, then walk around the nursery doing jobs in preparation for the next day. She'd re-pot plants knocked over by the wind or by children running down the pathways. Sometimes she'd find a raccoon or fox scavenging and shoo it back into the bamboo. The bamboo attracted a lot of rats, too, as they liked to bed down in the dense undergrowth. Occasionally, if Jules were home and wasn't drunk, he would come out and help her align the saplings and shrubs, and then, if the day had been dry, they'd water the plants together. Then Jessica would put on the garden lights and sit back in her favorite chair. She loved the night-sky over the Gulf of Mexico. In the moonlight, the water was emerald green, the sky a deep lapis lazuli blue.

Jessica went to the trays of new shoots and began to carry them towards the store. Before she'd shifted the second crate, Ashleigh came out of the house and began to help. Jessica saw that the girl was strong, built like a boy, broad and thick at the shoulders. Ashleigh carried the trays to the porch where Jessica wanted them laid out in a line so that they could be priced up and ready for sale in the morning.

"Don't you have a boy, Mrs Lawson?" Ashleigh asked.

"I do, but he's out of town. You'll meet him soon enough, though *boy* he is not."

"What's his name?"

"Jules."

"If I had a place like this I'd never leave."

"It's good to travel to places, Ashleigh. Jules – my boy – he likes to get out, that's all."

"You travel much, Mrs Lawson?"

"A little. I wanted to do more. But with the business, I guess I didn't get the chance", Jessica replied.

"Maybe you thought there wasn't much reason. I saw the way you like the evenings out here." There she goes again, Jessica thought, spouting her insight and her wisdom.

"You got a daughter, too. I know coz I seen her pictures. That must be her room with all the covers in it."

"It is", answered Jessica, quietly.

"You waiting on her to come home, too?"

"I am", Jessica replied, swiftly pulling on her damp garden gloves. She tugged at the tiny sprouts of weeds peeping up through the clay. She felt a surge of anger course through her that she could not reasonably explain to herself. Except that she knew this blood-rush always came whenever anyone would try and talk her out of waiting for Tina to come home. Not that Ashleigh had done that. But had she, Jessica would have sorely wanted to rip the child's heart out.

"What are these things anyway?" Ashleigh asked, turning to the crates with their inch-high shoots.

"These? Why, these are my Christmas roses. Except they're not really roses. That's just a nickname they got."

"What are they then?" Ashleigh asked.

"Hellebores. They bloom early. Around January. They're poisonous. But I don't grow them to eat them", Jessica replied.

———

Ashleigh and Olivia had been signed up by Bobby Jean for a term at Bay City High. Three days into term, Cole Spencer, the Head, called Jessica.

"No, it's not Olivia, Jessica May. It's Ashleigh. Look, I just think you should come down here, soon as you can."

When Jessica arrived at Bay City High it was quiet. All the times she'd been in that school for Tina or Jules she'd never seen it as calm. It was like it was shut for Christmas. Cole Spencer rushed into the foyer and asked her to hush as he led her into the assembly hall. All the students sat around quiet as mice, the teachers behind them, arms folded. She noticed that Miss Quigley was crying. Miss Quigley was as stern as iron so Jessica thought that maybe someone had died. Until she saw who it was they were sitting around listening to.

Up front, by the stage, on a small classroom chair, her long pale legs all tied up around each other like pea vines – Ashleigh, talking animatedly about the hurricane.

"It's not just Katrina", whispered Spencer.

"What else is there?" asked Jessica.

"A whole lot of what else. She says ... well ... she says she's ... *the daughter of God*". A cold shiver ran down Jessica's back. Mad as the words Spencer had said sounded, they went a long way towards explaining the unnerving self-assurance she herself had observed in Ashleigh.

"Don't be crazy, Cole. She's a kid. It's just a turn of phrase."

"Listen to her, and watch their faces. She's hypnotic. I'm telling you, the child is gifted. From the beginning of lessons this week she's been dazzling every teacher in her grade. She says she got the gift out in the floods. From the hurricane itself."

Jessica looked around at the rapt faces of the children. They were all engrossed in Ashleigh's tale. Which seemed to be about how when the whirlpool started up in the river, Ashleigh had stood up and demanded it fall away, and how it did just that, and how when the waters parted she walked on dry land to the other side of the river to rescue her sister, Olivia.

In the following weeks the store was the busiest Jessica had ever seen it. People came to buy flowers and wreathes and winter shrubs, but mostly they came to see the girl who had been touched by God in the hurricane. Even when they didn't ask directly to see Ashleigh, or point her out to each other, Jessica knew that that was why most people came to the store. On Saturdays, when Ashleigh would help out, Jessica would see old women or sick-looking people whisper into the girl's ear to see if she could help them.

Sometimes they touched her arm, or brushed passed her clothes, and Jessica knew it was so they could get something of Ashleigh into themselves. Some kind of hope or healing. Jessica wanted Ashleigh to settle down to a normal life, as much as she could offer the child while under her roof.

One evening Jessica asked Ashleigh to sit with her out on the porch.

"Sweetie, I know what you been saying at the school."

"I know, Mrs Lawson, I saw you." Jessica lit up a cigarette. She hadn't wanted to discuss the matter. It was Ashleigh's personal business, and soon the child would be gone from the house and Panama City anyway. But after seeing how people were with her in the store, how they looked at her on the street and in the bank, Jessica felt she had to speak up.

"This has got to stop, honey. You don't realize how people can react to this kind of talk. It's dangerous."

"You don't believe me, Mrs Lawson?"

"It's not about whether I believe or don't believe. Look – Eric – you remember Eric from the hospital?" Ashleigh nodded.

"Well, Eric said you and Olivia need to come by one day soon. He'd like you to speak to someone. Counselling it's called. You know what that is, Ashleigh?"

"I'm not crazy, Mrs Lawson. I already spoke to doctors."

"You did? When?"

"In the 'dome. After a couple of days they had doctors talk to the children who lost their folks. They thought I maybe got hit on the head. But I didn't."

Jessica looked long and hard at this skinny girl with the white braids and grey-blue eyes. She was convinced now that the loss of their parents had caused Ashleigh and her sister such untold pain that they were, indeed, as Eric had said, suffering from some kind of delayed reaction.

"Pineville is a long ways from New Orleans. How'd you get to the Superdome?" Jessica asked.

"Red Cross picked us up on some dirt track", Ashleigh replied.

"By then your parents had …"

"Yes, Ma'am."

"The house went too?"

"Yes Ma'am. See, it came real early in the mornin'. I remember the air filled up with grey and dark, and pieces of our rooms, my dolls, my books, were swirlin' around, gettin' flung down onto trees and other houses. We ran out of the house and jus' as we did it folded up behind us like firewood.

Olivia cried for Beau, our dog, and Ma and Pa went lookin'. They were jus' gone a couple of minutes when the river burst out of the earth and swept everythin' forward. We all got separated so quick. I remember my breath – coz it got took clean out of my body, and my nightdress swelled up and I thought I would take off and fly. But then I got swept along so I clung tightly to Olivia. We seemed to be in the water hours and hours. But nothin' fell on my head, Mrs Lawson. I just made up my mind to pull the strength out of myself, and I did."

"And all of this 'daughter of God' business?"

"Olivia got pulled to the other side of the river and this force started to build up inside the water and I couldn't cross. I tried and tried. That's when I heard a voice, and I recognized what it was sayin'. It was from Exodus: *And the children of Israel went into the midst of the sea upon the dry ground: and the waters were a wall unto them on their right hand, and on their left.* So I jus' did what Moses did, which was what the voice told me to do."

It occurred to Jessica, then, that maybe Ashleigh was right. Maybe nothing had fallen on her head. Maybe she just hadn't been well to begin with. After all, what did Jessica really know about these young people living in her home? So much data had been destroyed by Katrina; Ashleigh could be as ill as her sister for all Jessica knew.

"Ashleigh, Bobby Jean and me, we mostly go to Unity Church. And Unity is non-denominational. You know what that means?" Ashleigh nodded. "It means a mixture of everything and nothing in particular. You see, we don't do much Bible study at Unity. And we don't believe hurricanes have anything to do with God. Maybe you believe it's his wrath, do you?"

"What I believe, Jessica, has nothin' to do with religion."

"Your daddy. Was he a Baptist preacher?"

"Episcopal."

"Episcopal? Well, they aren't fanciful. So how come you got to thinking you're the daughter of God?"

"My daddy said."

"What do you mean, 'he said'?"

"My daddy told me. He said I was special. He said it every night he come in my room. And it was only the moment I saw my sister on the other side of the water, that I truly believed him."

Eric brought both girls out to the waiting room where Jessica waited with Bobby Jean. Then Bobby Jean stayed with the girls in the bright, sea-lit room as Jessica went into the consultation room with Eric. Jessica sat. The female psychiatrist entered and sat down opposite Jessica and opened a file.

"Olivia's epilepsy is congenital, but with the right treatment she will most likely stop having seizures by her teens. She is slightly traumatized, but it seems Ashleigh covered Olivia's eyes from a lot of the horrors they might otherwise both have seen."

"Horrors like what?" asked Jessica.

"Well, there were a lot of bodies on the river. Drownings. A lot of loose animals, too. And it was hot, so you can imagine what state those bodies were in. Ashleigh believes she saw things."

"What things?"

"Like I said. Drownings. Animals gnawing at bodies."

"What else?"

The doctor hesitated: "Well, if you must know, for instance, like a Guardsman airlift a woman then drop her to her death. Like soldiers opening fire on a neighbour of the Williams' who, Ashleigh claims, was procuring food from his own store. These are serious allegations. So for the minute it's Ashleigh we're mostly concerned about, Mrs Lawson."

Jessica decided at that point not to inform Eric, or the doctor, that there were people in Panama City who believed Ashleigh had divine lineage. But somehow Jessica thought that maybe they knew something about this already. The beach town was, after all, as provincial as any small village – which, indeed, it used to be – and, in a way, still was – despite its recent sprawl out onto the highways of Wal-Marts, malls and Po-Folks restaurants. People on this part of the Gulf knew the exact movements of the tide; they knew when new retirees arrived into this or that complex, or when they died. At the Unity Church there would be a coffee-hour after Service each Sunday and everyone would talk. Jessica had the feeling that everyone in Panama City (including the people from Unity) pretty much believed she had the daughter of God living under her roof. So it would be a lot easier for Jessica if it turned out the child had concussion; then everything could calm down before the two girls finally left for Atlanta or somewhere else. Just about anything (except that thing Ashleigh had alluded to the night before) was better than the child going round with an inner power other people wanted a piece of.

"What's wrong with Ashleigh?" Jessica asked the quick-eyed doctor.

"I'd like her to have an MRI", the doctor replied. "Just routine. To rule out concussion or brain damage before we assess her further."

"You don't believe she saw what she says she saw?"

"We need to rule certain things out."

"Well, what do you *think's* wrong with her?" Jessica insisted.

"I think the child is traumatized. Quite seriously. She assumed a lot of responsibility."

Jessica mowed in: "Has she been abused is what I'm asking you?"

"I don't know", the doctor replied. "It takes time to find out."

Jessica called the hospital the following day for the result of Ashleigh's scan: all clear. Then she made an appointment for the following week for the commencement of Ashleigh's counselling. The evening Jessica got the news that there was no sign of damage or concussion, or any nascent tumors in Ashleigh's brain, Jules came home from Miami.

———

She had begun to organize excursions for the girls so they would see less of her unshaven son slouching around the house. Jules had been unusually quiet since he'd come home, broke, in debt, and deeper into the end of his bottle than ever. He didn't join them at mealtimes, and worked mostly alone in the yard.

One evening, Jessica asked Ashleigh and Olivia if they'd like to go to the theatre. The Bellevue players were staging *Come Back to the Five and Dime, Jimmy Dean, Jimmy Dean* at the Martin Theatre, and her friend, Doreen, was playing a waitress.

"Who's Jimmy Dean?" asked Ashleigh.

"A famous actor who died tragically in a car accident", Jessica replied. As soon as she spoke the words she saw Ashleigh's face light up with understanding. She realized then that Ashleigh had somehow heard the story about Tina's car being left open with the radio on by the dunes and the lack of any body, or sign of it, for the best part of seventeen years. Before the girls had come, and before Ashley had stirred people up with her claims of divinity, Tina's disappearance had been the only story of note ever attached to the Lawsons.

After the play, Jessica brought the girls into Panama Java for hot chocolate. She looked at the two girls so joyous in the busy café with the fan swirling crankily above their heads like some kind of wounded bird. She knew that soon she would lose them both.

That night Jessica heard screams and thought Olivia was having a seizure. She ran quickly to the girls' room and opened the door. Olivia sat bolt upright, frightened, white as a sheet.

"Where's Ashleigh?" Jessica asked.

"She ain't here", said Olivia. The moans and cries continued as Jessica walked along the corridor. She saw a light on in Tina's room. She opened the door and saw her son standing by the window, smoking. Ashleigh lay on the bed. There was blood all around the girl's groin, and Tina's sheets were stained.

Jessica put on the main light. She was so dazed by the scene before her she could barely make out a word Jules was saying. All she could focus on was the blood, and Jules' foul smoke-breath filling up her daughter's room. Suddenly her voice seemed to take on a life of its own and she began to shout. She continued until she felt her son shake her violently by her shoulders.

"Are you listening to me?" he said. "I said, I heard crying. I thought it was Tina."

Jessica broke free and went to the bed. She covered Ashleigh with her robe.

"It came just like a flood", Ashleigh said. "I got so scared I came in here so as not to frighten Olivia. I'm sorry about the blood, Jessica. But Jules never touched me, not like you're sayin'."

"Why you just didn't let her have her own room, this room, I don't know. It's obvious what's happening to her!" Jules screamed.

"This is Tina's room. And you know I don't let anyone sleep here."

"Well, why's that I wonder?"

"You know damn well why. Now shut up and get me some towels."

"Tina's dead and she ain't ever coming back. And you know it."

"How in hell do I know that, huh? Am I psychic or something? Are you? They never found a body. Case. Not. Closed."

"Tina's case was closed the night she went out and ..."

"Shut the fuck up!" screamed Jessica. "She liked the nights on the beach. Just like we all did. You, me, her, your father – we often took you both out in the moonlight, you motherfucker. You know that. Now you just like the nights out drinking."

"Come on, Mama", Jules pleaded.

"She left the radio on in the car! Suicides don't leave the radio on in the car!"

"Yes they do!"

"She met someone and took off. She was like that. Flighty. She would just take off."

"She's dead, Mama. I know she is." Jules moved slowly towards his mother.

"Why d'you rush in here if you're so sure about it? Huh? You said you thought you heard her."

"I just wanted it to be true."

"You still came. You're as unsure as I am. Why don't you just admit it?" Jules left the room with his head bowed. Jessica curled up around Ashleigh on the bed and held tightly to the menstruating child. After a while Ashleigh turned to Jessica and said: "It seems to me you had two children and you never noticed but one. And not the one that stuck around neither. Jesus says to love all the children."

"I know", Jessica replied.

"Tina ain't coming back, Jessica May. Not ever. You jus' been clingin' to that radio."

"I know", Jessica replied.

———

When Bobby Jean came to pick up the girls Jules was out in the yard taking the lights off the Christmas tree. He hadn't had a drink in over a month and Jessica was glad to see him busy. A couple of girls from Bay City High had come to say goodbye to Olivia and Ashleigh, and Jessica was leaving them to it. Then, as Jessica tended to the last of her hellebores, their five-petal heads all drooping to one side, Ashleigh came up quietly behind her. Since the night in Tina's room Ashleigh had not spoken again in assembly and had gotten quiet all round. Cole Spencer had even called to ask what had happened to the dazzling student. Jessica was just glad that the circus that had built up around the child had finally packed up and left. And now that the Atlanta authorities had tracked down a relative, an aunt, Jessica had no more cause to worry about Ashleigh. The girl's counselling was to continue in Atlanta, the details of which would now pass exclusively to her aunt.

"Why do they droop their heads like that?" asked Ashleigh.

"I guess they're just protecting themselves."

"From what?"

"From things that might otherwise destroy them. The wind and cold and such like", Jessica replied, and looked up at Ashleigh, puddle-eyed.

"I'm going to miss you Jessica May."

Jessica held her close. The scent of camomile from Ashleigh's hair hung in the air as she moved off. Jessica watched her stop by the Christmas tree and speak to Jules. Something electric passed between them, and she saw her son suddenly become younger-looking and less bound up with his own inarticulate feelings and thoughts.

As Bobby Jean's car drove off with Olivia and Ashleigh in the back, Jessica thought her heart would break. She cleared up the plates of half-eaten lemon cake and tidied up inside. When she went out into the yard to turn on the evening lights, Jules was there. He had a towel rolled up under his arm.

"Where are you going?" Jessica said.

"I thought I'd take a walk on the beach. Maybe take a swim."

"You be careful. Don't go far out. Just as far as the rock."

"I will, Mama", he replied, and walked off towards the beach.

After her evening tour of the nursery, Jessica sat on her chair on the porch and listened to the sea. In the lull between the waves she could hear the low thrum of the humming birds in the bottlebrush. She looked up to the tops of her tall bamboos. The slim, dark leaves bubbled in the breeze all along like a wave. Jessica closed her eyes and pushed her face out into the mild evening. In the darkness she felt herself rising up over all the plants, flowers and trees of her gardens into the warm sea-air, becoming first, part of the lapis lazuli sky, and then the whole sky that looked down on all the travelled and untravelled earth.

(Editor's Note: Panama City is in the western panhandle of Florida.)

SAND

The sea's earth. But rootless and treeless due to the tide.
All crushed stones, pink shells, cockles, mussels
pestled by speed and water. Plus pieces of china:
Minton's blue willow, Wedgwood and Ming caught
in the sea's folds. The mainspring of glass, a hold
for the hours. A hard wash for feet. The material
of dreams; castles that will leave no trace, no colony.
Less fought over than land except where there's oil.
Fine as ash. Coruscates in sunlight, as stars on the black
rubber of sea-divers. Smells of bladderwrack, bladder wash,
all sunburnt and sea-flowery. In our hands like beach memories:
sandwiches with a tyrannical father, a sister's slit foot
on a sharp shell, air-travel and sangria. Its affinity: the stars.
Its elements: water and fire. Not wind. Not earth.

THE SELKIE OF DORINISH

*In 1967 John Lennon purchased Dorinish Island in Co Mayo. Before his death
in 1980 he and Yoko had discussed building a home there.*

She has come to love meadowsweet,
and rubs its Germolene smell
into her sallow skin.
In the evenings she gathers wingnuts
for her new artwork
and makes eyes and beady lines
from black bluebell seeds.

Around the cottage are the trees
I planted as seedlings in '67:
Spanish oak, a row of limes and elder,
and everywhere the stark green water –
on which, at night,
the mainland throws
its gold and amber elvers.

Sometimes ships will stop for stones
for ballast on the western beach.
Once a sailor saw me
changing from my wet-suit;
then Yoko came and we three sat together
drinking, then watching
the grey Atlantic skies
burst open with light.

There is an island for every day
of the year in Clew.
And here we should have come
after she'd had her New York premonition.

But better late than never.

She keeps the house now
and I the sea around it.

In winter she collects her kindling
in the morning,
wearing lambswool boots
that make no sound.
If out, I'll cast an eye across and at Croagh Patrick
then watch the mist fall over Inishcuttle,
thick as sealskin on the reeling sea.

*(Selkies are mythological creatures that swim as seals
but then cast off their seal-skins to take human form.)*

Jacqueline McCarrick is a graduate of Trinity College, Dublin. Apart from her work as a playwright, she has published short stories and poetry in journals such as The Dublin Review, Wasafiri Magazine, Poetry Ireland Review, Southword, Stony Thursday Book, Brace *(an anthology of short fiction published by Comma Press), and* The Frogmore Papers. *Her short story, "The Visit", is to appear in the* 2012 Anthology of Best British Short Stories, *edited by Nicholas Royle, and published by Salt.*

POEM

Vincent Woods

SEBASTIAN'S BUTTERFLY

The white butterfly hovered high
  in a small stone church
     near Barton-le-Clay.

High over the coffin of a boy
  whose father is my friend,
I see his pale face as I speak,
  quoting Dickinson, Rumi,
remember my words to him
  that morning, telling of
my mother's soul returning
as a butterfly, pink and black,
to settle on my hand
the night we put her body
    in the earth,
of how I held her to the night sky,
  starlit-vast and blew my breath
three times before she'd go.

He asked: is this true?
Or are you trying to give me hope
when I feel as if I myself have died.

I said it happened:
That is all I know.

Now I see this small winged life
  brief-bright in the air,
and say Sebastian's name.
We falter prayer and song.

Later I ask Michael
Did you see it —
The white butterfly?

He says no, is hurt, I think,
to think that I'd invent again
for sake of solace.

But a few others saw it.
That is all

And not enough, my friend,
to help you bear the weight
of your dead boy

The grief, you say, an icehouse
around your heart.

You say:

"Let me crawl to a mountainside
and die."

A poet and playwright, Vincent Woods was born in Co Leitrim in 1960. He has lived in the United States, New Zealand, and Australia. He is the author of two volumes of poems, The Colour of Language *(Dedalus Press, 1994) and* Lives and Miracles *(Arlen House, 2002), as well as seven plays. He has worked for RTÉ for many years, and is currently the presenter for RTÉ's flagship radio arts programme, "Arts Tonight". He is a member of Aosdána.*

FROM THE IRISH ARCHIVE

Ben Maier

THE FARM AT MILLISLE

Playing my harmonica.

During the night of 9 November 1938, a series of anti-Semitic attacks was carried out throughout Nazi Germany and parts of Austria. Jewish homes, shops and places of worship were ransacked and destroyed. Vast numbers of Jewish men were taken to concentration camps. In the days following the attacks, the world, largely ignorant up to this point about the extent of anti-Semitism condoned by the Nazi government, started to take note. A reporter for *The Times* in London wrote that "no foreign propagandist bent upon blackening Germany before the world could outdo the tale of burnings and beatings, of blackguardly assaults on defenceless and innocent people, which disgraced that country yesterday". One matter which perhaps touched outsiders most was the prospect of the children of the persecuted families, whose relatives had been snatched away, leaving them defenceless and alone. On 15 November, a committee of Jewish figureheads, Quakers and other benefactors in the UK approached Neville Chamberlain with plans to secure refuge for Jewish children from Germany and the Nazi-occupied countries of Austria and Czechoslovakia. It was finally agreed that a number of transports would be arranged, allowing children of up to 17 years of age to flee the threat of the Nazis in their respective homelands, dependent on a secured bond of £50 each. This mass evacuation became known as the *Kindertransport*, and in all approximately ten thousand unaccompanied children made the trip to the United Kingdom.

In Belfast, the Jewish community and a host of other multi-denominational benefactors had set up a Home for the Aid of Jewish Refugees at Cliftonpark Avenue. However, this and other emergency hostels quickly became cramped with new arrivals. Three members of the Hebrew Congregation were assigned the task of finding further accommodation. In

1939, the president of the Congregation was Burney Hurwitz, a Dubliner who managed his own linen business. In May of that year, he met up with his friend Lawrence Gorman, owner of Mooney's bar in Belfast's Cornmarket. The historian Michael Brennan writes that "Barney probably knew well that Lawrence owned a derelict seventy-acre seafront farm near Millisle ... one can only speculate about the warm and friendly discussion which ensued, but what is known as fact is that the outcome of their discussion was the signing, that day, of a twenty-year lease on the property at Millisle". On 13 May, the *County Down Spectator* reported the lease.

MOONEY'S

Picture a hand-shake above two glasses
of Guinness on a marble table top, gas-
lit. See the two drinking companions,
their words perforating the bar smoke.
As the event takes shape, reach in
and spill a little of the stout, then return
to your place as observer. Watch
as one of the men dips a finger
in the puddle you have orchestrated.
He draws four quick lines and
a spark of Mooney's marble
catches gas-light, filtered
through dark drink. Pan out
to Millisle, where a slip of sea
water, nightly beached
by the retreating tide,
catches the long ray
of the lighthouse
at Donaghadee.
The pool holds
the light, then
the beacon leans
back, limning
sand dunes,
sweeping cool
breezes in
its beam.
May, 1939.
The tense
length
of light
hurtles
out
to
sea.

The *Kinder* came from the Bahnhofs of Berlin, Vienna and Prague, with labels on their chests and a single suitcase each. *We Came as Children*, a collective autobiography of refugees edited by Karen Gershon, tells of the parents of two young boys who followed their sons from station to station through Berlin, "just to get a few last glimpses of our faces". In the absence of adults, the elder children were forced to act as wards of the younger. Many of the youngest were placed in the luggage rack to sleep. Robert Sugar, interviewed in the BBC documentary *The Farm*, recalls the sensation, "like rocking in the arms of Abraham". From the Nazi-occupied territories the trains crossed over into the Netherlands, and to the port of the Hook of Holland, where the children were given lemonade and sandwiches, fruit and sweets. From there they boarded boats to English ports, such as Harwich. Once there, those who were fortunate enough to have someone waiting for them were met, while others were taken to reception centres – out-of-season holiday camps such as Dovercourt in Essex. Some went on to London and other English cities. However, thirty children made the further sea-journey to Northern Ireland. The reasons were mainly arbitrary. In an article published in the *Journal of the Association of Jewish Refugees*, Gerald Jayson writes that "my final destination, Belfast, was decided by the fact that the Turkish lady who sold nightdresses to my father in his Berlin shop had a sister in Northern Ireland who pleaded with the Jewish community". When the *Kinder* first arrived in Belfast in 1939, most were housed in the Hostel for Young Refugees on Cliftonpark Avenue in North Belfast.

ANNA KOESTLER AT CLIFTONPARK AVENUE

My mother sent me here and came no further.
On the platform she left these traces:
a hair-line kiss and a piece of raisin-cake
in paper. I have not seen her since.

Once, my mother bought me dresses.
Coloured like cake and wrapped in paper,
they would not fit me now. The tailor's tape
unfurled, then wrapped back around his finger.

My mother sent me here, but left me traces:
three photographs, three addresses.
I had no one to tie my laces
so they went undone.

When she can, my mother writes me letters.
At breakfast this morning, I opened the latest.
A small piece of lace, embroidered with her name,
fell without a sound from its pages.

In this house, another lies beside me.
An older girl, she talks in her sleep and paces
up and down the room. I listen
to the familiar names and half-phrases.

She murmurs "mother" as I sit her down.
I take out the piece of lace and place it
in her hand and still asleep, she strokes it,
gently smoothing out the creases.

In the early 1980s, the historian Harold Smith published two articles in the *Belfast Jewish Record* concerning the "Millisle Refugee Farm". In the latter, "Setting Up House", he has this to say:

> On the morning of the 14th May, 1939, five Jewish teenagers
> stepped ashore from the Heysham boat and out on to the rain-sodden
> square setts of Belfast. All had arrived in the British reception centre
> from all parts of German Europe within the last fortnight. At "home"
> they had been committed to the Chalutz movement and had attended
> Bachad training centres … another stretch of water had been crossed.
> They were further than ever from all communication with what was
> left of families and friends and no nearer any Promised Land. Morale
> could not have been lower.

These were the "Chalutzim" (literally "pioneers" in Hebrew): highly religious young men and women who had been trained by the Bachad fellowship for Religious Zionist Youth, in order to gain farming skills which they could then take to Israel. The first arrivals on the Farm at Millisle, they were to use the farm as a "Hach'sharah" (literally "preparation"). With Eugene Patriasz – a Hungarian agronomist recently arrived in Belfast and selected as manager of the farm, Herr Patriasz to the Chalutzim – they drove the 20 miles from Belfast to Millisle.

At the end of the beach at Millisle, before the road curves round past Old Woburn House, there is a long path stretching inland with a wood at its side. At the top of this path is the Farm. To the left is a squat row of stables. To the right is Ballyrolly House, a mid-nineteenth-century Victorian farmhouse, which still stands. Patriasz's vision was to get the farm up and running as soon as possible, with the goal of self-sufficiency on the Kibbutz model. This was not to be a way-station, but a community. The Chalutzim spent four days clearing rubbish out of the buildings, returning to Belfast only to sleep. They rested on the Sabbath, but were back on Sunday with brushes and whitewash, hammers and nails. Over the ensuing days, one half of the stables was converted into temporary living accommodation with two-tier bunks and rudimentary storage. Thirteen days after their arrival, the first five Chalutzim moved in.

The following day, another dozen arrived. Among them was Israel Rednor, a technical engineer, who set his efforts on the neglected drainage system, fitting a brand new hand-pump. Wolf Zeiss, a young man in his early twenties, was appointed as head gardener and, with a team of helpers, he cleared the first small plot of land for the cultivation of whatever seeds they could acquire.

A PIONEER SETTING OUT

"Old man", said a fellow pilgrim near,
"You are wasting your strength building here,
Your journey will end with the closing day,
You never again shall pass this way.
You've crossed the chasm, deep and wide,
Why build you this bridge at eventide?"

from "The Builder" by Will Allen Drumgoole, published in "Our Poet's Corner", the
County Down Spectator *on 13 May 1939 — coincidentally, the day before the*
Chalutzim *arrived. In the same paper was the notice of the lease of the Farm, agreed*
at Mooney's.

Take this end of string and walk away from me. Stop.
The wooden peg – push that in the earth with the heel of your foot.
There. We have a wall.

When I say "wall", you frown. You say
you see a level field stretching East in endless ruffles of mud. You say
that my wall – *our* wall – is "air".

Come with me to Donaghadee. We'll peer back
with the eye of the lighthouse, over steam packets, over the arc of the
harbour
and the intervening sea

at a distant map of string;
at each individual taut line of *shtrikl* and the position held
by every peg.

And from that template, you can predict
a gable-ended world. A visionary in the lighthouse, you can cast
structures up out of the mud.

So begin by conjuring white-washed walls,
then home-made breeze-blocks, firm beneath the byre; the arched lip
of fascia and soffit;

the affirmation of un-sanded wood
with its patterns of knots. Form this scaffold, this rudimentary
constellation in a dirt sky.

And do not stop there
but look beyond the preparations; beyond the bare bricks, the steel tacks,
the concrete and the paint,

to images of future use: your little brother
holding a bucket, his hand on the handle of the fresh-water pump
whose deep draw you yourself dug

(keen to get out of the rain,
he rushes back to the kitchen, running tilted with the weight of water.
He gives the tin brimful to the cook, who

lifts and pours
into a pan of potatoes, peeled and sliced; the second harvest
we planted.)

Look again: this time
at the steady legs of the bunk-beds, the two-tiered dreams of sleeping
                                                                friends,
a single pearl of Barley on a pillow.

Feel the rain
on your bare head in this empty field, and then think of a warm space with
                                                                a roof
and four walls

which house the sound of the music:
your voice, my violin. See how the others are dancing in a ring, tightly
                                                                holding hands.
Then tell me all you see is air.

Now that the foundations had been laid, the Farm was ready for its youngest inhabitants. On a summer night in 1939, the first thirty *Kinder* arrived from Belfast in the middle of a terrible storm. Tents were set up. All night the rain lashed against their canvas sides. The children woke up soaking wet. The next night they were moved into one of the cowsheds whitewashed by the Chalutzim. Rudimentary privies were dug. An old stable served for a dining room.

All *Kinder* on the transports were allowed only a single suitcase with the most basic of provisions, some of which were confiscated by the Nazi guards who inspected the trains on their way out of the occupied territories. On arrival at the farm, these suitcases were stored. The word "stanza", as used to refer to the verse of a poem, comes from the Italian *stanza*, meaning "room". The next poem is a *stanza*, a verbal store-room, formed of two lists. On the right is a list of items which might have been found in the suitcases. On the left is a list of provisions which would have been acquired for the initial farm work. The items here were chosen from various "Classifieds" and "Auction Notices" placed in the *Belfast Telegraph* and *County Down Spectator* from May to November 1939, at the time when such provisions would have been bought.

INVENTORIES

a dozen day old table chicks

a tin of watercolour paints

quantity of hay (with rake & rick)

half-eaten piece of raisin-cake

quantity of seeds (oats & barley,

posie book inscribed with name

also perennial, Italian & Timothy)

silver pocket watch and chain

steering gloves & rubber boots

wooden ruler, pencil set

length of wire for chicken coop

and a wooden alphabet

5 young cows, springing

set of crayons (missing green)

stools & buckets (for milking)

no. of tickets (steamship and train)

potatoes (Accord & Kerr's Pink)

piece of white embroidered lace

draining board & porcelain sink

violin with bow and case

& other miscellaneous articles

After a break of a few weeks, the children were given chores. The fields were cleared. The youngest pulled up weeds and thistles and gathered stones, while the older, together with the adults on the farm, dug and hoed, preparing the fields for the planting and sowing of grain and vegetables. Progress was lightning speed. A local man, Bertie Muckle, was employed to train the refugees how to handle horses, how to plow and sow.

There were now three groups on the farm: the Chalutzim, the *Kindertransport* refugees and the adults who had also come from the continent. Of these latter, there were Eugene Patriasz, the Hungarian agronomist, and Dr Franz Kohner and his wife Edith, a Czech couple who had fled across Europe by train with their two young daughters. Kohner became the farm's administrator. Others included Adolf Mundheim, a German engineer in charge of the farm's workshop – a hulking man reported to have taken shoe-size sixteen.

When the *Kinder* first arrived, most could not speak any English. Reverend Thomas Kilpatrick, Minister of the Presbyterian Church in Millisle, and Mrs Leech, a local housewife, volunteered to teach them the basics. After a short time, a dozen of the youngest started at the local primary school. They would walk from the farm each morning, dodging the waves which broke over the sea wall covering the coastal road in spray. The schoolroom, now a Methodist church in the centre of the village, was split down the middle by a sliding partition, with senior infants' first and second class on one side and third to seventh on the other. The headmaster, Mr Palmer, organized the classroom so that each Jewish pupil sat next to a local child. He instructed the latter that if the newcomers were unsure of the meaning of a word, the utmost was to be done to teach them.

SCHRITT FÜR SCHRITT

YOLLAND Yes? Go on.
MAIRE Earth.
YOLLAND "Earth"?
MAIRE Earth. Earth.

Yolland still does not understand.
Maire stoops down and picks up a handful of clay.
Holding it out

Earth.

from Translations, *Brian Friel*

In the early days, side by side, we'd sit and read
long lists of words you'd never spoken.
I held your hand. You took my lead.

I measured out each word, so you could see
that it's a *wing* that helps a bird fly and can get *broken*.
In the early days, side by side, we'd sit and read

that by the beach, there are tunnels of *reeds*
and that *calamine* is a special kind of lotion
which heals the hands. I took your lead

and with a few more words, you and I made
a story of a ma and da and little boy in *lederhosen*.
In those days, side by side, *wir saßen und* ... read?

I showed you how to throw chicken feed;
with a flick of the wrist and the palm almost open.
I held your hand. You took my lead.

And did you know, when we waded through *seaweed*,
that to me you were *ein Held*, at the edge of the ocean?
In the early days, side by side, we'd sit and read.
I held your hand. You took my lead.

By October 1940, the farm was self-sufficient, with two horses, seven cows, two thousand poultry, 16 acres of vegetables and the remaining 54 acres of land in cereal and grazing. Up to 80 people lived and worked there at any one time. On 29 November 1939, the *Belfast Telegraph* published an article, "An Ulster Haven from Hitler", which reported on the farm's progress:

> University students of medicine and law, boys from high schools, merchants, and professional men from Germany, Austria, Poland, and Czecho-Slovakia are amongst the band of workers engaged in digging trenches, building huts, planting crops, or looking after the cattle and hens on a County Down farm ... Acres of ground have been cultivated. Thousands of lettuces, radishes, onions, and other vegetables have been planted or sown, and next year there will be many others. In a well-equipped dairy, butter and cream are made, and as well as the cows 30 store cattle are fattening on the pastures.

New buildings had been erected, including "Mundheim House" – a two-storey breeze-block construction with cow byres and workshops, named after its designer. As the war went on and it became clear that the children would not be returning to their homes in any near future, efforts were made to make their accommodation more comfortable. A long wooden building was constructed with dormitories for boys and girls, and further bedrooms for adults. This building also housed a recreation room, with tables for billiards and table-tennis, and a synagogue. Despite the great shift in lifestyle, the Jewish religious life was kept up and strictly observed. There was no work on the Sabbath. At Passover, long trestle tables were set up for the group meal. There were also three weddings. At the ceremony of one couple, Mr and Mrs Bamberger, Adolf Mundheim, the engineer, recited a poem in German on the brilliance of young love.

There were dances and plays. The "Saturday Night Concerts" were "an established feature at the camp, and invitations sent to the residents of the district ... eagerly accepted" (*Belfast Telegraph*). Franz Kohner, the farm's administrator, was a fine violinist, and would often play. The children regularly walked the three miles along the coast to Nardini's Coffee House in Donaghadee. There were occasional excursions to the cinema in Belfast and visits from American GIs: some Jewish – all laden with chewing gum.

During the Belfast Blitz on 16 April 1941, Luftwaffe bomber planes flew over Millisle on the way to the city. Bobbie Hackworth, a local historian, recalls that, as the planes flew over the village, they dropped flares which lit up the fields like daylight. Despite the intervening 20 miles, it was possible to see the sky over Belfast burning red, the city aflame.

News of events on the Continent came in snatches to the farm. Initially, many of the children received letters from their families. The youngest would often walk down to the beach and watch the boats go by, certain that one would carry their parents to shore. As the war went on, and Nazi persecution of the Jews went to ever greater extremes, the stream of letters dried up. News now came in the form of Red Cross messages, each limited to fourteen words. The historian Jane Leonard recounts the arrival of one such message:

> In 1942, one child at the farm got a Red Cross telegram confirming that his father had died in Theresienstadt. He went down to the beach and played his mouth-organ.

LITTLE BIRDS

The little birds are paddling.
They have orange sticks for legs
and they squeak and squeak.
I tried to touch one, and the mother bird
was angry at me, so I didn't any more.

I like the grey shells
with nothing underneath.
There are also pink ones
with snails underneath. I pat them
but I always put them back.

The little birds are trying to sing
and they can, almost. The mother bird
is careful. She has put them in a circle
and there are some rocks – big ones
with green on them – that stop them getting wet
(but they are allowed to get a bit wet).

There are two towers.
There is a white tower.
The other tower is winking at me
like my friend Erik can do with a mirror.
I like the white one better.

The little birds wave their wings
up and down and they put their beaks
up in the air. The mother bird has gone again
but I will watch that the little birds are alright.
I am good at this type of thing.

I also have a harmonica in my sock.
My brother Isaac had it and now I do.
He told me how to breathe in and then out
and then he told me to keep it in my sock.
And sometimes it scratches, but I do.

The little birds have stopped hopping
and they are trying again to sing.
With my harmonica I can make the same sound
as they do. They cry "peep!"
then I cry "peep" too.

There are three glass pebbles in my pocket.
I found them yesterday near to here.
Green and then white and then another green.
And I put them in my pocket
because they are beautiful.

I am still playing my harmonica.
The little birds have stopped singing.
They are not jumping. They are
more still. They look and they are blinking.
I think maybe they are listening to me.

After the war, some children were reunited with their parents. The majority were not. Some settled in England. The Kohners stayed in Northern Ireland, establishing a successful textiles business. Others went back to the Continent. The last refugees left the farm in May, 1948. Well over 300 adults and children are believed to have passed through.

There is a plaque in the Belfast synagogue expressing the refugees' gratitude to the Belfast Jewish community. The Safe Haven Holocaust Memorial Garden at Millisle Primary School, commemorating the farm, was opened in December 2007. Gerald Jayson recounts his time spent at Millisle as a child in the article mentioned above: "that farm, in Northern Ireland, on which I spent eight years, has held me in thrall more than any other eight years of my life".

Of the farm itself, there is, at first glance, little to show for its ten years of occupancy. Both Mundheim House and the wooden complex have been demolished for health and safety reasons. Ballyrolly House is now crumbling, but contains clues as to its history. On the doorframes of each room are the marks of two screws at either end of a strip of paint slightly paler than that at either side – marks of the *mezuzot* (pieces of parchment from the Torah folded into decorative casings) which would once have graced every doorway. Against one wall is leant the uprooted hand pump installed by Israel Rednor. In one of the downstairs rooms a rusting shoe-mending machine can be found. In a crumbling breeze-block shed, tucked away in the far corner of a field, is a message, written with a finger when the cement was still wet:

> Here in this very place,
> the builders played
> > cards.
> They were supposed
> > to be working.
> The boss came down and kicked
> > up a row –
> Result: Eme Yerstein
> > flew out.
> > 15/11 – 4/12. 1941.
> > > Walter Korbsen.

Ben Maier was born in North London in 1987. He studied English at Durham University, before completing an MA in Creative Writing at the Seamus Heaney Centre for Poetry, Queen's University Belfast. He currently lives in Belfast, where he is reading for a PhD on "radio poetry". He also works as an actor and musician.

David Ludwig Maier, Ben Maier's Jewish grandfather, left Freiburg-im-Bresau for London in February 1937 at the age of fifteen. The following year David Ludwig's father was taken to Dachau concentration camp. While attending Holloway Grammar School, David Ludwig secured a local teaching job for his father, who had been a professor of mathematics at Freiburg University. In June 1939 David Ludwig's parents managed to join him in London. In 2001, Ben Maier and his family accompanied David Ludwig to his place of birth, where he accepted the Freedom of the City of Freiburg and spoke to a number of audiences about his experience.

TWO POEMS

Sarah Jackson

I HAVE NOT DISCOVERED YET
after Paul Celan

This morning, I went to bathe
and found the basin filled with blood, Father.

It shined.

In it I saw the round hole of my mouth.
I have a slow, dumb smile.

These days, I have no eyes.
The two men stood at the window and watched.

The men watched me, so I cupped my hands
and ladled the shining blood to my face.

I washed in the blood,
and the two men watched.

I do not know whose blood it is.
I have not yet discovered.

I washed my hands, my face, and my body,
especially my breasts. I washed out all my crying.

Listen: the morning bells were ringing, and I filled
the jug with blood, and poured it over my hair.

I combed my long, brown hair. I had grown it
for my wedding. So now, if I bend right back

it almost touches my heels. The men
leaned closer. I almost saw them, Father.

Truly, they shined.

I closed the shutters,
and dressed as slowly as I dared.

VOCAL CHORDS

I breakfast at the side of the house
where an old Breton plaque rusts

in the gravel beneath the window,
and there, flies worship the sparrow,

which lies, head bent right back
with its beak snapped clean off

like the lid of the margarine tub.
I bend down, lift the beak

between my finger and thumb,
look into the hollow of its throat

to see its vocal chords nestling
like a peach stone, wondering

where music comes from,
and where my voice has gone.

Sarah Jackson was born in Berkshire, England, in 1977. Her pamphlet of poems, Milk, was published in 2008 by Pighog Press, and she has a full-length collection forthcoming from Bloodaxe Books in 2012. She is a Lecturer in English and Creative Writing at Nottingham Trent University.

IN OTHER WORDS: FROM THE ROMANIAN

Mihail Sebastian

FOR TWO THOUSAND YEARS
(1934)

In the shadow of the ghetto, a small discouragement.

from *Part II*

I couldn't have bumped into Sami Winkler at a better moment. "Just the man I need", he said cheerfully, when I recognized from afar his massive square boxer's shoulders in the corner at the National, where he'd paused, to pass the time. I hadn't seen him since the beginning of December, the day I went to the student dormitories and found him arguing with S.T. Haim, his ideological enemy.

I like Winkler for his sturdy calm, for the stocky physical power his rough appearance conveys, which he really uses as a cover for so much that he has methodically and painstakingly learned by rote. Someone pointed out to me once, in a foreign Zionist magazine, a technical report which Winkler delivered on behalf of the Romanian delegation at the annual Zionist congress in Basel: the subject did not interest me, but I realized how much work he had put into it, his sense of order, his great ability to organize documentary material.

"A bureaucrat at heart", is how S.T.H. dismisses Winkler. S.T.H. is zealous and unfair. And in the end I think Winkler's value lies not in what he is but in what he is not. He's not a lunatic, he's not a metaphysician, he's not crippled with doubt, he's not poisoned by complex crises of conscience. To not be all these things, and yet be a Jew, there's a challenge. I have the impression that Winkler is well up to it.

So, I said to myself, seeing him again, perhaps he would know how to answer the questions disturbing me lately – and though I have neither the disposition nor experience in opening my heart, I talked about the events of the previous days, of all I had been thinking about the isolation of the Jew, and particularly of the intellectual Jew, his isolation from the masses, his lack of aptitude for social life, and finally life in general.

— You, who believe in Zionism and work for the establishment of a new country, has your conscience never grappled with this sterile feeling of Jewish aloneness? Don't you feel that this collective effort you're involved in is somehow against the nature of the Jew, who is destined to live an interior life and to be unable to break the ring of iron that separates him from the world?

Forgive me, I realize what I'm saying is too abstract and pretentious, but follow me anyway. I'll try to be more clear. Look, I think that in an enterprise like this, involving building a country, an absolutely epic adventure if you really think about it, what really matters are not the practicalities – industry, economy, finance, raw materials – but something else, something of the order of psychology or metaphysics, if that doesn't alarm you. A bit of madness, a certain self-ease, even a little irresponsibility. I wonder if we're bringing too many problems with us, to a place where you should go with two hands ready for work. I don't know, I'm not well-informed and don't try to be, because I don't have much faith in figures, but without having thought deeply about Zionism, I believe its starting point is an assault on our own sterility, as it's more of a tragic attempt at salvation than a natural return to the soil.

In recent days, I've felt so ridiculous in moments when I've been suddenly confronted by life and with the masses that, when I'm thinking that there are other young people today like me who've put their books aside and gone to work with a pick-axe, in some terrible Palestinian colony, I ask myself if this leave-taking is an act of heroism, as you probably believe, or just an act of desperation.

— I don't believe anything, replied Winkler. I listen to you and see you don't understand. Too much psychology, and I've no time for psychology. I've never had these kinds of doubts, to be quite honest with you.

I've always seen things clearly – I've always known what to do. I look at you, the way you get worked up, I look at S.T.H., how he chews things over, I look at lots of people and I just don't understand. About your worries about rebuilding a country, I don't know what to tell you. Maybe you're right, maybe not, I've no idea. To me, the matter is natural, healthy and clear. I don't have any doubt that it'll all work out, but I'm not in a hurry either. I work and wait.

He stopped speaking, as though the discussion had come to an end, then, several beats later, added:

— Listen, if you want to find out more, come with me on Thursday evening to Jabotinski's conference. He's a dissident Zionist who's terribly at odds with the central leadership, as a result of his violent activities. He's a strange sort, as you'll see for yourself. At one time, back in the war, he organized a Jewish military legion to fight to take Jerusalem. Come hear him, maybe he can clear things up for you.

———

I listened to Jabotinski, and he didn't clear things up for me. But Winkler was right: he's a sort. He has a clipped, unemotional style of speech, but is also lively and lucid, showing his vocation as a fighter. Not much in the way of gestures, few smiles or frowns. A certain roughness of bearing, a lack of expressiveness even, which could well be intentional. Lots of facts and figures, but wrapped in a few simple – vehemently simple – ideas. I'm no expert on Zionist politics, but I think I understood the main thrust of Jabotinski's position towards the movement's official leadership.

"The executive imagines", he said, "that Zionism can succeed through diplomacy. It starts with a legal fact: England's mandate to create a Jewish homeland in Palestine. This term 'homeland' strikes me as vague and unengaging. I'd prefer them to clearly say 'state'. But, moving on. The central Zionist office thus believes that this legal document may provide a basis for its dealing with England, perhaps enable it to gain land, receive certain advantages and gradually achieve the movement's political and national objectives. The method is simple: the Jews will behave nicely, and in return the English will be magnanimous.

"Well, this policy of haggling and hoping strikes me as the slow strangulation of the movement. Suicide. A national movement which hangs on a document is a recipe for death. We don't become strong through a diplomatic pact, but through an inner creative spirit. With Lord Balfour's letter or without it, with a British mandate or without, it's all the one to Zionism. But without the will to create, without willpower, Zionism is absolutely nothing.

"'But what is it you want to do?' ask the prudent Jews who've heard rumours whispered that I want to raise some sort of army and start a war, or something of the kind. 'Do you want to bring Great Britain to its knees? Do you want to destroy the English navy? Do you want to fight with submarines, torpedoes and the admiralty's battleships?'

"These Jews of ours are pretty smart, as you can see for yourself. But I can be smart too when needs be and this is the answer I give them: that I don't know what I want. I don't know and I'm not curious to know. I don't sit and wonder what will work out and what it will be like. I just feel that things aren't moving and the movement has to shift from international affairs to our own affairs. That we need purely spiritual rather than diplomatic efforts. That, in the end, the most adventurous effort at self-realization is a thousand times more fertile, even when it fails, than the politest call for foreign goodwill, even when it succeeds."

... And so on, for two hours. It was not a success. There were a lot of people, but they were disturbed, afraid even, of the speaker's boldness.

In the end, in the street, Winkler clapped my shoulder and said "Well?"

I didn't know what to say. The man interested me, but the issue remained just as clouded. As it happened, we bumped into S.T.H. in the hall, and the three of us went to a café in the boulevard to talk.

S.T.H. was relentless.

"A fascist, that's what he is. And don't ask me to consider him any less of a fascist because he's a Jew. The idea of a Palestinian Jewish state, created through an act of national will – what an absurdity! And at the same time, what savagery. Don't you see the machinations of the English in this whole business, a capitalist venture, which the massacred native Arabs and the Jewish proletariat of the colony will pay for, their very blood exploited in the name of the national ideal? Great Britain needs a right hand man to guard the Suez Canal, so it's invented this myth of a 'Jewish homeland'. 'Homeland' is too nice a word. No doubt some Quaker or Puritan came up with it. But several million sentimental Jews have taken it at face value.

"I can practically hear that Jabotinski. 'You don't make a country out of practicalities.' Oh really? What do you make it out of then? Out of spirit? Perhaps with spirit, but before spirit there is geography, which is a precise matter, which you can't charm away with lyrical words, the way you can charm a roomful of goodhearted Jews. Land has its own terrible demands: so many square kilometres of land, this many mountains, this much rain, this much drought. How are you going to colonize a land the size of three counties with 15–17 million people?

"And what will you do with the indigenous Arabs, who also have the right to a natural death, rather than abruptly, by Zionist extermination? How will you bring to life an artificial conglomeration of people brought from every corner of the earth through a so-called national process, while ignoring the most bloody problems of the proletariat, social class, falsified political economy? I'd like to know if this Mr Jabotinski has heard of Palestinian labour unrest, of a Palestinian proletariat, of Palestinian finance. And I'd like to know to know how he proposes to resolve them.

"Rather, I wouldn't like to know. Because I know without him having told me.

"I can almost hear: *'Any problem of social struggle is subordinate to the national imperative.'* Not even Mussolini talks that way. Not even German counter-revolutionaries. Not even Nicholas I, the Tsar of all Russians.

"Jewish national unity is an absurdity. I don't know any Jews: I know workers and bourgeoisie. I don't know a Palestinian national problem. I know a practical economic problem involving Syria, Palestine and Mesopotamia, which is not an iota more interesting than the problems of Cuba, Indochina and Eastern Rumelia. The rest is a myth, an idyll, a chimera."

S.T.H. is an incurable Marxist. It's gone beyond a system of political thought and is now a complete inability to understand life in any other terms. Anything that's not a figure is not for him reality. For every fact there is a document, every proof a counterproof, and beyond that everything else is – as he puts it with terrible finality – an idyll ...

I was afraid Winkler would not accept such an open discussion and would be compelled to make counter-arguments. I don't know if he'd have lost the battle – and it's a stiff fight with a polemicist like S.T.H. – but I know we would have spent a wasted evening. Winkler would have produced a set of figures, demonstrating the viability of a Jewish Palestinian state, and S.T.H. would have produced another set of figures to demonstrate the exact opposite.

Again I observe that Winkler, despite his obtuse exterior, can sense nuances when he has to and sizes up a situation. He replied to S.T.H. by shifting the discussion to another level.

– I'm not going argue with you about matters of Palestinian geography and economics, though I could do so. Nor will I attempt to show you that your arguments about the Arabs and the Jewish proletariat carry no weight. I don't deny their reality, but there's a hierarchy of realities which you refuse to recognize. So between two equally valid arguments, one can annul the other, because it has another meaning, is of another order. So let's leave it.

– The question for me isn't whether Jews can create a Palestinian state, but whether they can do anything but. Understand? The chances of the enterprise succeeding matter less than the fact that it is so pressing. If we don't do this, we die. If we do – according to you – we still die. I don't know. Maybe we will, maybe we won't. And for the sake of this "maybe" it's worth making the journey. Don't ask a nation on the road to creating a country to count its money, to take out an accident insurance policy and to make a hotel reservation. In the end, to be honest with you, I find this whole argument pointless. I'm a soldier, a bricklayer, a miner. I listen and work. The rest is an idyll – if I may quote you.

– No you may not. You reason like a girl. Why do you love me? "I just do." Why don't you love me anymore? "I just don't." Admit it, your argument isn't any better. You explain yourself with "just because". Why are you a Zionist? "Just because."

I wanted to make an interjection at this point, though the look of lightning in S.T.H.'s eyes made it risky.

– I'll ask Winkler to allow me to reply for him. I just want to tell you, dear S.T.H. that this "just because" that you laugh at, is still a decisive reply. To be a Zionist "just because" means to be a Zionist naturally, by destiny, like being white, or blonde, or dark, a Zionist because it's raining or snowing, because the sun's rising or setting … I think this is the point that the Zionist drama begins. In any case, this is where my doubts begin. Because I don't think Jews are ready to live such an act of collective life directly and naturally. I regret saying it – though it's not the first time the idea has occurred to me. I have the feeling that the Zionist movement is an expression of despair: a revolt against destiny. A tragic effort to move towards simplicity, land, peace. Intellectuals, who want to escape their solitude. And I believe, ultimately, that the Zionist project contains this tragic seed which we trample upon, hoping we just might be able to forget about it … But won't it rise to the surface some day? For me, this is the only question.

– No, Winkler replied, sure of himself.

S.T.H. was quiet for a while, and just looked from one of us to the other, with a certain compassion. Then he burst out with it.

"Let's go, we're wasting the evening. It's impossible to talk to you. Myths, superstition, poetry … Do you pair reason about anything? On what basis? You sing. A couple of tenors, that's what you are. Puccini, Giacomo Puccini – our master. Waiter, the bill."

I don't think Winkler wants to convert me to Zionism. But he has time for me, because I intrigue him a little. With his believer's calm, my psychological doubts about Zionism throw him off much more than S.T.H.'s political objections.

He sought me out yesterday evening to invite me to a meeting.

"Come on", he said. "You'll meet a Palestinian. A pioneer, Berl Wolf."

"Really, until now we've just been talking like in books, about ideas, impressions, arguments. But this is a living man, flesh and blood. You have to meet him. I told him about you and said I'd bring you."

Indeed, I went and, I don't know why, on the way I was very unsettled … I had cold feet. I had asked Winkler for a few details about this Berl Wolf, who I was going to meet and find out about. A fabulous tale, in short. At age 14, he fled on his own from Russia, in the early days of the Revolution, a docker in a southern port several months later, stuck in Kiel in 1918 when the sailors mutinied, student for a year at an English polytechnic, crosses the Atlantic, spends some time in the United States, where he's a successful scandal journalist, and one day drops everything and leaves for Palestine, as a simple worker in a colony. He remains there a year, working from dawn till dusk with pick and spade … One morning, at the hour when they set off for the fields, there's an Arab attack. He takes a bullet in the left arm, near the shoulder, breaking the bone. Crippled, there is nothing he can do on the plantation. He goes to the office of the Zionist executive and says: "I want to continue working, use me somehow, give me a task". So they sent him to Europe as a propagandist.

Climbing the stairs, I was sorry I'd come. If Winkler hadn't been with me, I might have turned back on reaching the doorstep. "Who knows what awaits me." A long conversation with an agitated prophet perhaps, another series of arguments, another string of misunderstandings, another S.T.H., a Zionist one this time and much more intolerant than the first one, because this one would speak, without wanting to, in the name of his sacrifice, with the silent prestige of an arm lost in battle. I felt already humiliated by any victory it would be possible to have over him through argument.

And what am I anyway? A machine for arguing? What will this man say to me? What will I say to him? Who will arbitrate between his truth and mine? What is the point of all this wasted time, all this hot air? What's the point, if in the end you come back against the same dead-end questions, that same stubborn sadness. An argument, a hundred arguments, a million – to hell with them all.

We went in. A big, empty room with a few wooden benches and – on the walls – a few photographs, Palestinian scenes probably. Some 20 girls and boys of between 14 and 16 years old were listening to a story an older boy in the centre was telling them. They were speaking fluent Hebrew, which surprised me at first (I hadn't known that this language could be spoken easily, colloquially) and then made me feel awkward. I understood nothing and felt like an uninvited guest.

However, the older boy, the one telling the story, made a welcoming gesture and, as we approached the group, I realized with surprise that this child, this adolescent, had to be our man, the Palestinian missionary. While he gestured expansively with his right arm as he narrated, almost singing, his right sleeve was empty to the shoulder, tight against his body and tucked into his pocket.

In amazement, I ran over everything Winkler had told me about him on the way, watched again as if seeing brief cinematic images of his flight from Russia, the prison in Kiel, the crossing of the Atlantic, refuge in Haifa, the years of work in the colony, and I asked myself where this man with the cheeks of a child kept his scars and memories hidden ...

When he had finished his story, he approached myself and Winkler, extending his undamaged left hand and asked in clumsy French if we didn't mind waiting half an hour until he had finished with the children.

– In the meantime, join the circle. I held back. The game seemed rather silly to me, but my hesitation seemed even sillier, intimidated as I was before the kids.

"What the hell, I'm not that old", I told myself, and two little pupils made space for me.

Our Palestinian friend, always in the centre of the group, was now teaching us a Yemeni song. He would say a verse and the kids had to repeat it after him, first speaking it out loud, then singing it together. I kept quiet at first, but he stopped the whole choir after the first few words.

– That's no good: everybody has to sing along.

I blushed, feeling myself singled out, but kept quiet. He insisted again, in a good-tempered, comradely way.

– Somebody here doesn't want to sing. It seems he's annoyed with us – what other explanation can there be for not wanting to sing? Let's all ask him to sing, then I'm sure he will.

Anything but that. I'll do what they want, sing if they want, do cartwheels, tumble head-over-heels if I have to, just don't all stare at me like that, like a bad student, caught copying and put in the corner in front of the whole class. So I sang.

S.T.H. should have been there to see me. He would have roared with laughter. Myself, recalling it, I feel rather embarrassed – wrongly in fact and fussily, for – why should I be embarrassed to say it? – it was a pleasant hour, an hour of holiday, in which I was conscious of doing a thousand silly irresistible things, things more powerful than "my critical spirit", more powerful than my fear of being ridiculous.

In the middle of the room, lock of hair falling over his forehead (as he conducted us by nodding to the beat), a big smile illuminating his adolescent face, our man managed to get us playing in the end. By the time we were leaving, I'd forgotten that we'd gone there to debate ideas. He came up to me and shook my hand again.

– I don't have anything else to tell you. I wanted you to sing and you sang. That's all there is to it.

And that really is all there is to it. Can you sing? You're saved, so.

Well, I for one can't sing. I am shy, critical, have a sense of the ridiculous, am self-controlled, and more tragic nonsense of that kind, as I possess the supreme folly of personal dignity. Yes, indeed, at precisely the moment you hide behind your own penmanship, writing what you think is a confession and a severe internal trial, there is somebody inside who congratulates you behind the scenes and decorates you with the order of merit, first class. I write here plainly and in good faith that I'm an unfortunate fool and meanwhile a voice secretly consoles me: "You're a martyr", it says, "the hero of your own destiny, the guardian of the purest values of human dignity".

The duplicity of humility and pride, which frustrates all my sincerity … There's no call that I haven't undermined, no revolt against myself that I haven't annulled with a small hidden reserve, with a prearranged excuse.

And still I believe, I want to believe, I am convinced that my inability to sing is an infirmity, not a mark of nobility, that this inability to join the crowd – any crowd – to cast myself into the throng, to forget myself and lose myself, is a sad surrender, a sad defeat.

Oh, if I could only not be proud of this, if I could at least manage that much …

I hadn't met Abraham Sulitzer, my old Ahasverus, since that meeting on the train in the Christmas holidays. And now, our paths cross. It's extraordinary how opportunely people enter and leave my circle, as if directed by a thread of dialogue that calls them closer or sends them away, depending on whether they are required or not. Life has this kind of aptness, which is impermissible in literature. If I were a man of letters, I think the hardest thing would be to mask the unbelievable twists of reality, which show such daring and initiative ... (But what is this thought doing here? I'll tell it to Walter. He, as a critic and newspaperman, could at least put it in an article.)

It turns out that Abraham Sulitzer is my neighbour. He lives a hundred metres away, to the left, in an alley that opens onto my street. But because he heads out for work at seven in the morning and I closer to nine, we've been able to let an age go by next to each other without meeting. Yesterday, though, I had to get to the train station at dawn (a package sent home through Lulu) and on the way back I turned a corner and bumped into my friend Abraham.

– I saw you last week at Jabotinski's conference and wanted to call out to you, but then thought better of it. Who knows? I thought, maybe he's forgotten me. A bookseller he met once on a train ... But I wanted to ask if you'd read Sapsa Zwi's history. It's a book I was fond of.

I calmed him somewhat, assuring him that it had interested me greatly. But I'm sure my reply did not please him. (What was "it interested me" supposed to mean? A book either knocks you down or raises you up. Otherwise, why pay money for it?) Abraham Sulitzer certainly thinks this way, but doesn't say it out loud. He just smiles, full of reticence and eager amiability. (Well? Didn't you like it? Let's say, as you do, that you found it interesting. Well? Aren't you entitled to? Perhaps I can do something for you ...)

We separated quickly – we were both in a hurry – but he invited me to visit him some evening – an invitation I accepted with pleasure.

———

Books, books, everywhere books. I've seen people talking to their cats, their dogs ... Abraham Sulitzer talks to his books.

"Come down here to Papa, third on the shelf. Easy, now, don't wreck the whole row. Who'll put you back in place if you do? You? The hell you will. It's always me. And who does Roza shout at? Also at poor me!"

Mr Sulitzer exaggerates. Roza, his wife, doesn't shout: at most she grumbles.

Lord, how she moans at me, in that same slightly Jewish sing-song Moldovan, like his, "I have brothers too, and brothers-in-law, who are salesmen. One sells bobbins, another sells boots. And? They spend the day at the shop, and shut up shop in the evening – and that's the end of it. Does anybody take their bobbins home to sit and talk to?

"It's a curse, life with this husband of mine. I'm so embarrassed when neighbours call by to borrow a little tea or salt when they run out, and come across him, a fully grown man, talking to himself, to the walls, to the books. Now, tell me if you think that isn't pure madness."

I avoid a straight reply, so as not to add to conflict in the Sulitzer household, but my friend Abraham, at his table, besieged by books, timid and wise, smiles at me from behind his glasses, from behind the covers of a book opened wide – a smile of complicity ("let her talk, that's how she is; women are like that; she'll get over it"), the smile of a child who has upset a jam-jar and awaits his punishment.

I look at this kindly old man, who loves books with a passion, like an addiction. I look at this patient philosopher, terrorized by the nagging of a terrible wife, against whom he has no defence but a hidden smile and I suddenly remember Mr Bergeret.

How well Abraham Sulitzer resembles him in this moment, surrounded by books. Abraham Sulitzer and Anatole France. A Yiddish-speaking Anatole France. What a blasphemer I am!

He shows me an entire library, full of surprises. A Yiddish translation of Cervantes. Moliere, Shakespeare. And, nearer to us, Galsworthy, Dostoyevsky, Turgenev, Thomas Hardy. I'm amazed, he triumphant. With every volume he places in my hands, he has a kind of smile of false modesty, like a host proud of the vintage wine he has served you, without announcing its quality, precisely in order to test you. However often I exclaim in surprise at a new discovery, he buries himself deeper between two covers, making a poor attempt at indifference which only half-hides his pleasure. And, when his triumph is decisive (a Jewish edition of Dante, printed magnificently on parchment, with tiny letters, as if engraved in wood), he can take it no longer and explodes almost furiously, struggling with I know not whom.

– Beautiful? Beautiful you say? Beautiful like a puppy? Beautiful like a tie? No, Sir, it's not beautiful: it's earthshaking.

His frowning eyes burn – frowning for the first time. Roza says nothing, a little frightened, unsure what is happening. Myself, I feel uncomfortable somehow. (You don't like me Abraham Sulitzer; I thought you were a serious skeptic, not an amateur, subject to tantrums.)

But he calms down quickly and becomes tolerant again. Now, with a little courage, perhaps my life may not even be in danger if I said – to test him – that I didn't like a particular edition which inflames him with feeling. I don't think he'd kill me; he'd settle for throwing me out.

The truth is that here I am not in a mood for joking either and the revelations of his library open for me a world I never guessed existed. A culture in dialect? European culture in dialect. Why? For whom?

I ask Abraham Sulitzer and his reply this time is no longer excited or furious. It is sad.

– I was waiting for you to ask. What surprised me is that it took you so long. When it gets down to it, you don't know any more about it than any kid in the street who runs after Jews with caftans, when one wanders in here, shouting at him "oi vei" and "achichi azoi". Dialect! Broken German! A ghetto language: that's what Yiddish is to you. If I told you it was a language, neither a beautiful or ugly one, but a living one, through which people have suffered and sung for hundreds of years, if I told you that it's a language containing everything in the world which has been pondered, you'd look at me, well, just as you're doing now. Dialect indeed! It's a living language, with nerves and blood, with its own troubles, its own beauty. With its own homeland, which is the ghetto – the whole world, in other words. It makes me laugh when I hear those Zionists talking Hebrew picked up from books. Do we need Hebrew, us, along with dictionaries, grammar and philology, or whatever they call it? God help them … Turning their backs on a healthy language to go searching in a tomb for a language that has passed away. God forgive me, I speak Hebrew myself after a fashion, having picked it up in my old age, but – what can I say? – to me it's cold, harsh and empty somehow, like wandering through a long, long deserted stone hallway, without a single person or plant or window. How do you say "it hurts", "I'm burning up" or "I miss you" in this language? And if you say it, does it do any good? Say "it hurts" in Yiddish – and you sense the pain. There's blood there, it's hot, it's alive …

– I don't know either of them well, I replied. I don't know, though, to what degree you're right, but – and I hope you don't mind me saying this – I don't think you're all that right. Yiddish is still a dialect – and that's a serious problem. It's a language resulting from the corruption of another. Isn't that a humiliating origin? I find it hard to believe that from the degeneration of one language you can create another.

– But that's where your Zionists get it wrong. It's not a case of a language that's degenerated. It's a case of another language altogether.

Yiddish is only ridiculous in the mouths of rich Jews with German nannies who think that by speaking bad Yiddish they're speaking good German. But real Yiddish, straight Yiddish of a Jew without Fraulein, is a living, hot-blooded language. Millions of Jews speak it, millions live through it. For these millions these books you see are printed, for these millions Jewish is written, translations are made into Jewish, and Jewish theatre is performed. It's a complete life, a complete mass, with its own elite, and without diplomas or universities this elite wants to be informed, wants to know, wants to reflect.

There are Yiddish novelists, poets, critics, essayists and if you could know what wonderful beauties are held within this dialect-culture, which you despise without knowing, you'd probably have many pangs of remorse. Not to mention the folklore of the ghetto – all in Yiddish – a still-living, creative folk-culture, with its roots deep in the periphery, with anonymous singers, unknown humorists, with heroes, with legends, with myths, doubly alive, once through the immediate presence of the life of the ghetto, and then through the more distant mystery of the life of the synagogue. The tense, gritty urban realism of the ghetto and the mysticism of the synagogue united in this folklore of the Jewish ghetto all together constitute something for which, if you have an ear and a heart, makes living and dying worthwhile.

– Dying, especially, I interjected, because living through it is rather difficult. I can't really see those millions of Yiddish-speakers. And I don't really see the Jewish ghetto either. But I do see a multitude of Jews passing definitively into the culture of the countries in which they live: French Jews, German Jews, American Jews and Romanian Jews. A hundred years ago they spoke in dialect. Today they've forgotten it. Tomorrow, their children won't even remember that it once existed. And to such a precarious thing – however beautiful it may be – you want to bind a culture?

– Have you forgotten that, luckily, there are still anti-Semites. And, thank God, that there are still pogroms from time to time? However much you're assimilated in a hundred years, you'll be set back ten times as much by a single day's pogrom. And then the poor ghetto will be ready to take you back in.

– Why a ghetto and not a Palestinian colony? You speak about the ghetto with so much passion, as though it were a place of exile, and with so much love about dialect, as if it were not a borrowed language. If it's a matter of returning to ourselves, why don't we return to where we first started, the place we left two thousand years ago? It's not easy, either way. But if it's going to be hard, it might as well be for once and for all.

– Two thousand years? Do you think Zionism has something of those two thousand years in it? Do you think that these boys of Jabotinski's who wear boots, who salute each other like soldiers, who ride bicycles on Saturday and can say "give me a cigarette" or "let's go to a football match" in Hebrew – do you think these boys have anything in common with those two thousand years of our blood? Two thousand years through flames, through disasters, through wandering come to us through the history of the ghetto. It's a history lived under lamplight. "We want sunshine", these ones shout. Good luck to them – and let them become footballers. They'll get plenty sunshine then. But this lamp by which I've read so many hundreds of years, this lamp is Judaism – not their sunlight.

– You're old, Mr Sulitzer. That's why you talk like that.

– I'm not old! I'm a Jew – that's what I am.

from *Part V*

Sami Winkler has gone. In a workman's shirt, bareheaded, a little knapsack over his shoulder, he looked through the window of the third class wagon like someone taking a trip to the mountains for a couple of days.

I asked him, jokingly:

– Aren't you equipped rather lightly for a man who's making history?

– No. It's exactly what I need. The rest stays here.

– Didn't you find that hard?

– Pretty hard. That's why I'm making it short. One more reason for a clean break. Better to say goodbye to the lot than to one thing at a time.

It was just me at the station. He'd forbidden his relatives from coming and his fellow travellers had gone ahead to Constanta, where they would await him on the ship. Next Thursday they'll be in Haifa.

– And then?

He replied by spreading his arms, probably suggesting a reply too great for a single word: "everything", "life", "victory", "peace" … He was very calm, unexcited. Unhurried.

Two boys came along, selling a Cuzist newspaper. "Take one, gentlemen, it's against the *jidani*." I smiled at them for being so opportune. Sometimes symbols come readily.

Winkler called out to the boys and bought a paper.

"I'd absolutely nothing to read on the journey."

Indeed, he'd brought no books with him. Not a single one. Then again, he never was much of a one for books.

We shook hands. I would have liked to embrace him, but I was afraid of the upset such a show of feeling would have injected in our self-controlled parting. We shook hands.

———

I would like him to prevail, but I find it hard to believe victory will be his. I would like him to find peace among his Palestinian orange groves, the peace we have sought in the way ordained for each of us; S.T. Haim in Jilava prison, Abraham Sulitzer through journeys and books, Arnold Max through poetry, me on the site, building. The boat that takes him to Haifa will cut a path through the waves that perhaps leads onwards to a new Jewish history. Will it take him towards a Jewish peace? I don't know, I don't believe so, I don't dare to.

Two thousand years can't be overcome by leaving for somewhere. They would have to be forgotten, the wound cauterized, their melancholy cut with a scythe. But the truth is there are too many of those years for us to be able to forget them. We live always with the troubled memory of them, coming from far back and hanging like a haze over the horizon of our future. Very rarely, the brightness from a history of warfare, victories and kingdoms pierces the mist. Can a history be constructed out of so little?

———

Winkler has many things to conquer – and he will conquer them. But there is something he must lose also, and I don't know if he will succeed in losing it. He must lose his experience of suffering, he must lose his vocation for pain. The aptitude is too well developed and instinct too entrenched to yield before such a simple life. This bitter root can withstand every season and it will never be too late for it to bear its sad fruit, even in the gentlest of summers, when the soul is lulled into the dream of eternal peace. Then you come face to face with yourself again in a moment of fear and will learn once again what you have always learned and have always forgotten: that you can escape from anywhere, but not from your own self.

I wish I could reproduce word for word, stenographically, the discussion I had yesterday evening with Mircea Vieru.

He had visited me at work. Blidaru's house is of interest to him too. Mostly he's interested in my building, it being the first one I've done alone. He doesn't want to make any criticisms. He very much wants to see me bringing it all to a conclusion, on my own — which both delights and intimidates me. I'm not certain that I'm really getting it right. Sometimes it all seems inspired, clear, expressive. At other times, the contrary; it's all uncertain, cold and schematic. I invited the professor, but he didn't want to come.

— No. Carry on, do what you want, work how you want. That was what we agreed. When you're finished, let me know. In the meantime, it's your house.

From the site, I went with Vieru to the main road, to Bucharest, to have dinner. It's been a full five weeks since I've been out of Snagov.

— I never see you in town any more. Why?

— Because I'm fed up with it. I find the tension there poisonous. At every street corner, an apostle. And in every apostle, an exterminator of Jews. It wears me out, depresses me.

He didn't reply. He reflected for a moment, hesitating, a little embarrassed, as though he wished to change the subject. Then, probably after brief private deliberation, he addressed me, in that determined manner people have when they want to get something off their chests.

— You're right. Yet there is a Jewish problem, and it needs to be solved. One million eight hundred thousand Jews is intolerable. If it was up to me, I'd try to eliminate several hundred thousand.

I believe I failed to prevent myself starting with surprise. The only person I had believed utterly incapable of anti-Semitism was him — Mircea Vieru. So, him too. He noticed my distress and hurried to explain.

— Let's be clear. I'm not anti-Semitic. I've told you that before and abide by that. But I'm Romanian. And, as such, all that is opposed to me is a threat to me. There is an aggravating Jewish spirit. I must defend myself against it. In the press, in finance, in the army, everywhere I feel its pressure. If the body of our state were strong, it would hardly bother me. But it's not strong. It's sinful, corruptible and weak. And this is why I must fight against the agents of corruption.

I said nothing for a few seconds, which he had not expected. I could have responded, out of politeness, to keep the conversation going, but I failed to.

— Do I surprise you?

— No, you depress me. You see, I know two kinds of anti-Semites. Straightforward anti-Semites — and anti-Semites with arguments. I manage to get along with the first kind, because everything between us is clear-cut. But with the other kind it's hard.

— Because it's hard to argue back?

— No, because it's futile to argue back. You see, dear master, your mistake begins where your arguments begin. To be anti-Semitic is a fact. To be anti-Semitic with arguments — that's a waste of time, a dead end. Neither your anti-Semitism nor Romanian anti-Semitism has need of arguments. Let's say I could answer those arguments. What then? Would that clarify anything? Taking into account that all the possible accusations against Romanian Jews are just local issues, while anti-Semitism is universal and eternal. Anti-Semites aren't only in Romania. They're also in Germany, Hungary, Greece, France and America — all, absolutely all, in the context of interests, with their own methods, with their own temperaments. And there haven't only been anti-Semites now, after the war, there were anti-Semites before the war, and not just in this century, but in the last one and all the others. What's happening today is a joke compared to what happened in 1300.

So, if anti-Semitism is indeed such a persistent general fact, isn't it useless to seek specific Romanian causes? Political causes today, economic causes yesterday, religious causes the day before that — they're too many and too particular to explain such a general historical fact.

— You're very crafty, interrupted Vieru. Aren't you trying to make anti-Semitism inexplicable by making it eternal? And Jews innocent.

— God forbid! Not only does anti-Semitism seem explicable to me, but I believe Jews are the only ones to blame. But I'd like only for you to recognize that the essence of anti-Semitism is neither of a religious, political or economic nature. I believe it is purely metaphysical in nature. Don't be alarmed. The Jew has a metaphysical obligation to be detested. That's his role in the world. Why? I don't know. His curse, his fate. His problem, if you like.

Please believe me, I don't say this out of pride or defiance. On the contrary, I say it with sadness, weariness and bitterness. But I believe that it's an implacable fact and know that neither you nor I nor anybody else can do anything about it. If we could be exterminated, that would be very good. It would be simple, in any case. But this isn't possible either. Our obligation to always be in the world confirms it over so many thousands of years, which you know have not been merciful. And then you have to accept – look, I accept it – this alternation of massacres and peace, which is the pulse of Jewish life. Individually, each Jew can ask in panic what he has to do. To flee, to die, to kill himself, to receive baptism. Resolving one's personal affairs involves endless pain which you, certainly, as a man of feeling, will not ignore – but this is nothing more, however, than "resolving one's personal affairs". Collectively, though, there is only one path: waiting, submission to fate. And I think this, rather than being an act of reneging on life, is one of reintegration with nature, with the awareness that life goes on after all these individual deaths, they too being part of life, just as the falling of leaves is a fact of life for the tree, or the death of the tree to the forest, or the death of the forest for the vegetation of the earth.

– Once again, you're very crafty, he replied. You're changing the subject completely. Forgive me, but the problem of the Jewish people doesn't interest me. Their own problem, as you put it so well. What interests me is simply the solution to the Jewish problem in Romania. Not from a metaphysical point of view, which I refuse to enter into, but from a political, social and economic point of view, however that may frighten you. I maintain that the Jewish threat in Romania is real – a reality which must be understood and contained with tact and moderation, but firmly nonetheless.

You reply by talking about pogroms in 1300. Well, that's running from the argument. That anti-Semitism, as a religious phenomenon, is one thing, and my so-called anti-Semitism, which is political and economic, is another. There's absolutely no connection between the two. They're on different planes. I'm surprised at you intentionally making such a logical confusion. Let's return to what is plainly called "the Jewish problem" in Romania. There are a million eight hundred thousand Jews in Romania. What are you going to do with them? That's all there is to it.

– Let's go back then, if you want, with a small, very small, observation on my logical confusion. If you'll allow me.

The nature of today's anti-Semitism seems so different to you to that of 600 years ago. Religious then, political now. Do you really think these phenomena are unrelated? How mistaken you are. Think about it and tell me that they're not two faces of the same thing. Of course, anti-Semitism in 1933 is economic, and in 1333 it was religious. But this is because the defining element of that society was religion, while in this century it's economics. If tomorrow's social structure centres neither on religion or economics, but instead around – let's say – beekeeping, the Jew will be detested from the point of view of keeping bees. Don't laugh, it's true. What changes in anti-Semitism, as an eternal phenomenon, is the plane on which it is manifested. Not its first causes. The viewpoints, yes, they're always different: but the essence of the phenomenon is always the same. And this is, however much you may protest, the requirement that the Jew must suffer.

– Forgive me, please forgive me, but I refuse to reply. Essences, first causes, metaphysics – I don't accept any of this. I'm calling you to order. I'm a thinker: it appears you're a visionary.

– We'll agree even less if you don't reply. Look, I'll indulge you and deal with your arguments. So you'll see how confused things have just got. What you call "arguments" are in reality nothing but excuses. You're not an anti-Semite because you believe in certain Jewish threats, you believe in certain Jewish threats because you're an anti-Semite.

– Observe how this rather resembles the story of the chicken and the egg. Which came first? Anti-Semitism or the Jewish threat? Talmudism, my friend, Talmudism.

– Then it's Talmudism, if you wish. But listen to me in any case. And, so as not to generalize, let's take a concrete example. A moment ago you said there were one million eight hundred thousand Jews in Romania. Where did you get that figure from?

– Where did I get it from? I know it. It's common knowledge.

– "Common knowledge" is rather vague. How was it arrived at? Who arrived at it? Who verified it? Nobody, obviously. According to the Jews themselves, there are calculated to be between 800 and 900 thousand. At most, a million. According to authorities, in taxation, local government, electoral registers – there are slightly more than a million: a few tens of thousand more. But you bluntly say, simplifying the controversy, a million eight hundred thousand. Why? Is it not perhaps because these extra seven or eight hundred thousand satisfies your anti-Semitic feelings, which precede any figure and any danger?

– It's wrong of you to abuse the argument in this way. I don't of course have the means to determine how many Jews there are. Let's say there are only a million. So what? Do you think if there's million, that's not enough for them to constitute a threat?

– You see, dear master, now it's your turn to be crafty. Because that's not the issue. It's not about how many of them there are, but how many of them you think there are. Why do you, so critical in architecture and so rigorous about every fact and affirmation, why do you, so severe in your own thinking and your own conscience, when it concerns matters of art, become suddenly negligent and hasty when you come to speak of Jews, casually accepting a 90 per cent approximation, when in any other domain you'd balk at an approximation of 0.01? Why does your intellectual probity, which I have so often judged to be too harsh, when you foolhardily stake everything you have for the tiniest truth, why does this probity no longer apply here, in our conversation about Jews?

He said nothing for several moments. He stood up, took several steps across the terrace, stopped before me, perhaps wanted to say something, thought better of it, and then continued pacing the terrace, steadily, lost in thought. Then he spoke, very calmly, without the usual abruptness to his statements.

—You were right just now. It's very hard for us to see eye to eye. All this can be construed and misconstrued in a thousand ways. For each fact there are ten interpretations, for ten there are a hundred. An argument construed in five ways, five arguments in five hundred. It'll never end.

— Well, if you reject metaphysical explanations?

— No, be serious. The truth is, we're not statisticians. If we were, it would be as easy as pie. We'd say: there are so many Romanians and so many Jews. So many good Jews and so many Jews who constitute a threat. And we'd be completely enlightened. But as we can neither count them nor judge them, we have to be satisfied with certain impressions, certain intuitions. I know, for instance, that there are two Jewish bankers in Romania who manipulate our politicians, our government, our apparatus of state. Well, I have the feeling that these two examples represent an entire intolerant and domineering Jewish mentality. You want me to give you figures, when it's a matter of intuition? Who are we? People who enumerate or people who think?

— Neither, in this case. We're people who feel. You said it yourself: "I have the feeling that … " Well, we're in agreement here. It's a matter of a feeling, not of reason. That's why the discussion seems superfluous to me. Bear in mind that I tried to avoid it. But I was accused of dealing in metaphysics. I'm so convinced that this feeling of yours, this "intuition" if you prefer, is unassailable, that I know in advance that every argument, good or bad, will fail. I could contrast those two Jewish bankers you spoke of with twenty or two thousand or two hundred thousand unfortunate miserable Jewish workers struggling against hunger to earn their daily bread. But what of it? Would this shake your faith in your intuitions? God forbid! Do you see that what you call "intuition" and what I call your "anti-Semitism" select examples which can nourish it and ignore those which can refute it?

There has always been something in the Romanian sensibility which has driven it to count the deserters and to disregard the dead and wounded. Out of bad faith? No. I'm convinced that that's not it. From suspicion and doubt, from being long accustomed to a feeling of repulsion.

Believe me, I'm not blaming you for anything. I tell you this with my hand on my heart: there's an inevitability to this against which there is nothing to be done. As it happens, your arguments are unjust. Even if they were excellent, we still wouldn't get anywhere. I very calmly believe, with a very sad calmness, that there's nothing to be done about any of this. That with all the goodwill in the world, on both our parts, it's a lost cause from the start. I feel awkward talking this way about myself, but, having arrived at this point, it's best to speak unreservedly. You know, I'm certain that some day, if necessary, I'll die on a Romanian front line. Heroism? Certainly not. But I don't believe I'm a shirker and that I'm not the kind to run from a place where something decisive is being played out. That wherever it may be, in life, in war, in love, I will stay and fulfill my destiny. Our many years of friendship and acquaintance permit me to tell you this simply. Well, do you think this last hour is going to prove anything? Because, one way or another, won't I always be an outsider, always under suspicion, always kept at arm's length?

No, no, believe me, it's all useless. And, anyway, my sense of this futility is my only consolation.

Again he was silent, for a long time, thinking. I couldn't tell if he had been able to follow all I had said or had absently continued his own line of thought. Then he addressed me, with a certain weariness.

– You dispirit me. I don't know why, but I have the impression that every door you close opens ten more. Certainly, I'd find it difficult to reply to you. We would move still further from the heart of the matter. The heart of the drama, if you like, if that pleases you. You're far too passionately Jewish and I'm far too self-controlledly Romanian for us to agree. In argument, of course, as elsewhere, in life, permit me to be less sombre than yourself and to say that with Jews like you peace will always be possible. Even more than peace: love.

IN OTHER WORDS: FROM THE ROMANIAN

– "With Jews like you ..." I've heard this expression before. "If only all Jews were like you ..." It's a familiar old way of being friendly. And so humiliating. I'm tired of it, believe me.

– Tired and intolerant. You don't let me finish, you don't let me explain myself. You'll admit you're a difficult person to converse with. I firmly believe that your "metaphysical" despair introduces too much complexity into what is a difficult practical problem but one to which a solution exists. The fact that I believe this is the beginning of the solution. It remains for you to believe it too – all of you – and the job is done.

– You have a naive spirit.

– Yours is tragic.

We both lit our cigarettes. We tried to talk, but it didn't work – and it was late when we separated, a little embarrassed, with a truly warm handshake.

———

Stefan D. Parlea's conference at the Foundation on "The value of gold and the value of blood". An enormous crowd, on the balconies, on the stairs, on the steps to the stage. Parlea had to struggle to the lectern. He was pale and resolute, as though bearing the burden of the masses, though from time to time he broke into such violent and direct gestures that everybody's breath seemed to hang on his outstretched arm, awaiting something.

I don't know what he said. I tried several times to shake free from drowning in the sea of people under his waves of words, some whispered, some shouted, I looked for a single island amidst the shipwreck, to stem for a moment the insistent thundering flow of questions, to retain a thought, a judgment, a direction. It all seemed overwhelming, urgent, unstoppable, like being in an earthquake. I could no longer recognize the person who was speaking. He was a glimpse from afar, a troubled apparition from a dream, something out of a legend.

I was brought back to the moment by the cheering and shouting and the thunder of applause. A song I recognized arose from the galleries:

The foreigners and the jidani
All suck us dry, always suck us dry.

Obviously.

———

A moment of spasm, a moment of spasm … A world that's dying, a world being born … History split in two … a dead epoch … a living epoch …

Don't be afraid, dear old gentlemen. You have nothing to lose, neither what you've been believing, nor your head, nor your money, nor your little certainties, nor your little doubts. Everything will remain in place, everything will stay as it was. As it happens, there is a cry that arises again on time to calm the fever of indignation and to take the sting out of great revolutions. There is an another death, which can be demanded more easily than your own dear death. There is a race of people ready to pay up on time for you, for the overfed, for the starved, for the white, for the red, for the thin, for the fat. Don't you say that they're a race of bankers? So, let them pay.

———

I asked Parlea:

— Aren't you afraid it's going to end again with cracked skulls and broken windows? Don't you ask yourself if it's going to end up with an anti-Semitic disturbance, and go no further? Don't you think that calling this thing of yours a "revolution" is using too new a word for such an ancient wretchedness?

He frowned, and answered.

— There's a drought, and I'm waiting for the rain to come. And you stand there and tell me: "We need a good rain and it'll be welcome. But what if it comes with hail? If it comes with a storm? If it ruins what I've sowed?" Well, I'll tell you: I don't know how the rain will fall. I just want it to come. That's all. With hail, storm, lightning, as long as it comes. One or two will survive the deluge. Nobody will survive drought. If the revolution demands a pogrom, then give it a pogrom. It's not for me, or you, or him. It's for everybody. Whose time is up and whose isn't, I don't care, even if I myself die. I only care about one thing: that there's a drought and rain is needed. Apart from that, I want nothing, expect nothing, ask myself nothing.

I could reply. I could tell him that a metaphor is inadequate for a bloodbath. That a platonic inclination for dying doesn't balance the grave decision to kill. That through the ages there has never been a great historical infamy committed for which there couldn't be found a symbol just as big to cover it. That, in consequence, we would do well to pay attention to great certainties, to great invocations, to the great "droughts" and "rains". That small discouragement would temper our most violent outbursts.

I could reply. What good would it do? I have a simple, resigned, inexplicable sensation that everything that is happening is in the normal order of things and that I am awaiting a season that will come and pass — because it has come and passed before.

Translated, from the Romanian, by Philip Ó Ceallaigh.

For Two Thousand Years is a novel set in the form a diary, as yet unpublished in English. The first edition was published by Editura Nationala-Ciornei in 1934. Parts II and V, quoted here, are set in 1922 and 1933, respectively.

Mihail Sebastian (born Iosef Hechter, 1907–1945) was a Romanian journalist, essayist, playwright and novelist, who came to public attention again in the 1990s with the publication of his diaries — which detail the intellectual climate in Bucharest, and Sebastian's daily life — as Romania slid into fascism and war with its Axis ally Nazi Germany. They were first published in English as Journals 1935–1944, *translated by Ivan R. Dee (Pimlico). Sebastian's novel,* The Accident, *translated by Stephen Henighan, was published by Biblioasis in 2011.*

A native of Co Waterford, Philip Ó Ceallaigh is the author of two short-story collections, Notes from a Turkish Whorehouse *(Penguin, 2006) and* The Pleasant Light of Day *(Penguin, 2009). He lived in Russia, the United States, Spain, Britain, Kosova, Georgia and Egypt, before settling in Romania in the 1990s. He recently edited the short-story anthology* Sharp Sticks, Driven Nails *(Stinging Fly Press, 2010). He now lives in Bucharest.*

POEM

Michael Coady

TIMELINES FOR NENAGH FACES

for Pádraig Ó Flannabhra, photographer, on the occasion of his exhibition of portraits, "Nenagh Faces the 21st Century", April 2010, Abbey Court, Nenagh

> *Who are you, and what were you before?*
> *What did you do and what did you think*
> Rick, in *Casablanca*, 1942

1

What makes a face? Always two others
must meet and merge, while linked to each
of these are others who once met, now
layered in the deep of all who've been
before we happened on the scene.

But each face is unique, continues
in its shaping to the end. Sometimes
in death the countenance reverts
to set serenely – or else gives up
the ghost in utter ravagement

but in life it's always a work in progress.
My mother at 87 still reached
for her Wrinkles Defence Cream
before her night prayers, somehow believing
in resurrection before death as well as after

for women fight on, supporting
vast industries of dream. Men on the whole
just go to pot. They're into vanities
of power. Sport as surrogate for fight
is their obsessive Oil of Ulay.

2

What then of this array of vibrant faces
found in time and looking out at us?
I don't know your lives though some
bespeak your avocations. You draw us
in as life does everywhere

in its inexhaustible invention
and inventory, with faces young
or old or middle-aged but all
still in the making – each a once-off
genomed map fine-tuned

by all its nights and days to date,
by all the weather that the human heart
happens to encounter on its way
to groom and hatch its textured shape
and realize the soul informing all.

3

There is some magic and some mystery
still with the camera. We speak
of *taking* pictures as we make them,
find them, shape them. In the Louvre
thousands of flashers are every day allowed

turn lenses on La Gioconda.
But try to stand and photograph
the faces of the ranks of flashers
in the act and you're severely
reprimanded. She herself

remains as ever enigmatic
though surely bored beyond all
countenancing. Life on the wall was far less
yawnable those years she hung out in
the bedroom of Napoleon.

4

Flash forward Nenagh, this new century.
Add in to every image here the mind
and unseen face, the art and skill,
the eye and heart of the lens man
who invited each one in to pose –

the alchemist, upfront but invisible,
conjuring place and mood and setting
measuring light and time, a wizard,
though never entirely in control
for chance too enters his arena.

5

Gach nua sean, is gach sean nua* –
amazing to think of other faces
chancing on yours in a hundred years
and raising that same old query
to interrogate your eyes

as time the mystery goes by
with (yes) that same old story,
that fight for love or glory
that case of do or die
as Rick puts it eternally to Ilsa –

Who are you, and what were you before?
What did you do and what did you think?
I put the same to each of you
in turn, in my time as I pause.
– Here's looking at you all.

* *Proverbial Irish.:* Each new is old and each old new.

Michael Coady was born in 1939 in Carrick-on-Suir, Co Tipperary where he has lived all his life. He is the author of six collections of poetry published by The Gallery Press, most recently One Another *(2003) and* Going by Water *(2009), which integrate poetry, prose and photographs in an innovative form he has made his own. He is a member of Aosdána.*

RUSSIAN DOLLS

Matt Kirkham

We must be clear that when it comes to atoms, language can be used only as in poetry. The poet, too, is not nearly so concerned with describing facts as with creating images and establishing mental connections.
Niels Bohr, physicist.

There are six different types of quark, usually known as flavors: up, down, charm, strange, top, and bottom. (Their names were chosen arbitrarily based on the need to name them something that could be easily remembered and used.) http://en.wikipedia.org/wiki/Quark.

An enormous palm tree that grows to dizzying heights before flowering itself to death has been identified as a new genus by botanists working in Madagascar. The Guardian, 16 January 2008.

ONE

Girl, daughter, answer. Get right down to the bottom
of this abiding dream: a palm tree, dolled up top
to fingertips to toe, blooming with open charm
as suits a muster of peacocks, then giving up
the sweet mother ghost inside after laying down
on your same desk her daughter seed-store. She's one strange

hennaed, perfumed, mascaraed mother, this tree. Strange
as spending these borders of time at the bottom
of one and the same tree and opening eyes up
to count with no questions the gold inside a charm
of another late March's goldfinches atop
denuded ashtree fingertips of County Down.

When google-eyed satellites, tin kites, spin, gawp down,
a tin watch of nighttime nightingales, they clock strange
sights and/or flavours, and at the very bottom
of each of Madagascar's shafts, wells, worlds pick up
another, a picture of our selfsame charmer,
dressed with her same three-four-five foot leaves. That's the top

of the great matriarch palm, so it is, one top
tree botanists have yes, only now written down,
sought and, inside quotes, "discovered", scared of one strange
congregation of crocodiles at the bottom.
They sleep. Wait. Open maws, feed, gobble science up.
Who taught us to open indivisible charms

against flying crocodiles? If you ought to charm
her undiscovered Higgs boson down from the top
of the same tree, bite its fingertips or bottom
inside her baby accelerators where strange
entities skit, dart back or forward like a down,
or cloned husk, of undefined hares, don't you give up.

Now, when walking out in County Down, you look up,
fingertips stroking her goldfish – coelacanth? – charm,
on past four, five hosts of sparrows to the treetops,
there, to spot another red phoenix bedding down.
Wait, ask this bird, this time: she won't think it's so strange,
by my eyes, ma palm tree giving up that bottom

line, her air, her eye teeth for the weans. Bottoms up.
Fill another glass to the top with the bride's charm,
her palm wine, drink it down, you, you, drink to the strange.

TWO

Open one and another waits inside,
four times, top mother or flying daughter,
same palms, same charm, same fingertips, same eyes,

same indivisible question: now, is doll five
the wean- or ma-nightingale who taught her
to open one when another feeds inside?

A picture, her girl, babymother of the bride.
Late nighttime clocks her dress, goldfinch borders,
with charms, with palms, with fingertips, with eyes

undiscovered, mascaraed. Yes, she's undefined,
a red and hennaed answer our botanist sought
when opening each world. Another sleeps inside.

Her trees won't ask of science, of crocodile kites
if she counts these congregations back or forward,
her dreams, her palms, her fingertips, her eyes

cloned, blooming. On you watch, daughter, abide,
on your desk it's ghost written you ought to,
by a muster of palms, charms, fingertips, eyes.
You open one and another waits inside.

THREE

She is a botanist, with her dream clock
opening to discover nightingales,
"bloomin' late, baby", a strange charmer of crocodiles.
Her daughter's picture's on her desktop.

Red dress. Flying her kite. Her same girl.
Inside your borders she taught her to sleep
counting cloned and indivisible trees,
these five mustered fingertips her one world.

The night watches, and science, and time.
When one congregation feeds another
with four hennaed palms, mascaraed eyes,

you won't ask who's defined by a question,
the answer, daughter or mother.
You wait on another "Yes".

FOUR

When these eyes won't define sleep
she waits inside the indivisible night.
Mother feeds on fingertips.
A daughter dreams she is a red kite.

FIVE

wait on the night's sleep
indivisible mother
dream a daughter's eyes

Matt Kirkham was born in Luton, England, in 1966 and attended Cambridge University. He first came to Northern Ireland for a year in 1989, and moved to Belfast in 1995. His first collection of poems, The Lost Museums *(Lagan Press), appeared in 2006. He lives on the Ards peninsula, near Belfast, and works as a teacher.*

THE VIEW FROM THE GLEN

Cathal Ó Searcaigh

1.

I'm enjoying a quiet, outdoors Sabbath. Alone I make my way through the bog along the sinewy trails of sheep. It's an evening of scudding clouds and murmuring water.

Out here where green life thrives I'm refreshed by birdsong and the scent of honeysuckle. I become attentive to wonders; to the white drift of hawthorn in a hollow, to patchy sunlight on a hill, to the chant of green foliage on Joyce's farm.

I thank an ancient elder tree for its nurturing breath and courtesy in front of a pink rhododendron. I'm grateful to have an intimate place in the midst of this bountiful community of grass, trees and soil.

My senses mingle with their essences. I know that to be is a blessing. In this sacred moment I want all things to be happy. The earth spins, the trees sway in the wind, the light glides along a hilltop, all is alive and all is dance. I pity those who are estranged from the earth. There is nothing more ennobling than to touch and be touched by this beauty.

Bound here between the ether and the abyss, on the edge of edgelessness, I give thanks to this earthly fate for giving me the gift to wonder, to be surprised, to tremble. My salvation is here and not in any other world.

Today my religion is a creed of amplitude; an open heart that asks the branching tree and the tunnelling earthworm for the truth. This clear mountain stream – steadfast, giving, spirited – tells me all I need to know about the Dharma. A moss-covered stone is as edifying as any sacred scripture. In the presence of still lake-water at Loch an Ghainimh I know the relevatory power of silence.

I feel a vibrancy in every atom of my being that brings me into alignment with blazing galaxies and with blades of grass. After all every particle of my body comes from that primordial orgasm of matter that begot the universe. I'm an exudation of that primal energy. Today it flows through me with an aching love to coalesce, to be whole again. Every part of me and every part of you, every grain of sand and every blade of grass, contains a configuration of the whole. All living matter, be it minute protozoa or a supernova, is intertwined in the bounteous weave of creation. Seán Ó Riordáin, the Irish-language poet recognized this cosmic dynamic in a poem called "Na Fan". "Níl an áit ar fud na cruinne nach ann a saolaíodh sinne", is I think, one of his most visionary insights.

We live in grim times. The intricate balance in nature, that interweave of parts, is coming undone. In the name of development, economic growth and progress, we are all complicit in the ecological holocaust that is laying waste our world. Countless species are being wiped out, radioactive waste and toxic exhausts foul our waters and spoil our air. The detritus of prosperity, the effluent of greed, is killing the earth. Only when we become one ecological congregation, a wholehearted fellowship of love, swearing allegiance to the branching tree and the tunnelling earthworm, will we bring the earth and ourselves back into a natural alignment of needs.

Lucky for me I can enjoy a quiet, outdoors Sabbath in a place where the ecosystem is still diverse and thriving. For that I am grateful. As morning dawns and as evening darkens I give praise for the bright spill of light that allows me to see the unfolding universe of wonder that is Mín a Leá, Mín a Craoibhe and Caiseal na gCorr.

2.

Teresa Kennedy is a citizen of a little republic of light called Caiseal na gCorr. It is one of the neighbourhoods of Heaven; a Montmartre of mystery; a Greenwich village of grace. She is Caiseal na gCorr's most regal resident, its most revered artist.

Over the past 30 years she has been consistently engaged in capturing the shifty spirit of Caiseal na gCorr in her luminous watercolours. She is marvellously adept at trapping those sudden shifts of light that occur in our hilly climate. Suddenly, a hill lights up mysteriously mauve or a field glows in an amber mist or a sunset flush brightens up the face of a gruff lake. Teresa is instinctually attuned to this vibrant light; this grainy, glimmery light that transfigures a morning or raises an evening to a divine perfection. She is held enthralled by this, our daily drama of light and, like Christina Rosetti, knows full well that "could we but look with seeing eyes, this very spot might be paradise".

I love the oriental stillness of many of her paintings. They are small illuminated moments that glow with a lyrical intensity. Suzuki, the great exponent of Zen Buddhism, remarked: "When you do something, you should burn yourself completely like a good bonfire, leaving no trace of yourself". This, I think, is about purity of attention. Attentiveness! Detachment and clarity. These are virtues I sense very strongly in the work of Teresa Kennedy. Being one with what she is doing. Careful attention to the immediate, to the significant detail.

She has always been a generous encourager of new talent in our glen. Like a latter-day Johnny Appleseed she has been scattering seedlings of suggestions and saplings of ideas in the soil of our creative consciousness. The present flourishing of the arts in the glen is due in no small part to her ministering presence over many years.

She is our seer of open spaces; our celebrant of the stellar light green hills. She has made us alive to the awe of landscape; the lingering touch of sunlight on the swell and curve of a cloud, the glimmer of moonlight on bog pools.

Brent Nookes is another local artist and a glen-dweller from time to time. He runs the Harbour Gallery in Dunfanaghy, an emporium of local art and crafts. He is a man of frank views and forthright thinking. This uninhibited flow is also the delightful impulse that runs through his art. It is there in the spill of colour, the rush of energy, the sweep of vision. The spin and swirl of his paintings remind me of a whirling dervish. You can almost hear the whoosh of them as they reel about in rapture. They leave me giddy with joy.

The most keenly lived life is, I believe, the one in which the door of the heart is always open to receive the present. Too many people keep their focus narrow, their windows of wonder curtained tight by habit and conformity. Brent Nookes is not one to shun the heady options of the present. He revels in the here-and-now of things. That spirited vibrancy imbues his art with colour and movement, vitality and radiance. "They catch the heart off guard and blow it open" is a line by Seamus Heaney that aptly catches the power of Brent's paintings.

Ian Joyce is my neighbour in Mín a Leá and an artist of international standing. He is someone who sees the abyss at his feet and yet manages to continue.

His landscapes take exciting risks, a silent daring to summon up and reveal the mystic reality of the familiar. This is not a banal venture into Blakean transcendentalism. In his art, Ian Joyce communes with the commonplace in a way that is neither trite nor predictable. He is a visionary of the real, a see-r who liaises with what is marvellous in the ordinary.

Whether it is a picture of an angel marooned on a wild twilit moor, a bog ablaze with autumn or a moon delicate as a seedling in an April sky, the ethereal is always conveyed with a close, earthy actuality.

A recent painting by this artist hangs in my ouse. The luxuriant yellow of a sunny evening in Fana Bhuí fills my room with an otherworldly brilliance. It shines with light, the kind of lustre that surrounds old saints and mystics, in the glow of icons.

Like Wendell Berry, a sublime poet of the great American outdoors who buries his cast-aside winter writings in the earth come springtime so that the old commingles with the new and the past submits to the future, Ian Joyce uses his rejected jottings and abandoned diaries as calligraphic components in his art, thus fusing the past with the future.

Using a light solvent and brushing it across page after page of the written minutiae of his life, his personal archive is washed out and defaced. However, it is a transformative act where the text is given an afterlife; a slow release of something other than its original intention. A veiled life of rare visual patterns is elicited from the ruins and residues of the faded pages. It is also, I think, an attempt to free language from its weighty load of linguistic sense and give it a new visual coherence. This approach gives his art the appearance of archaic tablets, ancient fragments of a language aglow with the lore of fresh beginnings. Whatever linguistic traces remain are transmitted into graphic runes; a *rúnscríbhinn* beautiful as the hieroglyphics of winter ice on bogpools. It is the inscrutable speech of things; the hoarse cry of wind across March hills; the moist, salty tongue of dripping rain; the cosmic pulse of stones.

As a writer I envy the painter. As I speak, as I write I'm giving birth to words. Words that are smeared with an afterbirth of ambiguity. Words that need to be nourished in the school of meaning. Words that eat, sleep and excrete in the house of sense. Words that scream and smile, laugh and cry in the lap of language.

A painter's little tube of colour speaks with a clear, pristine silence.

Raw umber, sap green, yellow ochre, cadmium red, burnt sienna are heedless of vocabulary, unmoved by utterance and yet they are eloquent. They convey their meaning wordlessly.

Writers have to confront their readers with words that carry the nightmare of their histories, the trauma of their origins on their backs. Words that are worn out by circulation, bewildered by spin, wearied by cliché.

A painting speaks volumes … in silence.

I envy the painter's brightly minted currency of colour. Indigo, vermillion, magenta, viridian can be worked and kneaded into an easy expression – a lucid speech untroubled by words.

3.

I'm rereading a book that was published by Jonathan Cape in 1993. Mary Morrissey calls her first collection of short stories *A Lazy Eye* but far from any sluggishness of sight all of these stories benefit from the author's perceptive, keen-sighted vision. In these unsettling stories the eclipsed eye – the lazy eye of the title story – is not torpid or unattentive. It just veers shiftily in its gaze and looks at things differently.

The characters in these stories, an assortment of displaced individuals – women mostly: betrayed, grieved, guilty – act out of a blighted view of things. The defect in their characters, the squint in their vision, gives them a lopsided, partial view of the world, a view that is deluded but nevertheless unsettling in its uncanny familiarity. We all know the infinite possibilities of the mind to invent strategies of self-deception.

The narrative ploy of these stories usually involve a woman or a girl who is publicly humiliated and then attempts to grasp the indignity of her situation in order to contain it or avenge it. Bella Carmichael, the young woman at the centre of the title story, is travelling by train somewhere in Europe. Setting out she had envisaged being caught up in a revolution, swept up in some large-scale event, something that would single her out, give her a chance to be heroic. Instead, here she was, awake on the top bunk of a sleeper to the grim realisation that her period has begun and with no tampons to stem the flow. "There seemed to be blood everywhere, a huge stain beneath her, a clotted pattern on the top sheet, smears on her thighs." Then there's a sudden shift to Bella's childhood with particular significance given to the spectacles she wore to correct her lazy eye, "the right lens patched over with sticking plaster … so that for one glorious year Bella was 'marked out'".

She is now marked out again, told bluntly to leave the train by an outraged attendant in a small two-minute-stop town somewhere in Belgium. "Don't they understand", she asked the other woman in her sleeping compartment, "don't they know that women bleed?" But this Kafkaesque episode does elicit its own skewed and chilling epiphany. "There would be no large singular event to validate her existence. There would only be more of this official retribution for bleeding in public."

Most of her stories end with this sort of grim, defeatist comfort. These characters have nothing but their deadening despairs, their unruly conflicts, their repressed anger, their frustrations and fatigues to console them.

Mary Morrissey's genius is to identify in her fiction with these aggrieved outsiders, these marked women who cannot conceal their flaws and who seek, to no great avail, a temporary deliverance from their ordeal; some sort of a lonely refuge, *a makeshift, momentary amends*. Her real strength is to allow us as readers to share with the characters their perilous states of instability, to get a glimpse of the gaping maw at the centre of their grim-faced lives. With consummate craft she allows us to live the lives, briefly of course, of these ordinary and yet luridly fascinating people whose quest for fulfilment will always be futile. *A Lazy Eye* is a dark, disturbing book, a sensitive study into the inner turmoil of these pained and thwarted destinies.

Mary Morrissey is a seasoned storyteller with a clear distinct voice. Unfortunately her low-keyed, engaging narratives go unheard in the shrill hubbub of the literary jostle.

Cathal Ó Searcaigh is the Irish language Editor of this journal. His most recent volumes are Seal i Neipeal *(Cló Iar-Chonnacht, 2004), an account of his time in Nepal, and* By the Hearth at Mín a' Leá, *a selection of English translations of his poetry. He lives near Errigal Mountain, Co Donegal.*

CEITHRE DHÁN

Colm Breathnach

AN GRÁ A THUGAIS DOM INNÉ ...

An grá a thugais dom inné
níorbh fhoirfe, níor mhilse, níor réidhe é
ná an grá dlúth te tiubh
a thugann tú dom inniu
nó an grá dúthrachtach gealgháireach
a thabharfaidh tú dom amáireach.

Ach mar a tharlaíonn
bímídne filí
ag féachaint siar de shíor,

mar sin
tabhair dom cairde lae,
a ghrá, gach lá
is gheobhair dán
gach lá, a ghrá
i dtaobh ghrá an lae inné.

AN LEABHAR ÁRSA

Tóg an leabhar ársa seo
go bhfuil an clúdach leathair air ag dul i léithe,
go bhfuil na ciumhaiseanna ar na leathanaigh ann ar scéitheadh
agus an dúch orthu, leis, ag tréigean.
Tóg an leabhar ársa seo agus léigh é.

Léigh pé méid do is áil nó is féidir leat.
Faigh peann is téigh thar aon litreacha ann atá ag éag.
Scrios amach aon fhocail atá míshoiléir
agus breac isteach focail de do chuid fhéin.

Mar chlabhsúr
cuir focail eile
as a dheireadh,
scrígh aon ní is áin leat
fút féin go hiomlán atá,
anois.

Dein an méid seo céim ar chéim
agus chífir de réir a chéile
liathadh an chlúdaigh
scéitheadh na gciumhaiseanna
agus tréigean an dúigh
ag dul ar gcúl
chífir an ghnáthmhíorúilt ag tarlúint,
don leabhar ársa déanfar tráchtas úr.

NÁ CUIR AINM AIR SEO, UIMH. 2

faoi mar a bheadh sileadh,
nach uisce go díreach,
ach slaod, abraimís,
go mbíonn a cháithní ag slíobadh
fan do shliasta
go súitear an sracadh asat

bíonn na báid níos doimhne sa bhfarraige ná mar is gnách
castar maircréil íliúla úsclána id líonta
le gach cor dá dtugann tú díobh

nó fuaim riastartha
go ndeineann a torann
fothram do cholainne a shochtadh
amhail lá go dtaoscann a sholas
folamh do dhán

bíonn spréach sa bhfód ar do phíce
bíonn aonach gach lá i gcontae an Chláir
is bíonn tú a trí déag is bíonn tú ann

nó … nó …

mar a bheadh cuimilt
nach cigilt i gceart
ar fuaid fad gach baill dod chneas,
teas ag spreagadh drithlíní
áineasa a chuireann deireadh
le gach aiste

bítear suíte do
gur mil ar uachtar atá ann
gur cathair í mar a tuairisc
gur slán leis an uaigneas é

ná cuir ainm ar an mothú seo

ná … ná … f*cain fiú cuimhnigh air
nó … nó leáfaidh,
mar atá leighte cheana ort
gach iarracht do shlaod
gach slíobadh eile id shaol …

Ó THUAIDH

Le linn an t-amhrán a rá
níorbh í an té ar ar glaodh
le *noble call*
chun amhrán do rá
mar gurbh í ab'fhearr
chun amhrán do rá
inár measc.
Níorbh í an traidisiún
á chur fhéin in iúl
trí mhaisíocht iomadúil
ná trí neamhchúis nósúil.

Le linn amhrán a rá
do b'í an t-amhrán í
á nochtadh fhéin
go teann gan ornáidíocht
idir fhocail agus fhonn
go lom ós ár gcomhair.

Do b'í conair *Na Connerys* í,
do b'í an mhuir mhór bhrónach í
idir *Santa Cruz* agus Contae Mhaigh Eo,
b'í a cheannaíodh slat is dorú dom
agus a chuireadh amach ar an gcuan mé,
do b'í an bóthar ó thuaidh í
agus
mo chóngar aduaidh í.

Colm Breathnach was born in Cork City in 1960, and studied Philosophy and Irish at University College, Cork. He is the author of six collections of poetry, most recently Chiaroscura (Coiscéim, 2006). *He works as a terminologist with the Department of Education, and as a translator with the Government Translation Service.*

GEARRSCÉAL

Gabriel Rosenstock

CAD A DHÉANFADH MAC AN CHAIT ...?

Gaeil gan Ainm.

Ach luch a mharú! Is ball den eagraíocht Gaeil gan Ainm anois mé le ceithre bliana déag anuas, a déarfainn. Nó níos faide ná sin, seans? Ba dhóigh leat go mbeadh an dáta agam go cruinn nuair a smaoiním ar cé chomh cinniúnach is a bhí sé mar lá. An chéad bhall riamh d'eagraíocht a bhfuil breis is 8,000 ball inniu aici.

Murach Gaeil Gan Ainm bheinnse glan as mo mheabhair ar fad faoin tráth seo is dócha. Ná bac is dócha. Le gealaigh a bheinn. Le craobhacha. Im ghealt chríochnaithe amach is amach. Craiceáilte. Im Shuibhne i measc na n-éan binn agus mé bodhar acu. Cleití ag bogadh amach as mo thóin.

Gaeil gan Ainm. Mura mbeidís ann chaithfí iad a chruthú agus pé rud a cheapann tú fúmsa is féidir an méid seo a rá i mo thaobh – ní bheidís ann gan mé agus ní le mustar a deirim an méid sin. Nach ormsa a deineadh na chéad tástálacha a chruthaigh go heolaíoch a leithéid d'andúil a bheith ann sa chéad áit agus í gach aon phioc chomh casta le handúil ar bith eile is mian leat a lua.

Tá a fhios ag an saol mór an mhaitheas go léir a dhéanann Alcólaigh gan Ainm, do na halcólaigh féin, Dia á mbeannachadh, dá gcairde is dá muintir is don tsochaí trí chéile. Is iomaí duine a bheadh béal faoi ar thaobh an bhóthair gan iad. Ar thaobh an bhóthair ar m'anam agus an drúcht á shú de na neantóga feoite acu. Sin í an fhírinne.

Is ag cruinniú d'Alcólaigh gan Ainm a chuala mé Gaeil gan Ainm á lua an chéad uair. Ní raibh aon trácht orthu ag an am (mar nach rabhadar ann). Níor chreideas-sa go mbeadh a leithéid ar an saol go deo ná go mbeadh páirt lárnach agam féin i mbunú na heagraíochta sin. Cé a chreidfeadh é? Alcólach gan ainm éigin le linn grúptheiripe, é ag smaoineamh os ard, Gaeil gan Ainm atá uaimse, ar sé. Sea, arsa mise láithreach, tá an ceart ar fad agat. Gaeil gan Ainm, tá géarghá lena leithéid.

Bhí an-chúnamh faighte agam roimhe sin maidir le réimse leathan andúile – andúil san ól, sa ghnéas, sa tseacláid, sa chearrbhachas, sa chócaon agus mar sin de go heireaball siar (Facebook fiú amháin, andúil eile acu) ach bhí a fhios agam nach leigheasfaí go deo mé mura dtabharfainn aghaidh ar an andúil ba mhó orthu, is é sin an Ghaeilge bhinn ársa ar milse liom í ná bainne cíche na mban basgheal, mar a dúirt Ian Lom fadó, sea go deimhin, níos milse ná neachtar na ndéithe má tá a leithéid de dheoch ann agus is cinnte go bhfuil.

Hello, I'm Tadhg, arsa Tadhg, nár Thadhg in aon chor é ach Conallach agus níor bhuaileas riamh le Conallach a raibh Tadhg air. *Howya Tadhg*, arsa gach éinne ar ais leis. *I'm Hiúdaí*, arsa Corcaíoch léannta. Gháireamar. Nach ait an rud é, bhí léann ar a leath dá raibh i láthair ag an gcéad chruinniú sin de Ghaeil gan Ainm agus ardléinn ar bheirt acu. Ceadaíodh ainmneacha Gaeilge a úsáid sa chlinic ar dtús ach níor ligeadh dúinn aon fhocal eile Gaeilge a rá ina dhiaidh sin. Oiread is siolla. Bhí sé faoi mar a bheifeá ar ais arís i laethanta an Bhata Scóir agus an teanga faoi chois.

Luíonn sé le réasún. B'ionann leanúint orainn ag stealladh Gaeilge agus scata Alcólach gan Ainm a thabhairt isteach go dtí an Stag's Head, abair, agus iarraidh orthu fiche saghas fuisce a bhlaiseadh ar mhaithe le taighde margaíochta. Chuala mé ina dhiaidh sin nach gceadóidís fiú Tadhg a rá a thuilleadh. *I'm Timothy*, a chaithfeá a rá, ar eagla go gcuirfeadh ainm Gaelach – Colmán, Sorcha, Luisne – sceitimíní neamhcheadaithe éigin ort.

Bhí go maith is ní raibh go holc. An rud is mó a chuaigh i bhfeidhm ormsa – nó an cúnamh is mó a fuaireas uathu – ná gur aithníos sa deireadh nach galar éinne amháin é. Ní bheadh a fhios agat cé air a mbeadh galar na Gaeilge, duine a bheadh suite trasna uait ar an traein cuir i gcás. Ní haon deimhniú é an galar sin a bheith ort fáinne na Gaeilge a chaitheamh, abair, nó – an rud is annamh is iontach – dá bhfeicfí thú agus leabhar Gaeilge á léamh agat in áit phoiblí. Ní haon chruthúnas é a leithéid sin gur maith leat an Ghaeilge fiú amháin; cruthaíonn sé go bhfuil Gaeilge agat, nó go bhfuil tú ag ligean ort go bhfuil, sin uile; ní hionann san is a rá go bhfuil do chroí is d'anam ar fad inti, gur luachmhaire ná do smúsach féin gach siolla di, gach amhrán a cumadh riamh sa teanga, gach seanfhocal, gach ciúta cainte, gur luachmhaire ná d'anam iad gach ainmfhocal, gach aidiacht … an gá dom dul níos faide? An gá dom an Uimhir Dhé is an Modh Foshuiteach a tharraingt isteach sa scéal?

Éinne a chuaigh leis an eagraíocht sin Gaeil Gan Ainm is mar sin a bhí sé, scafa ar fad chun na Gaeilge, nó "scúite" mar a deir daoine áirithe. Cad a theastaigh uainn? Cad a chomáin isteach sa chlinic sinn? Chun go leigheasfaí sinn, ab ea? Ní hea in aon chor ach chun go mbeadh cothromaíocht éigin sa saol arís againn, nach ag smaoineamh ar an teanga ó dhubh go dubh agus i lár na hoíche féin a bheimis ar feadh ár saoil go léir is ar feadh na síoraíochta, seans. Teacht ar an tuiscint de réir a chéile go raibh saol eile ann lasmuigh den Ghaeilge.

Glac uaimse é, bhí sé sin dian orainn, an-dian ar fad. Geall le bheith dodhéanta. Níos deacra ar dhaoine áirithe seachas a chéile, ar ndóigh. Thuigeamar nach mbeadh faoiseamh ceart i ndán do mhórán againn go deo. Bhíomar mallaithe ag milseacht na teanga, tumtha ródhomhain inti. Dulta chun ainsil.

Cathain a fuairis amach go raibh greim ag an nGaeilge ort, an chéad cheist a cuireadh orainn ag an ngrúptheiripe. Samplaí de na freagraí a tugadh:

Nuair a léigh mé dán le Cathal Ó Searcaigh. Gafa a bhíos ón nóiméad sin ar aghaidh.

Bhí mé ag freastal ar choláiste samhraidh i Ros Muc agus bhraitheas tarraingt éigin aisteach idir mé féin agus an Piarsach. Is lasmuigh de Theach an Phiarsaigh a fuaireas mo chéad phóg.

Freagra uaimse: Bhí cóip d'Fhoclóir an Duinnínigh ag m'athair. Andúileach ab ea é siúd chomh maith, gan fhios dom. Gan fhios dom mháthair. Gan fhios don saol, gan fhios do shaol na Gaeilge fiú amháin. Im dhéagóir a bhíos nuair a chuas ag léamh an Duinnínigh, an chóip de a bhí ag m'athair, beannacht Dé leis. Táim á léamh ó shin. Tá sé cois na leapa agam. B'fhusa éirí cortha den saol ná éirí cortha den Duinníneach. Braithim ceangal diamhair éigin le m'athair nuair a léim na focail a bhí marcáilte aigesean ann: focail ar nós *buarach bháis*, *seicimín*, *ullastráth*, *móg*. An éifeacht atá ag na focail sin ormsa, an raibh an éifeacht chéanna acu ar m'athair?

An freagra a thug Hiúdaí: "Ní ag iarraidh a bheith smairteáilte atáim, ach ní cuimhin liomsa cathain nach raibh greim ag an teanga orm. Géillim don athionchollú. Bhíos anseo cheana. Im Ghael. Aimsir Chromail. Chonac cad a bhí ag titim amach. Níor tugadh saol sách fada dom ag an am chun uisce mo chinn a shileadh ná chun aon ghaisce ceart a dhéanamh ach an oiread. Gheallas dom féin go dtiocfainn ar ais. Seo anois mé agus ní ligfidh mé lá tharam gan an Ghaeilge a labhairt fiú má chaithim labhairt liom fein!"

Fastaoim! Ní dhéanfaidh sé sin cúis in aon chor, arsa an teiripeoir. Athionchollú? Níl ansin ach leithscéal agus baothchaint. Cathain a fuair an Ghaeilge greim ort? Tá greim aici orm ó rugadh mé, arsa Hiúdaí. Lig sí osna fhadaríonach. Conas a chuirfinn síos ar an teiripeoir áirithe sin? Bhí sí ar nós an chait úd sa seanfhocal: "Chonac cheana thú, mar a dúirt an cat leis an mbainne beirithe." B'in an saghas í. Gach rud cloister aici, gach rud feicthe aici, dar léi féin. Ainbhiosán! Ní raibh puinn Gaeilge aici ná aon mheas aici ar an teanga ná aon tuiscint in aon chor aici don ghrá as cuimse a d'fhéadfadh mo leithéidse agus leithéidí Hiúdaí a bheith againn don séimhiú, don urú is don síneadh fada. (Dá mbeadh síneadh gearr ann bheadh grá as cuimse agam dó!)

Ba leasc léi a admháil go raibh a leithéid de ghalar ann in aon chor. Ach bhí – gus tá – agus nach mise mé féin a chruthaigh gurbh ann di mar andúil sna tástálacha stairiúla a deineadh orm i gClinic na Carraige Duibhe, scéal a chuaigh timpeall an domhain ag an am. Scéal is ea é (ar nós a lán lán scéalta nuachta eile) atá dearmadta ag daoine anois ach dóibh siúd nár chuala trácht riamh air is mar seo a tharla:

Iarradh orm sliocht as leabhar Béarla a léamh agus díreach ina dhiaidh sin deineadh scanadh inchinne orm. Ba é an leabhar a tugadh dom *The Conscience of the Rich* le C.P. Snow. Is maith is cuimhin liom an sliocht a roghnaíos mar is mion minic a léas ina dhiaidh sin é:

> As soon as I got back to London after that week-end, Ann asked me to dine with her. Once more she took me out in luxury, this time to the Ritz. I took it for granted, going out with her, that the waiters would know her by name: I was not surprised when other diners bowed to her. As usual, she set herself out to buy me expensive food and wine ...

Nuair a bhí an méid sin léite agam cuireadh isteach i meaisín mé, saghas spásárthaigh mheasas-sa, agus deineadh scanadh inchinne orm. Ní raibh puinn de na sceitimíní sin ar a dtugtar ionoirfíní ag snámh thart i m'inchinn. Oiread is frídín amháin. Patuar, ar nós cuma liom, a bhíos i ndiaidh Snow. Amach liom as an spásárthach. Tugadh gloine uisce dom agus an chéad rud eile síneann an bhanaltra cóip de *Eachtra Phinocchio* chugam, leagan Phádraig Uí Bhuachalla. D'osclaíos ar Chaibidil 27 é:

> Nuair a shrois Pinocchio an tráigh d'iniúch sé an fharraige go géar, ach má dhein ní fheacaigh sé Míol Draide ná éinní mar é. Bhí an

fharraige chomh sleamhain le gloine.

"Cá bhfuil an Míol Draide?" ar seisean lena chomrádaithe.

"Ní foláir nó tá scroid bheag aige á chaitheamh," arsa duine acu agus é ag gáirí.

"Ní dóichí rud a dhein sé ná é féin a chaitheamh sa leabaidh chun greas beag a chodladh," arsa duine eile, agus sceart sé ar gháirí.

Thuig Pinocchio go rabhthas tar éis bob a bhualadh air. Ní dheaghaidh san síos rómhaith leis agus duairt sé go teasaí:

"Cad 'na thaobh díbh an cleas san a imirt orm? Ni fheicimse go bhfuil aon tsulth ann."

"Tá, agus sulth go tiubh," ar siad san d'aon ghuth …

Leanfainn ar aghaidh go brách ach cuireadh stop liom. Ar ais sa mheaisín ansin liom. Scanadh eile. An uair seo bhí m'inchinn ar maos le hionoirfíní. Ar maos, a dhuine. Ionoirfíní ag teacht amach as an bhfaireog phiotútach, isteach i gcorda an dromlaigh agus suas leo go breá meidhreach ansin go dtí an inchinn. Ba bhreá leat féachaint orthu, chomh sona is a bhíodar. Caithfidh gurb é an focal "sulth" faoi ndeara é!

Dheineadar a thuilleadh tástálacha ormsa agus ar go leor daoine eile i mo dhiaidh. Gaeilge na Mumhan amháin a dhúisigh na hionoirfíní ionamsa aisteach go leor. Is beag éifeacht a bhí ag na canúintí eile orm.

Ar aon chuma, cuireadh go dtí clinic eile mé chun mé a leigheas ach caitheadh amach mé nuair a fuarthas an dá imleabhar de *Caint an Chláir* faoim philiúr. Ní rabhas thar n-ais ann ó shin. Ach táim im bhall den eagraíocht i gcónaíagus is breá liom a chlos nuair a thagann brainse nua ar an saol, i Singeapór nó i Shanghai cuir i gcás.

Nach ait an diabhal ruda é. Ta Gaeilge an Chláir marbh le fada ach fós cuireann abairtí as *Caint an Chláir* na hionoirfíní ag preabadh ionam: "Ní raibh aon deisínteacht i bPádraig riamh; ní féidir leis an teine féin a chur síos." Pádraig bocht!

Luaigh mé gur tháinig mé agus mé i mo dhéagóir ar chóip m'athar d'Fhoclóir an Duinnínigh a chruthaigh go raibh seisean ina andúileach millteach gan fhios do chách. Conas a choimeád sé ina rún é? Tar éis a bháis, ransálas trína chuid leabhar go léir féachaint an dtiocfainn ar leid éigin a d'inseodh dom cén saghas duine ab ea é. Sciorras tríd an gcóip d'Fhoclóir Uí Dhónaill aige féachaint an bhfaighinn roinnt focal ann a bhí marcáilte aige, focail b'fhéidir a thabharfadh léargas breise dom air. Focal amháin a bhí marcáilte aige ann: *canúnaí*, "person interested in, addicted to, dialect." Bhí dhá líne faoin bhfocal "addicted" aige agus comhartha ceiste ar imeall an leathanaigh.

Lean sé ar feadh i bhfad ina dhiaidh sin mé, an comhartha ceiste sin. Cad a bhí á cheistiú ag m'athair, n'fheadar? Sainmhíniú an fhocail sin, *canúnaí*? Nó a shaol, saol a chaith sé faoi choim?

WHAT WOULD THE SON OF A CAT DO ...?

Gaels Anonymous.

... except kill a mouse! Of course!

I have been a member of the organization Gaels Anonymous for 14 years now, I'd say. Maybe longer than that, even? You'd think I'd remember the date by now considering how fateful a day it was – the day I joined up. I was the very first member to register with an organization which now numbers in the region of 8,000 members. If it wasn't for Gaels Anonymous I'd have gone round the bend by now, I'd say. Never mind "I'd say". I'd be gone loopy and that's as sure as I'm standing here. I'd be a complete loon. I'd be like Sweeney, sitting there high up in the branches, deafened by song-birds. There would be feathers growing out of my rear by now. Gaels Anonymous. If such an organization didn't exist, somebody would have to create it. No doubt about it.

Whatever you think of me, you can't deny this much – there would be no such thing as Gaels Anonymous if it wasn't for me. I don't say this out of pride, it's a simple fact. Wasn't it on myself that they did the first tests which proved scientifically that such an addiction existed in the first place? Wasn't it tests on me that proved conclusively that this condition is as complex an addiction as any other?

Everybody knows the great work that Alcoholics Anonymous does for alcoholics and their families. Society would be in a far worse state than it already is if it wasn't for Alcoholics Anonymous. There would be people left homeless if it wasn't for them. Poor unfortunates lying by the side of the road, traces of nettle juice on their lips. As true as God.

Funnily enough, it was at a meeting of Alcoholics Anonymous that I first heard tell of the concept that is Gaels Anonymous. (Obviously, there was no further discussion of the topic seeing as Gaels Anonymous didn't actually exist at the time.) To be honest, I didn't think that such a group would ever see the light of day, never mind that I myself would have a central role in its foundation. Who would have thought it? An anonymous alcoholic thinking aloud during therapy and he comes up with this? People wouldn't believe it even if you told them. Gaels Anonymous is what I want, says he. "Yeah", says I immediately. You've got it spot on there, friend. Gaels Anonymous, I cried out. Exactly what we need. Previous to this I had got great help with a range of addictions – alcoholism, sex addiction, chocolate addiction, gambling addiction, cocaine addiction and all the rest. (I was even addicted to Facebook at one stage.) I knew deep down that I would never really be healed of any of these cravings if I didn't deal with the biggest addiction of them all. This was my addiction to the Irish language. I couldn't get enough of this ancient language; it was a compulsive craving. I loved it more than the child who loves the breast milk of white-palmed women – as the Scottish poet Ian Lom once put it. In mellifluous Gaelic, needless to say. I loved it more than nectar of the gods – if such a drink exists – as I'm sure it does.

Hello, I'm Tadhg, announced Tadhg who was no more a Tadhg than the man in the moon. This man was from Donegal and there wasn't a Donegal man born yet whose name was Tadhg.

Howya Tadhg, everybody in the group said back to him in unison.

I'm Hiudaí, announced a Corkman with an educated tone of voice. We all laughed. Wasn't it strange too – the people gathered for that first meeting of Gaels Anonymous were a clever bunch? In fact, two of the group were highly educated academics.

Irish-language names were permitted in the clinic for purpose of introducing ourselves but after that, the use of Irish was banned. Not a syllable of Irish could be uttered; its use was subject to penalties and prohibited at all times. We might as well have been back again in the days of the Tally Stick, an era in which the language was completely outlawed; that's how repressive they were about it.

This made sense, of course. To continue spouting Irish to each other was similar, say, to a group of alcoholics heading for the Stag's Head in order to sample twenty different brands of whiskey as part of a market research exercise. I even heard afterwards that they had banned the Irish name Tadhg. *I'm Timothy* was the permitted form of address from the first day in the clinic onwards.

They were afraid that the utterance of even one Irish word – a forename like Colmán, Sorcha or Luisne – would exacerbate our withdrawal symptoms and send us over the edge.

Things went on like this for a while. Time passed. The biggest lesson I learned during therapy – the biggest help they gave me – was in accepting the fact that I wasn't the only one who was cursed with this affliction. This disease could affect anybody. The person sitting across from you in the park could be a sufferer and you never could tell. The outward manifestations – say the wearing of the "fáinne" – or even stranger still, the sight of somebody reading an Irish-language book in public – these were in no way a reliable guide to who had the Irish disease and who didn't. Just because you liked Irish or could speak it – or even if you let on that you could speak it – none of these traits were indicative of a full-blown obsession, the dependence that is characteristic of the true Irish-language addict. The true addict was the person who was completely hooked – the person who couldn't get out of bed without inhaling every single breath of the language – every syllable, song and idiom ever uttered, every adjective and noun ... do I really need to go any further? Do I really need to drag in the Subjunctive Mood and all the rest of it? You get my drift ...

Anybody who joined Gaels Anonymous was like this. Every pore of their being reeked of Irish. They ingested it and excreted it every moment of the day; they breathed it in with every breath that they took from cradle to grave. It was their very blood and sweat.

And what had driven us to that clinic in the end? Did we hope for a complete transformation of ourselves, a complete cleansing or catharsis? Did we expect to find a cure for our affliction, a cure as complete as it would be miraculous?

Not at all. All we wanted was to recover some form of equilibrium in our lives. We wanted a new balance to our days, some way of controlling the obsession with Irish that tormented us from morning to night – and through the night even. We sought to withdraw somewhat from our compulsive behaviour in relation to Irish. Without achieving some form of balance, every day of our lives would be a form of one-pointedness; we might even be obsessed with Irish for all eternity.

It might be a gradual process but we had to undergo it; there *was* another life out there; there was a life that lay outside the Irish language and we *had* to find it. A difficult process; take it from me.

Incredibly difficult. Difficult beyond belief. Almost impossible.

Some people found it more difficult than others as you would expect, of course. None of us were under any illusions. We all knew that most of us would never achieve a real sense of inner peace. Our addiction was too strong; we couldn't escape the iron hold that the sweet Irish language had over us; we had gone too far already and it was too late for any real turning back. We were chronic cases; it was as simple as that.

When did we first realize that we were infected with the Irish language disease? That was the main question we tried to answer during group therapy sessions. Here are a few responses to this question as provided by some of the patients:

When I first read a poem written by Cathal Ó Searcaigh. I was completely hooked from that moment onwards.

I was at Irish College one summer when I felt a strange telepathic connection between myself and Patrick Pearse. It was right outside Pearse's Cottage that I got my first kiss.

Here's my response: My father had a copy of Dinneen's Dictionary. Unknown to me, he too was an addict. Even my mother was unaware of his addiction. Nobody knew that he was addicted, not even other Irish-language enthusiasts. I was a teenager when I first began reading Dinneen – my father's copy (God rest him). I've been taking Dinneen ever since. I get my fix regularly. I always have it by my bed. I would give up life itself before I could wean myself off Dinneen. Every time I use the dictionary, I feel some sort of mysterious connection with my father; every time I read the words that he marked … Words like *buarach bháis, seicimín, ullastráth, móg.* Those words have such an effect on me. They give me such a high. Did my father have the same trip?

Here's Hiúdaí's response: "I'm not trying to be a smart-ass but I really can't remember a time when I was not completely and utterly addicted to Irish. I fully accept the theory of reincarnation. I was here before. I was a Gael. I lived through Cromwell's time. I saw what happened. Unfortunately I didn't live long enough to make any impression on that realm of existence. I didn't get a chance to be brave, to resist. And so I promised myself then that I would definitely come back again some time in the future. And here I am. And I can tell you one thing … I won't let a day go past in this present life of mine without speaking Irish – even if that means that I end up speaking to myself!"

"Hang on a minute now! That won't do at all", interrupted the therapist on hearing this. "Reincarnation is it? Pull the other one! That's a load of old codswallop. That's just an excuse not to deal with your addiction. Now tell us straight – when did Irish get a firm grip on you?"

"I've been addicted to Irish since the day I was born", said Hiúdaí. The therapist emitted a long and weary sigh. How can I best describe that particular therapist? She was one of those types ... she was like the cat in that old saying: "I've met you before, as the cat said to the boiled milk". That's the type she was. One of those people who are tired before they are born. She had heard it all and seen it all before – according to herself, that is. An ignoramus if there ever was one! She hadn't a word of Irish. She had no interest in the language and even less respect for it. She couldn't understand for a minute how the likes of myself and Hiúdaí were addicted to the all the nuances and flavours of Irish – she could never comprehend the hit we got from the *séimhiú*, the *urú* and the *síneadh fada* (if there had been a *síneadh gearr*, I would have got a serious high from that too!).

In fact, she was reluctant to acknowledge that a condition such as ours existed at all; she was in denial about the disease that we had contracted. But such a disease exists and continues to exist and I'm living proof of it – ever since those tests they undertook on me in Blackrock Clinic all those years ago. This was a news story which made headlines all over the world back then but like many news stories it has been largely forgotten today. For those who never heard about it, this is the gist of what happened during the tests ...

Firstly, I was asked to read an extract from an English-language book after which they gave me a brain-scan. The extract I had to read was from *The Conscience of the Rich* by C.P. Snow and I remember the extract very well as I've read it quite often since:

> As soon as I got back to London after that week-end, Ann asked
> me to dine with her. Once more she took me out in luxury, this
> time to the Ritz. I took it for granted, going out with her, that the
> waiters would know her by name: I was not surprised when other
> diners bowed to her. As usual, she set herself out to buy me
> expensive food and wine ...

Once I had finished reading, I was directed into a machine (which looked like some kind of spacecraft) for a brain-scan. They found no trace of any endorphins in my system after the scan. Not the slightest. I was completely impassive and unmoved after reading Snow; not a flicker of excitement registered itself. I was taken out of the spacecraft and given a glass of water to drink. Next thing, the nurse handed me a copy of *Eachtraí Phinocchio* (*The Adventures of Pinocchio*). It was Pádraig Ó Buachalla's version of the story, straight from the Italian. I opened it at page 27 where I read the following:

Nuair a shrois Pinocchio an tráigh d'iniúch sé an fharraige go géar, ach má dhein ní fheacaigh sé Míol Draide ná éinní mar é. Bhí an fharraige chomh sleamhain le gloine.

"Cá bhfuil an Míol Draide?" ar seisean lena chomrádaithe.

"Ní foláir nó tá scroid bheag aige á chaitheamh," arsa duine acu agus é ag gáirí.

"Ní dóichí rud a dhein sé ná é féin a chaitheamh sa leabaidh chun greas beag a chodladh," arsa duine eile, agus sceart sé ar gháirí.

Thuig Pinocchio go rabhthas tar éis bob a bhualadh air. Ní dheaghaidh san síos rómhaith leis agus duairt sé go teasaí:

"Cad 'na thaobh díbh an cleas san a imirt orm? Ni fheicimse go bhfuil aon tsulth ann."

"Tá, agus sulth go tiubh," ar siad san d'aon ghuth ...

I would have continued reading all day only that they told me to stop. Back into the machine I went for another brain-scan.

This time my brain was hopping with endorphins. I was on fire, man. They could be seen everywhere on the scan those same little endorphins; buzzing through me, zipping out from the pituitary gland and making their merry way into my spinal cord. It was a wonderful sight to behold, those ecstatic endorphins jumping for joy, all across the surface of my brain. It was the use of that beautiful word "sulth" that really kicked everything off, I think!

They did further tests on me and on a good many of the other patients also. Funnily enough, it was Munster Irish that induced the endorphins. Other dialects did nothing for me. In the heel of the hunt, I was sent to another clinic for treatment. I was expelled from there, however, when two volumes of the Irish of County Clare, *Caint an Chláir*, were found hidden under my pillow. I never returned to that clinic again although I am still a registered member of Gaels Anonymous. I follow the organisation's progress closely and I'm always thrilled to hear of new developments in the field, the opening of a new branch of the organization in Singapore or Shanghai, for example.

Isn't it a strange one too? Clare Irish is dead for years and yet whenever I read a few sentences from *Caint an Chláir* the hairs stand up on the back of my neck and the endorphins go mad inside me.

I mentioned earlier that I came across my father's copy of Dinneen's Dictionary when I was still a teenager. This discovery confirmed for me that my father was very seriously addicted to the Irish language even if he managed to keep his addiction hidden from others. How the hell did he manage to keep it under wraps for all those years? That's what I want to know. After his death, I ransacked his book collection to see whether I could find deeper clues as to his personality. I carefully scanned another dictionary, Ó Dónaill's, to see what it could tell me about him. He had only marked one word in the entire dictionary as it turns out – the word "canúnaí": "person interested in, addicted to dialect". He had underlined the word "addicted" twice and placed a question-mark next to this word at the edge of the page.

That question-mark haunted me for years. What did my father mean by placing that question-mark in the margins like that?

Was it the definition of the word "canúnaí" that intrigued him, or was it something far more profound than this? Was it his own existence that he was questioning, a secret life he had kept hidden from the world?

Translated, from the Irish, by Micheál Ó hAodha.

A poet, short-story writer and translator, Gabriel Rosenstock was born in 1949 in Kilfinane, Co Limerick and is a graduate of University College Cork. One of the "Innti" poets that transformed Irish-language poetry in the 1970s, he writes primarily in Irish and is the author or translator of over 150 books. His most recent collection of poetry is Bliain an Bhandé *(Year of the Goddess,* The Dedalus Press, *2007).*

DHÁ DHÁN

Cathal Ó Searcaigh

ANTINOUS: AMMON, FILE,
A CHAOINEADH IN ALEXANDRIA, 133 AD

Buachaill bocht as Bithnia
ach faoi bhláth agus faoi mhaise na hóige
b'eisean an té a ba deise
dá bhfacthas ariamh in Alexandria.
B'eisean Antinous na háillleachta
ar thug an tImpire taitneamh dó agus grá.

Bhéarfá mionna gur gineadh é gan smál,
bhí sé chomh dea-chumtha sin
i ngach ball, chomh caoin ina mhéin,
chomh séimh ina ghné. Dá mba toil liom na déithe
déarfainn gur iadsan a mhúnlaigh é
as cré dhiaga na gnaoiúlachta.

Chífinn é ó ham go ham sa giomnáisiam
agus sa leabharlann ach ní raibh sé de dhánaíocht ionam
labhairt leis. B'eisean an comrádaí ríoga
is ní raibh ionamsa ach cléireach uiríseal
i seirbhís na hImpireachta. Mar ba dual do mo chinéal
bhí orm urraim a ghéilleadh dó i gconaí.

B'eisean mian súl an tslua, fir agus mná,
b'ionann a gcás, b'áil leo bheith i gcaidreamh
leis an bhuachaill seo a b'áille dealraimh.
I dtaca liomsa de, ní raibh a thaibhreamh domh ach é,
a bhéal le mo bhéal, a ghéaga i mo thimpeall;
bhéarfainn a raibh i mo chnámha ach dlúthú leis.

I gconaí buan agus daingean ina dhílseacht
dá leannán, nuair a tháinig am na hachainí
gan ghearán, d'íobar sé é féin sa Níl i ndúil
is go ndéanfaí an tImpire a shábhail
ó thubaiste éigin a bhíthear a thuar dó.
Dá mba rud is go dtiocfaí an chinniúint a ordú!

Anois tá a dhealbh le feicéail i mbailte na ríochta
is tá a íomhá buailte ar bhoinn airgid na hImpireachta.
Le hómós dó d'fhógair an tImpire ina Dhia é agus cé
gur eol dúinn nach bhfuil sna déithe ach miotas ár mianta
is aoibhinn linn go bhfuil Antinous, buachaill a ghéill
do chlaonta na Gréige, ár ndálta féin, anois ar ard na glóire.

Antinous na háilleachta! Antinous na grástúlachta!
Sa cháil sin, buan beo a bheas sé anois agus go deo.
Sa staid dhiaga úd, fiú mura bhfuil ann ach samhail,
buanóidh sé ar feadh na síoraíochta
ionas nach dtig leis an bhás, fiú amháin, díobháil
a dhéanamh dó nó é a chur ó dhealramh.

Antinous: Rogha an Impire Hadrian, saolaíodh an buachaill álainn seo i mBithnia sa bhliain 110 AD, báthadh é sa Níl in aice le cathair Alexandria i 130 AD. Deirtear gur íobair sé é fhéin ar mhaithe le deashláinte an Impire. Bhí Hadrian croí-bhriste ina dhiaidh.

GINSBERG I MOROCCO

Bhain sé de
a raibh air
is sheas sé lomnocht,
nadúrtha gan náire
i mo láthair.
A gháire,
a bhéal déadgheal,

a chneas gan teimheal
chuir said loinnir
sa tseomra brocach, tais.

Nuair a shú mé
an síol as
bhlais mé na glúnta
dá bhunadh;
a athair is a sheanathair
agus níos faide ar gcúl
berberaigh urranta
an tsléibhe
ó bhunchnoic na hAtlas
Ó Tafroute, ó Taliouine
agus ó Tata.

Bhí mé lán daofa
de chogarnach na haoiseanna
ó Ahmetanna, ó Mhustafanna,
ó Abdullahanna, ó Mhohamadanna;
a ndúchas is a dtréithe
ag cuisliú ionam
i mo neartú.

Beidh lorg na hoíche seo
ar a bhfuil romham amach;
iadsan nár casadh orm go fóill,
iadsan nár mhuirnigh mé
i leabacha an tsómais,
beigh an oíche seo liom
chun na leapa leo;
a mbeannú, a gcumhrú,
is a dtabhairt chun aoibhnis.

See the biographical note for Cathal Ó Searcaigh on page 180.

DÁN

Niamh Ní Lochlainn

GORT THOMÁIS

Mar a bheadh bád á thabhairt i dtír,
Thurlingíomar,
Chaitheamar dínn screamh na cathrach
Is screamh na bliana,
Thumamar aríst i gcaint is i gcadráil muinteartha,
Béimeanna troma is gutaí leathana,
Gaineamh órga trá, ceol is ragairne
Is bhí gort Thomáis fé bhláth.

Airgead luachra go fras, a shásódh draoithe,
Eireaball caitín go spuaiceach tríd,
Duilleoga an fheileastram, Bealtaine na súl buí,
Luachra na Féile Bríde,
Mallacht Phádraig a sheargaigh,
Neantóga cealgacha is cupóga sráide,
Barra coiríneach an raithinigh
Táipéis ildaite romhainn.

Duilleoga ar an gclaí anois
Ins an áit ina raibh samhaircíní,
A mhaisigh táirseach is a thimpeallaigh tobar,
Siní an bhainne bó bleacht ina bhfochair
Caonach is féar, cóilinithe tosaigh an chlaí,
Saighdiúirí mar ghárda,
Síneann crobh éin is tím,
Crochtar peasair, lóchrann síneach.

An dris a d'éalaigh isteach
Meallann an bheach, ach tachtann crann
Is an táith-fhéithleann righin, mileanna gabhar,
Cúmhracht mhilis an Mheitheamh,
Méaranna sí a dhíbir iarlais,
Seasann os cionn cách.

Ó ghort Thomáis go barra chnoic,
Cocaí féir is stacaí mar chompánaigh,
Tré aitinn ghallda is an fhraoch cloigíneach,
Osna ó thalamh ag fáiltiú romhainn,
Scamall diamhair ar bharra,
Caipín ar chruach.

Niamh Ní Lochlainn grew up in Dublin with Irish as her first language, spending her summers in the West Kerry Gaeltacht. Her collection of poetry Guth ón dTobar *(Coisceim) was published in 2005. She now lives and teaches in Connemara.*

DHÁ DHÁN

Caitríona Ní Chléirchín

DOIRE NA SEALG

Rachaidh mé síos go Doire na Sealg,
áit a mbeidh mo ghrá,
faoi chiamhair chraobh.

Beidh dearcáin faoi chos is caonach,
i lár na coille cumhra,
caora cuilinn, cnó agus úlla
go fairsing ann.
Biolar agus samhadh
i ngleann ceo.
Flúirse ina bhflúirse ann.
Fianna a ritheann i réimeanna is
Damh sa choill,
amuigh ar an cheo sa choill.
Buailfidh muid lenár dtaibhsí féin.

Luífidh muid faoin chrann caorthainn ann
ag éisteacht le monabhar an tsrutháin
is craobhmhúr agus craobhcheathanna
craobhchith tamall ón spéir.

Binn guth an smólaigh ar bharra craobh ann
binn guth na cuaiche
is an loin dhuibh.

Glaise ina ghlaise ann.
Duileabhar fúinn is luachra
go barra glún.

Éalóidh muid ón domhan seal.
Éalóidh muid uainn féinn
i lár na coille cnó agus úlla
go fairsing ann
biolar agus samhadh
i ngleann ceo.

Seinnfidh ceol do shúl im chroí, a stór
nuair a rachaidh muid síos go Doire na Sealg
le coimheascar lae.

Tá caonach faoi chos i nDoire na Sealg
mar a luíonn muid faoi chiamhar chraobh
i nDoire na Sealg, ba bhrídeach sí mé
is lean mé mo ghrá mar eilit sa cheo.

DEARNASHALLOG

I will go down to Dernashallog,
the wood of the hunting,
down to where my love will be
under the gloom of the branches

There'll be acorns underfoot and moss
in the middle of the fragrant wood
holly berries, nut and apples
in plenty there
cress and sorrel
in the mist-glen
plentifulness there
and deer running in leaps
and a stag out in the wood mist
We'll meet our own ghosts there

We'll lie a while under the rowan tree
listening to the stream's murmur
rain showers through the branches
awhile from the sky

The thrush's voice will be sweet there,
from the top of every branch
and sweet the cuckoo
sweet the blackbird

Greenness there beneath us,
leaves and rushes
up to our knees

We'll escape from the world awhile
escape from ourselves
in the middle of the fragrant wood
holly berries, nuts and apples
in plenty there
cress and sorrel
in the mist-glen

The music of your eye
will play in my heart, love
when we go down to Dernashallog,
the wood of the hunting
at dusky eveningtide

There's moss underfoot in Dernashallog
where we lie under the shade of branches,
In Dernashallog, I was a fairy bride
and I followed my love like a doe in the mist

TAR LIOM, A GHRÁ

Tar liom, a ghrá amach ar na bánta
amach ar bhánta an earraigh.
Déanfaidh muid leaba luachra sa ghleann
luífidh muid seal faoi chantain na n-éan

Tar liom, a ghrá amach ar na bánta
óir ní fothain dúinn
ballaí an tí seo, ní foscadh
is racht bróin dár pblúchadh

Cluinim ceiliúr do cheoil i mo chluasa
is mian liom imeacht leat,
druideanna is cuacha ag eitilt romhainn
Cluinim scairt na machairí orainn is na cnoic

Tar liom, a ghrá amach ar na bánta
mise a bheas mar bhrídeach sí agat
brisfidh muid amach as na slabhraí
óir ní tréise an bás ná an grá …

COME WITH ME, LOVE

Come with me love, out on the plains,
out on the plains of Spring.
We'll make a bed of rushes in the glen,
and recline to the birdsong.

Come with me love, out on the plains,
the walls of this house are no shelter
for you or me, no protection,
with this sadness choking us.

I hear your chanting in my ear.
I want to go away with you,
to fly like the starlings and cuckoos.
I hear the call of the hills.

Come with me love, out on the plains.
I will be your bride of the *sidhe*.
We'll break out of our chains,
since death is not stronger than love ...

Caitríona Ní Chléirchin was born in 1978 and grew up in Scairbh na gCaorach, Co Monaghan. She was educated at University College, Dublin where she is now Lecturer in Irish Language and Literature. Her first collection of poetry, Crithloinnir *(Shimmer, 2010) was published by Coiscéim.*

IN THE SPIRIT OF DINNEEN

Rody Gorman

(Editor's Note: Gorman's unique English translations of his own Scots Gaelic work go in a direction opposite to the usual procedure, towards "the multidimensional of the multilingual".)

GATHAN

A' siubhal air ais dhomh
Sa Chuan Sgìth,
Chunnaic mi mar lasair
Eadar dà thaigh-solais
Losgadh air an uachdar
Agus de ghathan a' boillsgeadh
Nam faileas
Ann am blobhsag a' bhodaich.

SHEAFSPOKESUNBEAMDARTS

deathseektravelling back in the tiredminchoceanbay, i saw like a
flashflame eitherbothbetween two moonphaseknowledgelighthouses
shootburning on the woofcreamsurfacetop and sheafspokesunbeamdarts
gaudyglittering like a shadow in the halfbottlespectreoldcodboy's
oilskinblouse

MONAIDHEAN

Feasgar air siubhal dhuinn
'S a' ghrian ri laighe
Seachad air na carbadan
Air an trèigsinn 's na tobhtaichean
'S an tràigh cho geal sèimh,
Cha robh agam ann
Mar a bha mi 'n dùil mar shealladh
An cladh ann an Cill Nèimh
Is gun sìthean ann
Is taigh-'n-aifrinn
fo chòinnich is dallan-cloiche
'S carraighean-cuimhne
'S aon chrois
Is na h-uile aig fois
Is na h-aon sloinnidhean
Is manaidhean a' togail ceann,
Gus am Bris an Latha,
Cha robh na, air a chaochladh,
Leis gun robh mi air mo mhealladh
Leam fhìn an sin gun ghuth
Ach treud a chaoraich bhàna
Air allaban air feadh an àite.

DESERTPASTUREMOORMOUNTAINS

vespersafternoon out away deathseekwalking and the seabottomsunland
liesetting past the chariotvehiclecars abandoned and the
turfwallthwartknollruins and strand so whitebright and calm, it wasn't
the dykespawninggraveyard in kilnave i saw without any
fairyhillockflowers or masschapelhouse under moss and a blind
standingstone and memorialrocks and one cross and all at rest and the
same patronymicsurnames and apparitionmantras headappearing, *until
the day break*, not at all, the deathchangeopposite, as i was deceived by
myself there without a bardtauntvowelvoiceword but a herdflock of
fallowgroundvacantwhitefaced sheep wandering all over the place

EADAR DRUSKININKAI 'S VILNIUS

A' tighinn à Druskininkai Didòmhnaich,
Dh'fhalbh sinn gu lochan air oir na slighe
Far am biodh an tuath còmhla
Ris na caileagan-achaidh
'S na sgùlain gus cur thairis —
Morel, chanterelle, helvella —
Nam falach am feadh nam beithean 's nan giuthas.

Agus nuair a bha mi fhìn rèidh
'S a rinn mi stad is tionndadh,
'S e na dh'fhairich mi ann ach sgal
Mar gum b' ann mar obair an taibh
'S e ri suathadh anns an tràigh
'S an làn ìseal
Feasgar fad' air ais aig baile.

EITHERBOTHBETWEEN DRUSKININKAI AND VILNIUS

coming fromoutof druskininkai on sunday we went for a pondpiss on the
    edge of the roadway where the northcountryfarmfolk used to be
    bothtogether with the fieldgirlmushrooms and the baskets about to
overflow — *morel, chanterelle, helvella* — hidden amongst the beeches and pines

and when i was readydone and i abodestopped and turned, i
smellfeltheard a calfsquallskirlyelp like the working of the western ocean
rubnearing the strand and the fulltide low a long vespersafternoon away
                back in townvillagefarmhome

MODH

'S nuair a bha sinn cruinn
Còmhla nar cloinn mun a' chaillich,
Ri faire, leth mar leth mar thional-claidh
'S a' coimhead oirnn fhìn gar breith,
'S an ionnas dèanamh às,
Dh'iarr i oirnn falbh
'S thuirt mi rithe:
Dè tha sibh 'g ràdh?
'S thuirt i: *Mas e ur toil e!*

'S nuair a dh'èirich na bh'ann
'S a leig sinn leatha laighe,
Don turas mu dheireadh,
Thuirt mi rithe:
'S dè tha sibh 'g ràdh a-nis?
Is thuirt i mu dheireadh:
Tapadh leibh!

ADDRESSRESPECTMANNERS

and when we were globepreciselygathered doorframetogether as
familychildren round heroldwifiewitchself, carewaking, half like a
funeralgathering and half preservewatching ourselves being
judgementborn and about to head off, she asked us to go and i said to
her: *what do you say?* and she said: *if you loveplease!*

and when all there got up and we let her lie, for the last journeytime, i
said to her: *and what do you say now?* and she said at last:
goodluckthankyou!

SAMHAIN

Seall am bodach againn
Anns a' ghàrradh leis fhèin
A' gearradh is a' bearradh
Agus an t-Samhain air lom —
An dùil am bi e smaoineachadh is ag ràdh
Ris fhèin: *Ciamar fo Dhia*
Nach eil e crìonadh is a' dol air ais
Is a' dol bàs
Mar bu dual am-bliadhna
Mar anns an aimsir a dh'aom?

NOVEMBERHALLOWEEN

showsee our halfbottlespectreoldcodboy in his dykegarden by himself
earmarkcarvecutting and ridgeshearing and novemberhalloweeen on the
barehorizon – i wonder does he think and say to himself: *howwhy the*
hell is it not depresswithering and going back and deathgoing as it
plaitshould this year like in the epochseasonweathertimes that are
bentgone?

Rody Gorman was born in Dublin in 1961. He has worked as Convenor of the Translation and Linguistic Rights Committee of Scottish PEN and as Specialist Adviser for the Scottish Arts Council. He has published twelve collections of poetry, most recently Beartan Briste/burstbroken judgementshroudloomdeeds *(Cape Breton University Press, 2011). His selected poems in Irish and Scottish Gaelic,* Chernilo, *was published by Coiscéim in 2006. He was recently Writer-in-Residence at the Scottish National College for Gaelic Language and Culture, Sabhal Mòr Ostaig, and lives on the Isle of Skye, Scotland.*

IN THE SCOTS GAELIC

Niall O'Gallagher &
Marcas Mac an Tuairneir

DOM GHAOL NA NIGHINN BHIG

Niall O'Gallagher

Nam b' urrainn dhomh na faclan
    seo a chur tha iomall tìm'
chuirinn thugad mo phògan
    nad nighinn òig, 's mi a dhìth;

ann an litir a dh'innseadh
    leis gach briathair òr is ùr
gu bheil mo ghaol a' feitheamh
ort ge ceillte e bhod shùil

's nach b' fhiach dhut a bhith draghail
    mun bhròn sealach a bheir an là
na dealgan beag' a phianas
    nach do mhair riamh mar an gràdh

agam, na chraobh a dh'fhàsas,
    dol fo bhlàth à freumhan fhèin,
nas motha is nas brèagha,
    na h-èarlaid air gàrradh cèin.

Bhithinn airson do stiùireadh
    air seòladh ùr gus as d'fhuair
thu thugam na bu tràithe
    a dh'aindeòin gach ràith', gach uair

's tu dealaichte bhom ghaol-sa;
    chuirinn gaoth mhòr na do shiùil
airson do bhàt' a luathadh
    thar gach cruadail fo mo iùl.

Leughadh tu na mo litir,
    anns gach lide na mo làimh
cearbaich (an tè a chleachdas
    mi, a' dealbhachadh an dàimh

a th' eadarainn) gur milis
    a' bheatha chlis a th' an dàn
don dithis againn còmhla
    's sinn ri ceòl a bhitheas làn

de chomhardadh 's ar binnean
    tighinn ri chèile gus fonn
ùr a thogail, a chluinneas
    sinne thar luinneag nan tonn.

Nam b' urrainn dhomh do ruighinn
    's tu ri cluich nad nighinn bhig
chuirinn am broinn a' phasgain
    mo dhàn banail cuide ris

an litir gus am faiceadh
    tu anns gach aicill gur mòr
mo chùram is mo dhìcheall
    's mi ga sgrìobhadh dhut, a stòir,

's an uair sin, aig an direadh
    chuirinn m' ainm, a nighinn chaoimh,
mar ghealltanas gum bithinn
    ann, gun tigeadh tu dom thaobh.

UISGE TETH

Marcas Mac an Tuairneir

Bidh m'fhearg a' losgadh an uisge-amair.
Fiù 's an luidhear na chànran,
Cha tèid e air an smuid.

Cluinnidh mi do mhùc-sa thairis air a' bhalla,
A' caoineadh bliadhna coirbheachd,
Nach gabh mi cùram a ràcadh.

Tha d' fhadachd air a' chlais,
Treadhte eadar mo flat is am bàr.
'S àgh a th' ort is d' fhuasgladh.
Snàig mi fhìn a-mach air ìnean.

Cha mhòr nach d' ràinig mi an uachdar,
Ro mo chuairteachadh leis na bruthaich.
Ballachan an tuill sleamhainn.

A Bhreabadair, am figheadh tusa beatha,
Le buill spìonte a chèile?
Cha ghabh mi grèim air a' ghreallach.

Cha d' rinn mi bhòidse, leis an amas de philltinn.
Tha mi, niste, nam mhurrag, air muir air a goil.

HOT WATER

This anger scalds the bath water.
Even the air-vent grumbles.
It cannot cope with this steam.

I hear you snivelling beyond the wall,
Mourning that year's decadence,
I don't care to repeat.

You long for the furrow,
Ploughed between my flat and the bar.
Lucky you, being extricated.
I crawled out by the fingernails.

By the time I had surfaced,
The slopes had surrounded me.
The walls of that slippery well.

Weaver, could you have knitted a life
Out of dismembered limbs?
I can't even grasp the entrails.

I did not voyage with the idea of return.
And now I am flotsam on this boiling sea.

Since 2007 Niall O'Gallagher has worked from the Scottish Parliament as a political reporter for the BBC. Previously, he taught at Glasgow University while writing his doctoral thesis on the work of Glasgow novelist Alasdair Gray. In 2009 he received a New Writers Award from the Scottish Book Trust / Gaelic Books Council and in 2011 took part in An Chuairt, *the tour of Scottish Gaelic Poets to Ireland. He has written for the* Guardian, *the* Herald *and the Catalan-language daily* Ara. *He lives in Glasgow.*

Marcus Mac an Tuairneir is a recent graduate of the University of Aberdeen, where he received both an MA in Gaelic and Hispanic Studies, and an MLitt in Irish and Scottish Literature. He has been writing poetry for some years and previously published poems in several magazines. He now lives in York, England.

THE GAMES

Liz McSkeane

Outwith a wrong and beautiful order.

The first time Kate ever saw a grown-up person cry was the day her mother dropped the bottle of whisky they were supposed to bring back to the croft for Donald. They were both tired out and bad-tempered by that time, Kate because of the blisters on her feet which were really starting to hurt and her mother for being sent on the message in the first place, a three-mile walk to the Co-op and back just to keep a man in drink.

They were almost home when it happened. First the bottle hit the ground with a crack, then Kate looked at her mother and her mother looked at Kate and together they watched the golden liquid soak into the sandy ground where it mixed in with bits of broken glass that glittered in the sunlight until there was nothing left but a wet patch on the gravel and the jagged half of a bottle. Then Kate's mother sniffled a bit and a few tears rolled down her cheeks which was quite scary. But she took Kate's hand and they set off on the last mile home which wasn't home at all but only where they were staying for their summer holidays.

Already in the few days since they'd got there, the island looked different from the great patches of empty fields and sky and sea they'd found when the ferry had let them off at the tiny harbour. Even if there were still hardly any houses to be seen and no trees at all because the last one was swept away in a gale that blew in from the Atlantic a long time ago, maybe six or seven years ago, before Kate was born, it didn't look exactly empty any more. Once you'd got used to the rocky fields and sandy roads and craggy mountains that stretched out and touched the sea and the sky above and all around you'd never again say that the island was empty. There, for instance, almost hidden behind a grey line of rocks was a sparkling blue ribbon of water and that hadn't been there yesterday. And if you let your eyes wander like that now and then, you'd always see something new or something in a different way. Like Ben Dubh, the Black Mountain which wasn't black at all but today was glowing purple and green with a few patches of white. The purple and the white were clumps of heather and Kate's father had promised that one day soon they'd climb to the top of the mountain and find some of the real lucky white heather which is very rare and grows only in the highest, farthest places where the golden eagle makes its nest and is nothing like the stuff you see in the shops which is the ordinary purple heather bleached white for the English visitors who cart it off by the ton and tell everyone on the mainland it's the real thing.

Already they'd passed by the blue ribbon of loch which Kate had spotted uncurling behind a grey line of rocks and very soon they were home. By this time Kate's mother had just about stopped crying and when she told Kate's father what had happened she even gave a little giggle and it was probably the giggle that annoyed him and not the whisky at all. But then uncle Donald laughed and Kate's father smiled though he tried not to and everybody laughed except for Maggie who scowled and spat and muttered something in the Gaelic which was all right because that was what she always did. And when she had finished spitting and shoving brown stuff up her nose she began to scold Kate as usual and sent her running off to do things that didn't want doing at all.

Tonight none of that mattered because at last, the Games were nearly here. Tomorrow, somewhere amongst the sandy hills that the islanders called the *machair*, looking out over the sea where the Atlantic meets the Minch with the wind in her hair and the murmur of the ocean in her ears, Kate would dance her first Highland fling. Many times before she had practised dancing a fling but far away in the city where the traffic rattling past Miss Campbell's living-room window almost drowned out the crackle from the gramophone and the sound of the slap from the old lady's bony hands on legs that weren't straight enough or arms that weren't held high enough.

Tomorrow, though, they'd make music with real pipes, like the set that Donald took down to look at every night before he went to bed. He never played them, only held them in his arms like a baby, stroking the black wooden chanter with his worn twisted old fingers and after a while his soft blue eyes would start to glitter and Kate's mother and father would look at each other and shake their heads, but carefully, so that Donald didn't see. Then Donald would light up some tobacco in his pipe and her father would light a cigarette and slowly they would puff out clouds and rings of white and yellow smoke that went up and disappeared into the blackened ceiling and the smell mixing with the smell of the peat in the range and old-man smell. For Donald wasn't her real uncle at all but her father's uncle and that was why he was so old. Then usually after a long time without saying anything Donald would reach up into the cupboard behind the television set and pull out a bottle of golden whisky but probably not tonight because of what happened this morning. Then he'd pour himself a dram and Kate's father a dram but not her mother, in two little glasses the size of a big man's thumb and the two men would sit talking and Donald would think for a long time before singing out the English words in a wrong and beautiful order.

It was a pity that Donald wouldn't play those pipes because it is very difficult, though not impossible if you know how to count it out properly in one-two-three-four-toe-heel-toe-heel, to practise dancing a Highland fling without music. There was an old wireless that might have done as well which Kate spotted on top of the dresser, but Maggie said that there wasn't a peep out of it. The television was no good because apart from certain important football matches and the Calum Kennedy show it was never switched on. Once Kate thought she saw john-paul-george-and-ringo through the crackle and the fuzz but Maggie switched them off straight away and only shouted at Kate not to be such a notice-box when she started counting out her dance steps by herself.

The only time that Maggie ever spoke to Kate was to bark at her not to be such a notice-box or else when she wanted her to do something or to go somewhere and then she would pinch her or thump her in the back. Sometimes, and this was even worse, she would bend her wrinkled yellow old face right down to Kate's ear and whisper to her loudly about the dangers of the croft. Every one of the fields that straggled out from the farmhouse or stretched over the mountain or out towards the *machair* was scored with long lines of rock that stuck out of the sandy ground and some of them were dotted with boulders that might be round enough and interesting enough for a small girl about Kate's size to want to climb. And it was not unusual for stupid people who went climbing on those rocks to fall and crack their skull and never be heard of again or only when it was too late. Most dangerous of all were the lochs that sprinkled the whole island with their blue glitter, a lot of them half-hidden by a thick covering of dark green reeds that swayed together in the breeze or got whipped in a gale and looked exactly like a dark green carpet that was about to take off any minute. Those lochs, and especially the one at the edge of the kitchen garden, were bottomless so that the bodies of disobedient boys and girls who fell in were never found, not even by the police.

All the lochs and fields and rocks as far as you could see belonged to Donald. That night, as he poured out the two drams for himself and Kate's father after all, while her mother pressed her blouse for the next day, he told them that the part of the *machair* where the Games were to be held belonged to him, too, and that they weren't to pay admission. He would see to it himself.

But the next day, Donald wouldn't come. Everyone was sitting in the old white van her father had borrowed from the MacDonalds who lived by the crossroads, Kate's mother and father in the front seats and Kate in the back, her costume in a bag at her feet except for her white blouse which her mother had spread carefully over her lap. The early mist cleared, the sky got bluer and still Donald wouldn't come. He was in bed and nothing would shift him. At last out came Maggie, her face darker than usual with her bad temper. She had on her tweed coat that she always wore on Sundays. As she climbed up into the van beside Kate she screamed out something at her brother who wouldn't get up, a Gaelic curse Kate's father said later. Donald didn't answer of course, he was probably still asleep. So they all set off.

Maggie never stopped talking the whole time. Because no one else would listen to her, Kate's mother and father having their own quiet chat in the front of the van while she was stuck with Maggie in the back, the old woman jabbered everything into Kate's ear. Every sheep and every stone that they passed by on the road to the *machair* had a story and Kate heard them all. So-and-so who always dipped his sheep in such a colour. Someone else who never mended his broken fences. And the Hamiltons who owned the big white house, the very last one before they turned off for the *machair*. Apart from the bits that belonged to Donald, the Hamiltons owned most of the island, even though Mr Hamilton was dead and Mrs Hamilton only came back once or twice a year with her sons and crowds of visitors who wore funny clothes and shot at the birds. But the people from the big house had always been good to them and gave jobs to the local girls, like Maggie's sister who was Kate's grandmother and died a long time ago. And sometimes when the girls got older, the people from the big house would find a place for them in some really big house in Oban or even in Glasgow where they went into service and other kindnesses.

The very first sign of the Games came floating to them on the breeze. Long before they'd rounded the last of the sand dunes that hid the *machair* from the road they could hear the low humming noise made by lots of people talking at once, the wail of the pipes and behind all that, the crashing of the waves drifting in through the window of the van which Kate's father had rolled down because of the heat. And all at once the voices were around them, separate voices that kept up a strange chatter she ought to understand, that any minute she would understand and then the words would fade and slip away from her altogether and she was alone. But it only felt that way because it was hardly possible to walk without tripping over someone or standing on somebody's sandwich or kicking over a cupful of Irn Bru or lemonade. Bit by bit, Kate and her mother and father and Maggie threaded their way through the crowd of men in kilts and women carrying plates of sandwiches and pots of tea and every so often someone would stop her father and shake his hand and her father would stumble out a few words in the Gaelic before introducing his wife and little daughter.

At last, they came to the place where Kate was to dance her Highland fling, a high wooden platform raised up over the grass. It was already occupied. Four tall girls were in the middle of a sword dance, at that exciting and difficult moment when you have to stamp and clap and let out a shout, all at the same time. The four of them leaped and turned, dancing in perfect time around the four points of the square that you make by placing the sword over its sheath in the shape of a cross, first stepping on the outside, not lightly on tip-toe like you might think but with a *thump!* and a *thud!* on the ball of your foot with each step and then again the same, but on the inside of the square so that you have to lift your feet very high to dance right over the sword but without touching it, which is much more difficult. And Kate knew that there was no greater shame than to kick the sword while you were doing this so that it lay crooked or even worse, skittered across the room and you'd be left with only two points to dance around instead of four and had to pretend.

As they still had to wait half an hour before Kate's turn for the dancing, they decided to go for a wander to see what else was going on. First there was the tug o' war when about twenty big men, ten on each side, hauled on two ends of a rope, groaning and spitting and straining while their friends called out jeers in the Gaelic. The whole thing didn't last very long, just until the ribbon that marked the middle of the rope passed some invisible spot on the ground and then, as if someone had given them a signal, all the men on one side of the rope let go of it and all the men on the other side fell to the ground in a heap. And it was the ones who fell on top of each other in a heap that were the winners. In another corner of the field a crowd was gathered around a big strong man who held in his arms a pillar of wood as big as a tree-trunk and after a lot of groaning and heaving, the caber, for that was what the pillar of wood was called, flipped over his shoulder and landed quite a way away. And that was it.

At last it was time to get ready. Kate was to be kitted out in full Highland dress. A kilt, of course, in the tartan of the MacLeods which was Donald's and Maggie's and her dead grandmother's name. Tartan socks and dancing pumps, properly laced right up to the knee. A white frilly blouse that peeped out at the neck and the cuffs. And last of all, a tiny black velvet waistcoat, complete with silver buttons and braid. As the music started up and a man with a microphone called out the names of the girls who were dancing Kate's fling, her mother wound a few of her curls around one finger, tied a tartan ribbon in her hair and before she knew it she'd been lifted up to the platform with the other dancers and they were off.

Right from the start there was something wrong. She didn't mind that the other girls were so much bigger but their costumes were different. Quieter, smarter than hers, with not a ribbon or a frill in sight. Just starched white shirts, kilts, pumps and one girl was wearing a tartan tie. And the music had an old familiar crackle to it, just like the scratches from the gramophone in Miss Campbell's living-room and when she was making her second turn, there it was at the side of the platform – a record player but with the music coming out of a box that was sitting beside it on the grass. And that made her miss her step and on her next turn she was looking right into the face of the girl with the tartan tie, which meant that one of them had it wrong because they had all started together, bowing in the same direction so they should all be turning together facing the same way and definitely not looking at each other. But the music was different and the beat was different and no matter how hard she counted she couldn't keep time. And even the final bow didn't work because the music didn't end properly but just sort of stopped when someone lifted the needle from the record and that meant that everyone had finished their bow when she was just starting hers.

Everybody said that she'd been very good. Maggie gave her a sweet and her father thought that she should keep her costume on for the rest of the day. But she didn't. By the time they'd called the names out for the next dance Kate had already squeezed into her slacks and pulled her jumper over the frilly white blouse, in case people would remember that she was the girl who got her turns wrong and missed her final bow.

They did remember her, though. As soon as she'd finished changing, the man with the microphone who had called out the names for the dancers waved at them and came running over. He had a cardboard box under his arm and after saying a few words to the grown-ups he handed it to Kate.

Everybody looked at her and waited while she opened it. Inside, under folds of white tissue paper, there was a Scotty-doll, a girl-doll done up in full Highland dress with a tammy and a kilt pin and a *scian dhu* inside one of her socks. And if the grown-ups had known, and if they had asked her why it was that she wanted to cry, she wouldn't have been able to explain it. So she just said thank you, nicely, and in a little while they all went home.

Liz McSkeane was born in Glasgow and has lived in Dublin since 1981. Her poetry and short fiction has been widely anthologized in Ireland and the UK, and her first full poetry collection, Snow at the Opera House, *was published in 2002 (New Island Press). She recently completed her PhD in Education, and is currently working on her first novel.*

FRIENDS OF IRISH PAGES

Supporting the culture of classic print.

The *Friends of Irish Pages* is a new and generous group of readers, writers and business organizations whose financial contributions help advance the work of IRISH PAGES: A JOURNAL OF CONTEMPORARY WRITING. The journal gratefully now acknowledges this financial assistance on one dedicated page of every issue.

Manus Charleton
Joe and Geraldine Duffy
Joseph Hassett
Philip Haughey
Enda McDonagh
John McGinley
McKibbin Commercial
Modern Office Supplies
Nicholson & Bass
Timothy Vignoles

In this difficult economic climate, not only the book trade, but the culture of classic print itself, is under pressure as never before. The new support of the *Friends of Irish Pages* is essential to the vitality and independence of Ireland's premier literary journal.

With the largest print-run of any Irish literary periodical, IRISH PAGES represents – uniquely for the island – the intersection of a large general readership with outstanding writing from Ireland and overseas. Each issue assembles a carefully-edited mix of English and Irish, prose and poetry, fiction and non-fiction, style and subject matter, in an overall fit aimed at a wide range of reading tastes. For the Irish resident, no less than the Irish expatriate or the overseas reader, IRISH PAGES offers an unrivalled biannual window on the literary and cultural life of these islands – and further afield.

Please send your contribution, photocopying the form overleaf, to IRISH PAGES at the address given; or ring our office directly at + 44 (0) 28 90434800, where your contribution can be taken by credit card. Alternatively, you can pay directly via PayPal at http://tinyurl.com/friends-of-irish-pages, making sure to notify us at sales@irishpages.org of your name and address.

SUPPORT US NOW

Friends of Irish Pages

NAME _____

ADDRESS _____

_____

COUNTRY _____ POSTCODE/ZIP _____

EMAIL _____

☐ I would like to become a *Friend of Irish Pages* with a contribution of £250/€300/$400 or more.

☐ I would like to become a *Supporter of Irish Pages* with the following contribution: _____.

Enclosed is my cheque/money order to IRISH PAGES for the amount of _____.

Please charge my ☐ Visa ☐ Mastercard

Card Number ☐☐☐☐ ☐☐☐☐ ☐☐☐☐ ☐☐☐☐

Expiry Date ☐☐/☐☐ Signature _____

Please post this form to:

IRISH PAGES
The Linen Hall Library, 17 Donegall Square North, Belfast BT1 5GB
Email: irishpages@yahoo.co.uk
Tel: +44 (0) 2890 434800
or visit our website at www.irishpages.org